REAL ESTATE MATH

DEMYSTIFIED

Steven P. Mooney

New York   Chicago   San Francisco   Lisbon   London
Madrid   Mexico City   Milan   New Delhi   San Juan
Seoul   Singapore   Sydney   Toronto

3 4 5 6 7 8 9 0   FGR/FGR   0 9 8 7

ISBN-13: 978-0-07-148138-0
ISBN-10: 0-07-148138-9

This publication is designed to provide accurate and authoritative information in regard to the subject matter covered. It is sold with the understanding that the publisher is not engaged in rendering legal, accounting, or other professional service. If legal advice or other expert assistance is required, the services of a competent professional person should be sought.
—*From a Declaration of Principles Jointly Adopted by a Committee of the American Bar Association and a Committee of Publishers and Associations*

McGraw-Hill books are available at special discounts to use as premiums and sales promotions, or for use in corporate training programs. For more information, please write to the Director of Special Sales, Professional Publishing, McGraw-Hill, Two Penn Plaza, New York, NY 10121-2298. Or contact your local bookstore.

This book is printed on acid-free paper.

Library of Congress Cataloging-in-Publication Data

Mooney, Steven P.
  Real estate math demystified / by Steven P. Mooney.
    p. cm.
  Includes index.
  ISBN 978-0-07-148138-0 (pbk. : alk. paper) 1. Real estate business–Mathematics. I. Title.
HF5695.5.R3M66 2007
333.3301'51–dc22

2007000525

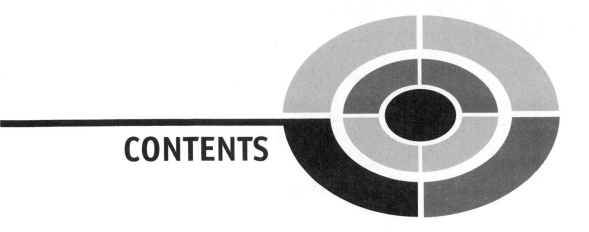

CONTENTS

ACKNOWLEDGMENTS

I would like to thank my wife Kate, for encouraging me to pursue an academic career in the late nineteen-seventies. I would also like to thank Jack Friedman for providing me a great role model during my doctoral program at Texas A&M University. Jack also recommended Kate as a potential author to Grace Freedson, who now serves as our agent, whom I would also like to thank. I would like to thank Julie Clasen for her hard work in creating many of the diagrams and lists used in the book.

Finally, I would like to thank every student I have ever taught at St. Cloud State University since it was our interaction that provided me with the material for this book.

Other Titles in the Demystified Series

Introduction

Real estate math is scary for some people. This does not have to be the case. In this book we revert back to some math principles we mastered in elementary school. In addition we brush up on some calculations we performed in junior high school and high school. Finally we address some topics that are usually discovered in college-level real estate courses. This book is not designed for people who have already taken those college-level courses; it is designed for the students who have forgotten some (or most) of the math they took as a student in the past, but are sincere in their desire to be able to analyze real estate from all the different viewpoints. This includes the viewpoint of the buyer, the seller, the lender, the appraiser, and the investor. I would certainly not discourage those who have taken college-level courses from reading the book, however. It will be an excellent review of some topics and may well introduce a couple of new ones to you.

This book is targeted at a broad group of readers. It will certainly be beneficial for those who are interested in obtaining their real estate broker's or salesperson's license. The individual investor would also be well advised to read this book.

Real estate students at the community college and university level would also profit from reading this book. Since I have been all of these people myself—a real estate salesperson and broker, a real estate investor, and a real estate student—I understand the needs of each of these groups of people. Now, as a real estate professor, I see the need for a book such as this to benefit the groups of people that I have belonged to.

There is much that is exciting about real estate analysis, and much of it is dependent on a firm math background. If you don't have that background right now, don't worry. You will have it by the time you finish this book. I have attacked this book not from the standpoint of a math expert. I am very much a practitioner when it comes to math, not a theory guy. In order for math to make sense to me, I have to be able to use it for something. If you are interested in math theory, you'd better find another book. If you are interested in how math can help you analyze real estate investments, find a quiet place, some paper, a pencil, and a financial calculator. Then hang on; it's going to be wild ride.

Review

You will find that this book is divided into 13 chapters that range from simple review to challenging new material. The first chapter is a review of math skills and addresses such concepts as equations and units of measure. We discuss what makes an equation an equation and also some relevant units of measure that are used in real estate. We close the chapter with a brief discussion of the financial calculator and how that will be used in future chapters.

Parts of a Whole

The second chapter addresses the concepts of fractions, decimals, and percentages. The manipulation of fractions, including the addition, subtraction, multiplication and division of those fractions is discussed in detail. This includes the manipulation of proper fractions, improper fractions, and mixed numbers. Later in the chapter we look at converting those fractions to decimals and percentages. These percentages are important since much of real estate math is dealing with commission rates, rates of return, interest rates, and discount rates, all of which are percentages.

Commissions

In Chapter 3 the topics of commission and growth rates are studied. This is an extension of the percentage discussion that begins at the end of Chapter 2. In addition to commission rates, which are of importance to buyers, sellers, brokers, and salespeople, growth rates are discussed. Both average growth rates and compound growth rates are analyzed. If you don't know the difference between average and compound growth rates, you need me; buy the book. If you do know the difference between the two but you don't know how to calculate them, you need me; buy the book.

Big Backyard?

The fourth chapter is called "Legal Descriptions and Lot Size: Does This Drawing Make My Backyard Look Big?" There are three types of legal descriptions that are the most commonly used in the United States. They are the metes and bounds system, the government survey system, and the subdivision plat system. The first one dates back to medieval England; the second, back to the days of the Louisiana Purchase; and the third, to relatively more recent times. In addition to these systems of describing land, we use some of the tools from the first chapter to calculate the area of a lot and the volume of a structure.

Real Estate Taxes

Chapter 5 is all about real estate taxes and covers such topics as ad valorem taxes, assessed value, estimated market values, mill rates, and state deed taxes. We address the concept of how value is determined for tax purposes. We look at the three approaches for appraising property, although in a much more cursory way than in Chapter 10 on real estate appraisal. Three different types of tax rates are analyzed—the nominal tax rate, the average tax rate, and the effective tax rate.

Time Value of Money

In Chapter 6, "Time Value of Money," we start to hit the mother lode of the book. As I tell my students, this stuff isn't important. It's critical! Once you understand time value of money, you understand finance, you understand investments, you understand appraisal, and you understand life. We will learn, mark, and inwardly digest the concepts of present value, future value, ordinary annuity, annuity due, net present value, internal rate of return, sinking fund payment, and payment to amortize. Your financial calculator will get its initial workout in this chapter. Don't worry if you don't understand your financial calculator yet. By the time you are done with this book, you will be playing that instrument like Johann Sebastian Bach played the organ.

Mortgages

We continue using the time value of money techniques when we move into the mortgage calculations in Chapter 7. Mortgage payment calculations and principal balance calculations will become second nature after you finish reading this chapter and working the associated problems. The impact of discount points and other prepaid items on loan yields are focused on. Those yields are important both from the lender's point of view and from the borrower's point of view. Loan-to-value ratios are discussed, and homeowner's equity is calculated. Finally, borrower qualifications and mortgage underwriting problems are tackled.

Appreciation and Depreciation

Chapter 8 is "Appreciation and Depreciation: You Win Some, and You Lose Some." The increase in property value over time is what we refer to as appreciation. The impact of appreciation on the cost of owning is one of the major factors leading over 67 percent of the population in the United States to own rather than rent their personal residence. We will look at estimating the value of a residence given a certain rate of appreciation. On the other end of changes in value is the concept of depreciation. Depreciation in two forms are addressed in the chapter. First of all the depreciation as it relates to real estate appraisal is discussed. This form of depreciation is a loss in value due to any cause, and it comes into play in the cost approach of the appraisal process. The second form of depreciation that we look at is the depreciation for tax purposes that is an important element in real estate investment analysis.

Closing Statements

The ninth chapter is about closings and closing statements. The closing statement is the actual accounting of the purchase/sales transaction. It tracks the expenses and the prepayments associated with the transaction. As much as it gives me the willies to talk about accounting (my wife is an accounting professor), in the closing statements we track both the buyer's and the seller's debits and credits. The bottom line in the buyer's closing statement is how much additional cash they have to bring to the closing. The corresponding line on the seller's statement will tell the seller how much money he or she will be taking home from the closing. Topics de jour include expenses, prepaid items, accrued items, and prorated items.

Appraisal

Real estate appraisal is the next topic in the book, and it appears in Chapter 10. The math portion of the sales comparison approach and the cost approach are pretty much a function of adding and subtracting. I feel confident you didn't buy this book in order to review adding and subtracting whole numbers and dollars and cents. That being the case, I focus most of my time and energies in this chapter on the different forms of the income approach. These include the gross rent multiplier, the income capitalization, and the discounted cash flow methods. Within the discussion of the income capitalization method are methods of calculating the capitalization rate in two different ways. One is through market extraction, and the other is called the band of investment method. Hopefully, when we finish up on the band of investment method, you will respond the same way I did when I first saw it. Wow! That is what I said, and that is what my students say, well the bright ones, anyway.

Real Estate Investment

An investor will only pay the present value of all cash flows to be received, discounted at the required rate of return. This is pretty much the heart of Chapter 11. It draws extensively upon Chapter 6, "Time Value of Money," and Chapter 10, "Real Estate Appraisal." The topics focused on are cash flow estimation, net present value, and internal rate of return as they apply to real estate investment. Once you have completed this chapter, you will be able to use these tools to analyze a student rental investment, a single-family home rental, a 4-unit building, a 5,000-unit apartment complex, or the Mall of America. The same concepts and analyses apply to all types of property.

Risk

Risk is, in effect, the probability of achieving an undesired outcome. From an investor's viewpoint that would be achieving a rate of return that is lower than the expected rate of return. For some reason investors don't mind achieving a rate of return higher than was expected. Rather, it is the downside risk they are concerned with. In Chapter 12 we take a close look at the impact that risk has on the investor, the appraiser, and the lender. We also look at the impact of risk on interest rates. Expected inflation is built into short-term and long-term interest rates, so we also look at the method of extracting expected inflation rates from those interest rates.

Leases

The chapter on leases gives the reader a picture of the importance of the lease in a real estate investment. Different types of rent are discussed including gross rent, net rent, percentage rent, overage rent, average rent, and effective rent. The final two that are listed, average rent and effective rent, are calculated in different lease scenarios. There are differences in how the rent is charged in residential property, office property, warehouse property, and retail property. The concepts and calculations of leasehold value and leased fee value are also addressed. You have no real estate investment until you have tenants sign a lease and start paying rent, so although this chapter is the last in the book, it could very easily be the first chapter.

The Financial Calculator

From Chapter 6 through to the end of the book, we are very dependent on the use of the financial calculator. When I tell my students in class that the world revolves around the time value of money, they question my sanity. As you will see from the latter half of the book, much of what goes on in the finance and real estate worlds is closely tied to this concept. Don't worry if you are uncomfortable with the calculator now. You will be close friends with it soon.

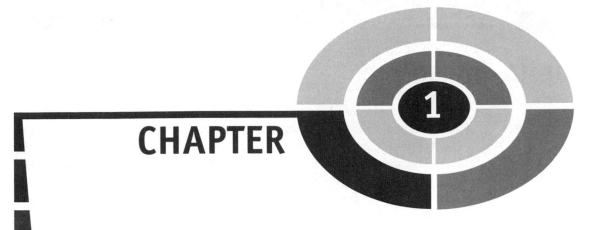

CHAPTER

Review of Math Skills

Math? I Took Math Once

Operations

As a quick review of your very first math course, there are four basic operations in math calculations: addition, subtraction, multiplication, and division. The author is confident that you are familiar with these processes, which are used repeatedly in this book. Knowing when to add, subtract, multiply, and divide is one of the keys to successful real estate math calculations.

Units of Measure

The units of measure used in real estate math calculations can be varied. Lot sizes and building sizes use feet, or more precisely, square feet as a basic unit of measure. If we take a storage shed measuring 6 feet by 6 feet, its area would be 6 feet × 6 feet = 36 feet^2 or 36 square feet. Notice that both the 6 is squared and the unit of measure, or feet, is squared. You will see both lot sizes and building sizes described in number of square feet, which is a measure of size for the area of a lot or building.

Some basic units of measure that are used in real estate include:

1 foot = 12 inches
1 yard = 3 feet
1 acre = 43,560 square feet
1 section = 640 acres = 1 square mile
1 township = 36 sections
1 mile = 5,280 feet
1 mile = 8 furlongs

As a subset of feet, we may look at inches, for smaller-sized objects. Surface area calculations result in answers with units of measure stated in square feet, square yards, or square inches. In the case of a rectangle you take the length times the width to get the area. If you are measuring the area of a square, as in the previous paragraph, you also take the length times the width, it just so happens these lengths are both the same. By definition the length and the width are the same in the case of a square.

When measuring volume, the unit of measure is not square feet, square inches, or square yards, but rather it is cubic feet, cubic inches, or cubic yards. That is because in order to calculate the volume of a three-dimensional object, you take the length times the width times the height. If our cube is 6 inches by 6 inches by 6 inches, the calculation becomes 6 inches × 6 inches × 6 inches = 216 inches^3 or 216 cubic inches.

Other units of measure that we may come across in real estate would include acres. One acre is equal to 43,560 square feet. Regarding the government survey system of legal descriptions, one township is made up of 36 sections of land. One section is 1 square mile and is made up of 640 acres of land. If that is the case, how many square feet are there in one section?

Equation 1.1

$$640 \times 43{,}560 \text{ square feet} = 27{,}878{,}400 \text{ square feet}$$

So there are 27,878,400 square feet in one section of land. Then how many square feet are there in a township?

Equation 1.2

$$36 \times 640 \times 43{,}560 \text{ square feet} = 1{,}003{,}622{,}400 \text{ square feet}$$

It appears that there are over 1 billion square feet in one township.

Equations

An *equation* is a mathematical statement that includes an equal sign. The values on either side of the equal sign must be equivalent to each other. If they are not equivalent, then the statement is not true. The following statement is not true: $35 = 5 \times 6$. That is, 35 is not the same as 5×6. When you take 5×6, you do not get an answer of 35; you get an answer of 30. In order to make the statement true, you would need to write $30 = 5 \times 6$, or you could write $35 = 5 \times 7$. In either case, the statement being made is true, so they are both valid equations. Thirty is equivalent to 5×6 and 35 is equivalent to 5×7.

Equations are the tools that are used to solve problems. The problem may be a long complex word problem, or it could be a short straightforward calculation. In either case an equation can be used to solve the question at hand.

In algebra we learned that an equation can be altered, and as long as we do the same thing to both sides of the equation, it will still be an equation. If we are using the equation from the first part of this section:

Equation 1.3

$$35 = 5 \times 7$$

and we divide both sides of the equation by 5, the result is:

Equation 1.4

$$35/5 = (5 \times 7)/5, \text{ which says, } 7 = 7$$

so our equation is still a true statement.

Some of these types of problems are addressed in this book. If *algebra* scares you, don't worry. That word will not be mentioned again … too much.

ORDER OF OPERATIONS

When there is a problem that requires more than one calculation, the order of operations can be dictated through the use of parentheses. The calculation within the parentheses is performed first, before the other(s). In the statement below:

Equation 1.5

$$(7 \times 5) + 5 = 40$$

there is a multiplication process called for as well as an addition process. Since the multiplication process is within the parentheses, that is the calculation that is made first. Thus make the 7×5 calculation and get an answer of 35, and then add the 5 for an answer of 40. If the statement did not have the parentheses and looked like this:

Equation 1.6

$$7 \times 5 + 5 = 70$$

the calculation may progress in a different manner. If we add the $5 + 5$ first, we get 10. And if we then take the 10×7, we get an answer of 70. As you can see, the parentheses are very important because they indicate which process, or calculation, should be performed first. Without the parentheses a completely different answer would result (in the example, 40 instead of 70).

EQUATIONS FOR AREA AND VOLUME

The calculations of area and volume are referred to earlier in the chapter. There are specific equations to use in the calculation of each of these items. The equation for finding the area of a rectangle or square is shown in Equation 1.7.

Equation 1.7

$$\text{Area} = L \times W$$

In Equation 1.7, L represents the length of one side of the rectangle, and W represents the width of the rectangle. To obtain the area of the rectangle, simply multiply the length times the width. (See Figure 1.1.) As mentioned previously, if we are finding the area of a square, the length and width are the same, so the area can be obtained by taking one side times itself, or the side squared. If the unit of measure of our rectangle or square is feet, then the answer to our calculation is given in square feet. If a lot measures 40 feet by 150 feet, the area of that lot is shown in Equation 1.8.

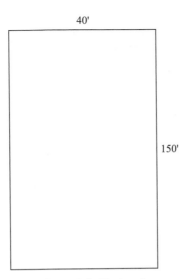

40'

150'

Figure 1.1   Rectangle

Equation 1.8

$$\text{Area} = 40 \text{ feet} \times 150 \text{ feet} = 6{,}000 \text{ square feet}$$

The volume of a rectangular box, or cube, is found by multiplying the length times the width times the height, as shown in Equation 1.9.

Equation 1.9

$$\text{Volume} = L \times W \times H$$

If the unit of measure in our calculation is feet, then our answer is given in cubic feet. If a shed is square in shape and is a single floor with measurements of 6 feet by 6 feet and it has a 6-foot-high ceiling, the volume calculation would look like Equation 1.10 (see Figure 1.2.)

Equation 1.10

$$\text{Volume} = 6 \text{ feet} \times 6 \text{ feet} \times 6 \text{ feet} = 216 \text{ cubic feet}$$

The area of a circle is only somewhat more complex in that we must use a number called pi, or the Greek symbol π. Pi (π) is equal to approximately 3.14. The area of a circle is as follows:

Equation 1.11

$$\text{Area} = \pi(r^2)$$

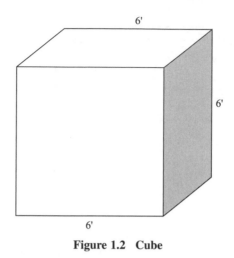

Figure 1.2   Cube

where r is equal to the radius of the circle and π, or pi, is equal to 3.14 rounded to two decimal places. (See Figure 1.3.) The radius is the distance from the center of the circle to the outside of the circle itself, or one half of the diameter of the circle. If we wanted to find the area of a circle that has a radius of 20 feet, the calculation would be as follows.

Equation 1.12

$$\text{Area} = 3.14(20^2) = 3.14(400) = 1{,}256 \text{ square feet}$$

The area of a circle does not come up too often in real estate, but it may arise in an agricultural setting where the square footage covered by an irrigation system must be found.

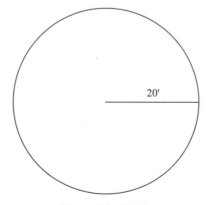

Figure 1.3   Circle

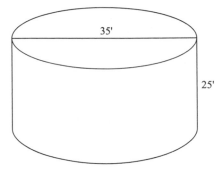

Figure 1.4 Cylinder

The volume of a cylindrical tube, like a silo, would be the area of the base times the height. (See Figure 1.4.) The calculation would look like this:

Equation 1.13

$$\text{Volume} = \pi(r^2) \times H$$

It is simply the area of the circular base times the height. If a silo is 35 feet from side to side (diameter = 35 feet) and stands 25 feet tall, what would its volume be? The calculation would look like this:

Equation 1.14

$$\text{Volume} = 3.14(35/2)^2 \times 25 = 3.14(17.5)^2 \times 25 = 3.14 \times 306.25 \times 25$$

$$= 24{,}040.63 \text{ cubic feet}$$

Recall that the calculation of the area of a circle calls for the radius squared times π, and in the preceding problem we were given the diameter. As a result, in Equation 1.14 we needed to take the diameter, 35, and divide it by 2 to get the radius of 17.5.

A trapezoid is a four-sided figure in which the corners are not all right angles (90 degrees) and the bases are not the same length but they are parallel to each other (see Figure 1.5). The calculation for the area of a trapezoid is as follows.

Equation 1.15

$$\text{Area} = 1/2 \,(\text{sum of the bases}) \times H$$

The H in this case is the perpendicular distance between the bases, not the length of the shorter sides. The area of a trapezoid (see Figure 1.5) that has bases of

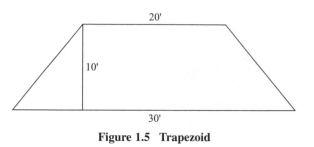

Figure 1.5 Trapezoid

20 feet and 30 feet and a height of 10 feet would be:

Equation 1.16

$$\text{Area} = \frac{1}{2}(20 + 30) \times 10 = \frac{1}{2} \times 50 \times 10 = 250 \text{ square feet}$$

The Financial Calculator

Starting with Chapter 6, "Time Value of Money," this book depends strongly on the use of the financial calculator. This time-saving device has replaced the cumbersome time value of money tables that had been used in the past. In real estate, the tables were referred to as the *six functions of a dollar*. The subtitle of Chapter 6 makes reference to the equations that made use of the tables, "Six Equations That Will Change Your Life." The calculator solutions that are used in the book have reduced the dependence on the equations. However, for someone who truly wants to understand time value of money, understanding the equations is a prerequisite.

THE TI BUSINESS ANALYST II PLUS CALCULATOR

A number of the calculations that are addressed in this book are simplified through the use of a financial calculator. Chapter 6 depends extensively on this calculator. Subsequent chapters also make much use of the financial calculator. While the calculations can be made using a standard four-function calculator and a set of present value/future value tables, the financial calculator makes the job much easier. In those chapters that make use of the financial calculator, you will see the solutions to the problems spelled out in calculator keystrokes. The calculator that is used is the Texas Instruments Business Analyst II Plus financial calculator. It is probably the most cost-effective financial calculator in use today. It is readily available in office supply stores and college bookstores. Some of the important keys for us are described in the following section.

IMPORTANT CALCULATOR KEYS

The BA II Plus calculator has many abilities that we do not address in this book. The ones we primarily focus on are the time value of money keys and the cash flow keys. The time value of money keys are in the third row from the top of the calculator and are as follows: [N] [I/Y] [PV] [PMT] [FV]. The [N] key stands for the number of compounding periods in the calculation. The [I/Y] key is the interest

Figure 1.6   The Texas Instruments BA II Plus calculator

Texas Instruments BA II Plus^{TM} image used with permission

rate per year. The [PV] represents the present value in a problem. The [PMT] is the payment in an annuity calculation, and finally the [FV] is the future value calculation. These keys are put into context in the time value of money (TVM) discussion in Chapter 6.

Other keys that we make use of are in the first row. These include the [cpt] key, which tells the calculator to compute a value. The [enter] key is used to enter a value. The up and down arrow are used to move up and down within a cash flow worksheet that we use in the real estate investment chapter (Chapter 11). The [on/off] key is fairly self-explanatory.

The second row of keys is also used in the investment chapter as well as others. The [2nd] key moves us up to the second level of many of the keys. You will notice in the photo of the calculator in Figure 1.6 that the second level of the [FV] key says CLR TVM. If we hit the [2nd] key followed by the [FV] key, that clears out the TVM registers. In other words that process puts zeros in those TVM registers so that we can start from scratch on a new problem. If you don't clear out those registers and you move from one type of problem to another, an old number from the previous problem will try and work its way into the new problem and end up giving you a bogus answer. The [CF] key stands for cash flows, and we use that key to get into the cash flow worksheet in our investment analysis. The [NPV] key is used for calculating the net present value of a series of cash flows. The [IRR] is used when we want to calculate the internal rate of return of a series of cash flows. (The terms *NPV* and *IRR* are defined further in Chapter 11.)

The worksheet can be cleared after an NPV problem or an IRR problem by hitting the [2nd] key followed by the [CLR WORK] key in the lower left-hand corner of the calculator. Additional keys are described as their use becomes necessary.

Quiz for Chapter 1

1. The home you are selling has a rectangular lot with dimensions of 75 feet by 150 feet. What is the area of the lot?
   a. 10,750 square feet
   b. 12,000 square feet
   c. 11,250 square feet
   d. 11,750 square feet

2. Your driveway is 20 feet by 20 feet. How many square feet of pavement will you have if you have the driveway tarred?
   a. 400 square feet
   b. 4,000 square feet
   c. 600 square feet
   d. 400 cubic feet

3. If your garage has a flat roof, what is its volume if its dimensions are 22 feet by 24 feet and it stands 8 feet tall?
   a. 528 square feet
   b. 528 cubic feet
   c. 4,224 square feet
   d. 4,224 cubic feet

4. What is the answer to the following calculation? $7 + (3 \times 2) - 4 = ?$
   a. 16
   b. 9
   c. 10
   d. 14

5. Your neighbor's lot is trapezoidal in shape. The two bases are 50 feet and 80 feet in length. The perpendicular distance between the bases is 100 feet. What is the area, in square feet, of your neighbor's lot?
   a. 400,000 square feet
   b. 13,000 square feet
   c. 6,500 square feet
   d. 13,000 cubic feet

6. You are planning to make a skating rink in your back yard. You put a stake in the center of the yard and by using a rope you measure a circle

with a 15-foot radius. What will be the area of your skating rink in square feet?

a. 225 square feet

b. 706.5 square feet

c. 225 cubic feet

d. 94.2 square feet

7. A farmer is building a new storage bin for grain storage. The base of the bin will be a circle with a 28-foot diameter. If the bin is 30 feet tall, what will its volume be?

a. 2,461.8 cubic feet

b. 615.4 cubic feet

c. 18,463.2 cubic feet

d. 615.4 square feet

8. The floor plan on your new house looks like the one pictured below in Figure 1.7. What is the square footage of the first floor?

a. 1,300 square feet

b. 1,200 square feet

c. 1,600 square feet

d. 1,500 square feet

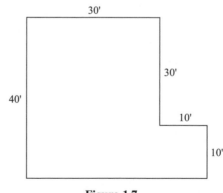

Figure 1.7

9. Your son and daughter are coming home from Iraq this weekend, and you would like to tie a yellow ribbon around the entire house shown in Figure 1.7. How much ribbon do you need to buy if you think you will need an extra 6 feet to tie the bow?

a. 1,306 feet

b. 156 feet

     c. 166 feet

     d. 126 feet

10. The lot you recently sold had a sale price of $65,000. The lot had a front footage of 80 feet and a depth of 165 feet. What was the price per square foot it sold for and the price per front foot?

     a. $4.92 and $393.94

     b. $393.94 and $812.50

     c. $80.00 and $393.94

     d. $4.92 and $812.50

CHAPTER

2

Fractions, Decimals, and Percentages

Which One of These Is Not Like the Others?

A large portion of math is involved with calculating and manipulating parts of a whole. These parts may be fractions, they may be decimals, or they may be percentages. Real estate is no different. You may be dealing with 1/2 of an acre, or an operating expense ratio of 0.35, or calculating 6 percent of the sale price. In each case we are dealing with a part of a whole something. The greater

your ease in moving from one measuring unit to another, the greater is your chance of success in working in real estate.

Fractions

There are a couple of different ways to look at a fraction, and the best way for you to look at a fraction is the way that makes the most sense to you. The first way to look at a simple fraction (a fraction with a value of less than 1) is by analyzing both the numerator (top number) and the <u>d</u>enominator (bottom or "<u>d</u>own" number). The denominator tells us how many parts our whole is divided into. If the fraction is 3/4, that tells us that our whole item is divided into four parts. The numerator tells us how many of those parts we are actually dealing with. Again if our fraction is 3/4, the numerator of 3 tells us that we are only dealing with 3 of those 4 parts that the whole is divided into. If the fraction is 1/2, it says that our whole item is divided into 2 parts and that we are currently looking at only 1 of those parts. If the fraction is 2/2, then the item is divided into two parts, and we are looking at both of them. So if the fraction is 2/2 we are looking at 2 of 2 parts, in other words we are looking at the whole item, so 2/2 = 1. Whenever the numerator and denominator are the same, the value of the fraction is the whole number 1. Thus, the value of each of these fractions is 1: 2/2, 3/3, 5/5 and 1,000/1,000.

MIXED NUMBERS

Another way to look at a fraction is that a fraction is a division problem waiting to happen. If the numerator is greater than the denominator (or the value is greater than 1), the solution or answer to the division problem will be a mixed number. By performing the operation that is called for, we are beginning to manipulate a fraction. In Equation 2.1,

Equation 2.1

$$5/4 = 5 \div 4 = 1 1/4$$

you divide the 5 by 4, and a you get the whole number 1, plus a remainder of 1 which becomes the numerator, and 4 is your denominator, so the answer is 1 1/4. This is referred to as a *mixed number,* because there is a whole number and a fraction. If we want to convert this back to a fraction, we take the denominator, 4, times the whole number, 1, and add the numerator 1 and we get $5/4$. If we take the fraction $7/2$, we could convert that to a mixed number by dividing 7 by 2 and get the answer 3 plus a remainder of 1 (which becomes the numerator over the denominator of 2) to give us the mixed number $3^1/2$. That $3^1/2$ in turn could be converted to a mixed number by taking the denominator of 2 times the number 3 to get 6, plus the numerator of 1 gives us $7/2$.

REDUCING FRACTIONS

A fraction can be reduced to simpler form. The fraction $4/8$ can be reduced to $2/4$, and $2/4$ can be reduced to $1/2$. For the fraction $4/8$ divide the numerator by 2 and the denominator by 2, and that yields an answer of $2/4$. Do the same to $2/4$, that is, divide both the numerator and denominator by 2 and get the answer $1/2$. Alternatively, just dividing the numerator and denominator of $4/8$ by 4 will also give the answer of $1/2$. This is called *reducing a fraction to its simplest form.*

MANIPULATING FRACTIONS

Adding fractions is just like adding whole numbers. In order to add $1/4$ plus $3/4$, simply add the numerators, $1 + 3 = 4$, and put the answer back over the denominator, $4/4$. In like fashion $3/8 + 7/8 = (3 + 7)/8 = 10/8$. That answer could be converted to the mixed number $1 2/8$, which can be reduced to $1 1/4$. In similar fashion $3/4$ minus $1/4$ would result in an answer of $2/4$, or $1/2$.

The requirement that must be met before adding or subtracting fractions is that they must first have the same denominator. If there are fractions with different denominators, they can still be added or subtracted, but they must first be converted to a *common denominator*. A common denominator is a denominator that the two fractions would have in common with each other, given a little manipulation. The simplest way to find a common denominator would be to multiply together the two denominators. For example, to add the two fractions $1/4 + 1/3$, multiply the 4 times the 3 and get a common denominator of 12. In effect we multiply each fraction by 1. In the case of the fraction $1/4$, we will multiply it by $3/3$ to get an answer of $3/12$. We multiply the $1/3$ by $4/4$ to get an answer of $4/12$. The result is $1/4 + 1/3 = 3/12 + 4/12 = 7/12$.

Following the steps from the previous paragraph, take a minute and add the fractions $1/2 + 3/7$. Let's see what you might have done.

Equation 2.2

$$1/2 + 3/7 = (7/7 \times 1/2) + (2/2 \times 3/7) = 7/14 + 6/14 = 13/14$$

The common denominator for the two fractions would be $2 \times 7 = 14$. Multiply the $1/2$ by $7/7$ and get $7/14$. Then multiply $3/7$ by $2/2$ and get $6/14$. Now add the $7/14 + 6/14$ and get $13/14$ as an answer. By multiplying $1/2$ by $7/7$ and $3/7$ by $2/2$, we multiplied each fraction by 1 and any number multiplied by 1 gives us the same number. Just like $1 \times 5 = 5$, $1/2 \times 7/7 = 1/2$, only this time we are calling $1/2$ by the name $7/14$ so that we can add it to $6/14$.

If this didn't make sense when you read it the first time, read it over again and jot down the fractions on a sheet of paper as you go. There is no penalty associated with reading some material twice.

Converting Fractions to Decimals

The division problem that is being called for in a fraction might not deal with a remainder, as in the explanation of Equation 2.1 above. Rather, it may make use of a decimal point, and the answer may be in decimal form. Let's look at the fraction $3/4$ again. The fraction asks us to divide 3 by 4. If we were to do this in long division, or more likely today, punch the numbers into a calculator, $3 \div 4$, the answer to the calculation is 0.75. Thus 0.75 is the decimal equivalent of $3/4$, or $3/4 = 0.75$. (See Chapter 1 for the calculator key strokes for the TI Professional Business Analyst calculator.)

Your calculator key strokes should look like this for the TI calculator:

Equation 2.3

$$3\,[\div]\,4\,[=]\,0.75$$

This is the type of answer you will get when the fraction is a simple fraction with a numerator that is less than the denominator; in other words it has a value of less than 1. The answer will begin with a decimal point, again indicating a value of less than 1. If the division problem has a numerator that is greater than the denominator, then the answer will begin with a whole number with a decimal point

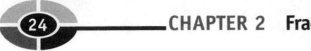

somewhere in the middle of the number with additional zeros or numbers to the right of the decimal point. If the fraction is 5/4, the TI calculator key strokes would look like this:

Equation 2.4

$$5 [\div] 4 [=] 1.25$$

The decimal equivalent then of 5/4 is one point two five (1.25). You will recall the mixed fraction answer to this problem was 1 1/4. The decimal equivalent of 1/4 is in fact 0.25 or 25 one-hundredths. The first place to the right of the decimal point is tenths, the second is hundredths, the third is thousands, the fourth is ten thousandths, and so on.

If Equation 2.1 is true and Equation 2.4 is true, then it must be true that:

Equation 2.5

$$5/4 = 1 1/4 = 1.25$$

To verify that, take 1/4 and punch it into your calculator, 1 [÷] 4 [=] 0.25 plus 4/4 which is equal to 1, so 1 + 0.25 = 1.25. So Equation 2.5 is indeed an equation because the elements on either side of the equal sign, in this case two equals signs, are indeed equivalent to each other.

We have discovered two ways to find the decimal equivalent of 5/4. Either take 5 [÷] 4 = 1.25 or take 1 [÷] 4 [=] 0.25 and add it to the 1 to get 1.25.

As practice, find the decimal equivalents of each of the fractions in Table 2.1. Cover up the right-hand column as you calculate the decimal equivalent of each of the following fractions.

Table 2.1   Fractions to decimals

Fractions	Decimals
1/2	0.50
1 3/4	1.75
2 2/3	2.67
3/5	0.60
20 4/10	20.4
10 65/100	10.65
5 1/4	5.25

Converting Decimals to Percentages and Back

The second decimal place to the right of the decimal point represents hundredths. A percentage is a statement in hundredths of a whole, or 1 hundredth = 1 percent = 0.01. Sixty-five hundredths stated as a decimal is = 0.65. To convert that decimal value to a percent, simply move the decimal point two places to the right and add a percent sign, so 0.65 = 65%. This is again an equation because the value to the left of the equal sign is equivalent to the value to the right of the equal sign. The decimal value may be stated in thousandths rather than hundredths. It doesn't matter; we still move the decimal places two places to the right to get the percentage value. That being the case, a decimal value of 0.855 is equivalent to 85.5%.

The need to convert decimals to percentages arises all the time in different real estate settings. For example, your taxes went up from $3,000 per year to $3,500 per year, and you want to know what percent increase that was. The taxes started at $3,000, and they went up to $3,500. The ending value of $3,500 minus the beginning value of $3,000 gives us an increase of $500 per year. Taking the $500 increase and dividing it by the $3,000 beginning value gives us an increase of 0.167 ($500 ÷ $3,000 = 0.167). Now convert that to a percentage by moving the decimal point two places to the right and adding a percent sign, and we see that your taxes went up by 16.7%. Alternatively we could take the ending value ($3,500) divided by the beginning value ($3,000), $3,500 ÷ $3,000 = 1.167. We then subtract the 1, shift our decimal point two places to the right, add the percent sign, and we get 16.7%. Either method is acceptable.

Another situation may involve an investor. She has purchased a duplex for $285,000 and the assessor has told her that the land value is $57,000. She would like to know what percentage of the total purchase price is represented by the land value. She should take the land value and divide it by the total purchase price, $57,000 ÷ $285,000 = 0.20 and then move the decimal point two places to the right and add a percent sign. This answer indicates that the land value represents 20% of the total purchase price.

Maybe your city planner tells you that the maximum coverage your new building can have on your lot is 55% according to the city building requirements. You know that your lot is a rectangle of 125 feet by 150 feet. The building you are planning to put up has a footprint, or a first floor square footage, of 9,750 square feet. Do you fit within the city's requirements? First find the area of the lot. Take 125 feet × 150 feet and get 18,750 square feet as the area of the lot. Then take the square footage of the first floor of the building and divide it by the area of the lot; 9,750 ÷ 18,750 = 0.52 = 52%. Your building will cover 52% of the lot, so you are within the city code for area coverage.

Table 2.2 Decimal to percent

Decimal	Percent
0.75	75%
0.22	22%
35.9	35.9%
1.255	125.5%
0.999	99.9%
0.01	1%
2.02	202%

Cover up the right hand column of Table 2.2 and convert the decimal values to percentages. Uncover the right-hand column to check your answers.

Just as frequently in real estate transactions there is a need to convert percentages to their decimal equivalents to facilitate, or make easier, a calculation. You are a broker and have just sold a house for a seller; the sale price was $355,000. You told the seller he would have to pay you a 6% commission. What is the dollar value of the gross commission? Take the 6% and shift the decimal point two places to the left and drop the percent sign and get 0.06. Now take the 0.06 × $355,000 and find the gross commission value which is $21,300.

Maybe you are working as a property manager and your boss told you that you are being given a lot more responsibility and you will now be managing four buildings instead of the three that you have been working on in the past. As a result you will receive a raise of 8%. You are currently making $42,000 per year. How much will your raise be? How much will you be making next year? Take the 8% and shift the decimal point two places to the left, drop the percent sign and get 0.08. Now take the 0.08 × $42,000, and your raise is $3,360. Add that $3,360 to the $42,000 to find you will be making $45,360 next year. As an alternate method take the $42,000 and multiply it times 1.08. You also get $45,360 as your next year's salary.

In Table 2.3, cover up the right-hand column and calculate the decimal equivalents of the percentages that are given. Once you have finished, uncover the right-hand column, and the correct answers will again magically appear.

Part, Percent, Whole

Many real estate situations call on the use of the part, percent, whole concept. It is an example of simple algebra, but don't let that word scare you. Look at Figure 2.1.

Table 2.3   Percent to decimal

Percents	Decimals
6.5%	0.065
20%	0.02
135%	1.35
15%	0.15
55.5%	0.555
110%	1.10
7%	0.07

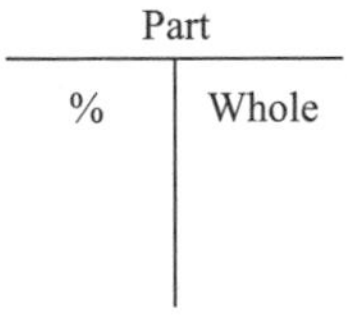

Part

% | Whole

Figure 2.1   Part, percent, whole

You will notice that the part is above the horizontal line and the percent and whole are below the horizontal line. Think of that horizontal line as the line in a fraction. In effect we are creating two different fractions and one multiplication problem. The first fraction illustrated is part/whole. To make this an equation, we simply plug in the percent, as shown in Equation 2.6.

Equation 2.6

$$Part/whole = Percent$$

This tells us that if we take a part of the whole and divide by the total whole, it will give us the percentage of the whole that the part represents. Let's say that we have a whole sale price of $125,000 and we know that the commission that is being paid on the transaction is $7,500. The question is, what was the commission rate on the deal? We simply plug our number into Equation 2.6 and get $7,500/$125,000 and get 0.06 or 6%.

The second equation that Figure 2.1 is begging us to create is Equation 2.7.

Equation 2.7

$$Part/percent = Whole$$

This equation tells us that if we take the part and divide it by the percentage that it represents, the resulting answer will be the whole that we are dealing with. If our net proceeds from the sale are $134,850 and that is after paying a 7% commission, then the net proceeds actually represent 93% of the whole, so we take $134,850/0.93 and get a whole sale price of $145,000. If, on the other hand, we had been given the commission amount of $10,150 and had been told that it was 7% of the sale price, we would have taken $10,150/0.07 and gotten the same whole sale price of $145,000.

The third equation that is being called for in Figure 2.1 is multiplying the two items below the line to get the value above the line.

Equation 2.8

$$\text{Percent} \times \text{whole} = \text{Part}$$

This calculation is probably used more often than the other two. This time we can take our commission rate times our sale price and get the dollar amount of the commission. Given a sale price of $325,000 and a commission rate of 6%, this should result in a commission value of $325,000 \times 0.06 = $19,500$.

You will find a variation on the part, percent, whole equations used extensively in Chapter 10 on real estate appraisal. The equations in appraisal are referred to as the IRV formula, where I is equal to the NOI (income) of the property, R is the capitalization rate and V is the value of the property. The resulting equations are I/R = V, or income over rate equals value; I/V = R, or income over value equals rate; and R $\times$ V = I, or rate times value equals income.

Percentages and Mortgages

Mortgage amounts are typically stated in terms of loan-to-value ratios. A *ratio* is one number divided by another. In the loan-to-value ratio, the loan or mortgage amount is divided by the value of the property, like this—(loan ÷ value) or (loan/value)—and the answer is given as a percent. If we are purchasing a home for $100,000 and we are getting an $80,000 mortgage, our loan-to-value ratio is $80,000/$100,000 = 0.80 = 80%. In similar fashion only this time working in the other direction, if we are purchasing a home for $145,000 and we are getting a 75% loan to value mortgage, $145,000 \times 0.75 = $108,750$, we will be borrowing $108,750 in the form of a mortgage loan.

One minus the loan-to-value ratio is the equity-to-value ratio. If you think of the total value of the home as 1, or 100%, and your loan to value ratio is 80%, then your equity-to-value ratio must be 20%, 100% − 80% = 20%. This emphasizes the concept that the market value of the property is made up of equity and debt, where debt is the mortgage on the home. The difference between the market value of the home and the mortgage balance is your equity, as stated in Equation 2.9.

When you just purchase the home, your equity is the same as your down payment, and your mortgage balance is the amount you just borrowed from the bank in the form of a home mortgage.

Equation 2.9

$$\text{Equity} = \text{Market value} - \text{mortgage balance}$$

As time goes by, your equity increases because of two changes (see Equation 2.10). First of all, your equity increases because of any appreciation that takes place in the value of your home. This increase in market value gives you more equity. Second, your equity increases because the principal balance on your mortgage decreases over time because the principal is reduced each time you make a mortgage payment. (See Chapter 7.)

Equation 2.10

$$\uparrow \text{Equity} = \uparrow \text{Market value} - \downarrow \text{mortgage balance}$$

Equation 2.10 states that an increase in equity can come about as a result of an increase in market value and/or a decrease in mortgage balance. As long as your housing market experiences no housing price bubble, the first caveat will be true. And as long as you have an amortized mortgage and you continue to make your mortgage payments, the second caveat will be true.

Quiz for Chapter 2

1. Add the following sets of fractions. Where necessary, find the common denominators before adding. Reduce the answers to their simplest form where necessary.
    a. $1/4 + 3/4 = ?$
    b. $2/3 + 2/3 = ?$
    c. $1/5 + 3/5 = ?$
    d. $3/8 + 1/4 = ?$
    e. $5/4 + 1/3 = ?$
    f. $1/2 + 4/6 = ?$

2. Following the instructions from question 1, perform the following subtraction calculations.
    a. $3/4 - 1/4 = ?$
    b. $2/3 - 1/2 = ?$
    c. $6/7 - 3/4 = ?$
    d. $3/8 - 1/4 = ?$

3. Perform the indicated multiplication calculations.
    a. $3/4 \times 1/4 = ?$
    b. $2/3 \times 2/3 = ?$
    c. $3/8 \times 1/4 = ?$
    d. $5/4 \times 1/3 = ?$

4. Perform the indicated division calculations.
    a. $3/4 \div 1/4 = ?$
    b. $2/3 \div 2/3 = ?$
    c. $1/5 \div 3/5 = ?$
    d. $3/8 \div 1/4 = ?$
    e. $5/4 \div 1/3 = ?$
    f. $1/2 \div 4/6 = ?$

5. List the decimal equivalent of the following fractions and mixed numbers.
    a. $3/4 = ?$
    b. $2/3 = ?$
    c. $1/5 = ?$
    d. $1\,1/2 = ?$

e. $2\,1/4 = ?$

f. $4\,3/4 = ?$

6. List the percentages represented by those same fractions and mixed numbers in question 5.

7. Sylvia purchased a home earlier this year for $167,750 and took out a mortgage for $142,375 at 8% for 30 years. What was the loan-to-value ratio on the mortgage, and what was her down payment as a percentage of the purchase price?

   a. 75%, 25%

   b. 85%, 15%

   c. 90%, 10%

   d. 85%, 10%

8. How much equity did Sylvia have in her home on the day of closing in question 7?

   a. $142,375

   b. $167,750

   c. $25,375

   d. $16,775

9. Your brother Jake just sold his house for $220,000 and netted $206,800 on the sale. What was the commission rate that he paid his broker?

   a. 5%

   b. 6%

   c. 7%

   d. 7.5%

10. Jake, in question 9, had purchased his house only one year earlier. He purchased the house for $215,686. What rate of appreciation had he earned in that one year?

    a. 5%

    b. 4%

    c. 3%

    d. 2%

3 CHAPTER

Commissions, Growth Rates, and Net Proceeds

Every Seller Has a Price

Commissions, growth rates, and net proceeds all have one thing in common. They either begin with or end with some sort of percentage. A percentage is a value given in an amount per hundred. One percent is 1 of 100 parts. Five percent is 5 of 100 parts. Fifty percent of a candy bar is 50/100ths, or 1/2 of the candy bar. A 7% commission is 7/100ths of the selling price of the house. In this chapter you will become familiar with decimals and percentages (including commissions and growth rates) and with calculating the net proceeds from a sale.

Broker/Salesperson's Commissions

The classic percentage calculation that most people can relate to, whether you are a broker, salesperson, buyer, or seller, is the commission. The sales commission is generally a percentage of the sale or exchange price of a piece of real estate. The commission could also be a percentage of the monthly or annual rental rate of a piece of property in the case of a property manager.

To facilitate the commission calculation, it helps to convert the commission percentage to its decimal equivalent.

PERCENTAGE TO DECIMAL

A percentage can be converted to its decimal equivalent, as explained in Chapter 2, by taking the decimal point and shifting it two places to the left and dropping the percent sign, as shown in Equation 3.1.

Equation 3.1

$$6.5\% = 0.065$$

Once the percentage has been converted to its decimal equivalent, you can begin to calculate the dollar value of the commission, given a certain sale price.

MULTIPLICATION USING DECIMALS

To calculate the dollar value of the commission, you simply multiply the decimal equivalent of the commission times the sale price, as illustrated in Equation 3.2.

Equation 3.2

$$\text{Commission rate} \times \text{sale price} = \text{Commission amount}$$

If the sale price of a home is $175,000 and the commission rate is 7%, convert the commission to the decimal equivalent, 7% = 0.07 and multiply the decimal equivalent times the sale price as shown in Equation 3.3. Use Equation 2.8 (from Chapter 2):

Equation 3.3

$$\text{Percent} \times \text{whole} = \text{Part}$$

$$0.07 \times \$175,000 = \$12,250 = \text{Gross commission}$$

Given a commission rate of 7% and a sale price of $175,000, the resulting commission is equal to $12,250.

NET PROCEEDS

To arrive at the net proceeds (before mortgage payoff and other expenses) that the seller would receive after the commission is paid, simply subtract the commission amount from the sale price, as illustrated in Equation 3.4.

Equation 3.4

$$\text{Sale price} - \text{commission amount} = \text{Net proceeds}$$

Using the dollar amounts and commission rate that were used in Equation 3.3, the net proceeds are stated in Equation 3.5.

Equation 3.5

$$\$175,000 - \$12,250 = \$162,750$$

Given a sale price of $175,000 and a commission rate of 7%, we have illustrated that the commission amount would be $12,250 and the net proceeds to the seller after the commission has been paid would be $162,750.

SHORTCUT TO NET PROCEEDS

A second method of calculating the net proceeds from the sale is to take 1 minus the commission rate and multiply that resulting percentage, or decimal equivalent, by the sale price. Again, using the sale price and commission rate used above, the shortcut calculation of the net proceeds is illustrated in Equation 3.6.

Equation 3.6

$$(1 - 0.07) \times \$175,000 = 0.93 \times \$175,000 = \$162,750$$

As the equation states, take 1 minus 7%, or $1 - 0.07$, and multiply that resulting 0.93 by the sale price of \$175,000, and you get exactly the same net proceeds of \$162,750 that you calculated in Equations 3.3 and 3.5. In effect, the multiplication problem from Equation 3.3 and the subtraction problem from Equation 3.5 have been combined into the single Equation 3.6.

Commission Splits

When real estate brokers and salespersons have a cooperating sale with another brokerage firm, the commission is typically split between the two firms. That split may be 50-50, with 50% of the commission going to each firm, or it may be 55-45 with 55% going to one firm (usually the listing firm) and 45% going to the other (or selling) firm. The commission split arrangements can vary depending on local custom.

If you had a cooperative sale with a \$195,000 sale price and a 6% gross commission, and the firms were on a 55-45 split, the commission would look like this. Multiply the sale price of \$195,000 by the commission rate of 6% and get a gross commission of \$11,700, as shown in Equation 3.7

Equation 3.7

$$\$195,000 \times 0.06 = \$11,700 = \text{Gross commission}$$

As shown in Equation 3.8, the listing firm would receive 55% of that, or \$6,435.

Equation 3.8

$$\$11,700 \times 0.55 = \$6,435$$

The selling firm would get 45% of the gross commission, or \$5,265. This amount may be obtained by multiplying the gross commission by 0.45 or simply subtracting the listing firm's commission from the gross commission. Both calculations are illustrated in Equation 3.9.

Equation 3.9

$$\$11,700 \times 0.45 = \$5,265 = \$11,700 - \$6,435$$

The commission split does not affect the homeowner typically. The brokers would work out those details.

Let's try a practice problem. You have just received your real estate salesperson's license, and your first day on the job you sell a small house for $125,000. The house was listed by a broker across town at a 6% commission rate. Brokers in your community are on a 50-50% commission split arrangement on cooperative sales. Your broker pays you 60% of all commission dollars you bring into the shop. How much will you earn from this transaction? First you find the gross commission amount by multiplying the sale price by the commission rate, $125,000 × 0.06 = $7,500. Then you multiply the gross commission by the 50% for the split with the listing broker, $7,500 × 0.50 = $3,750. You then multiply that amount by the 60% that your broker has agreed to pay you, $3,750 × 0.60 = $2,250. So you have earned $2,250 from this particular transaction.

Graduated Commissions

For transactions involving larger property values, the commission will sometimes be calculated on a graduated scale; this is sometimes called a *tiered commission*. That is, the first so many dollars of sale price will have a commission rate of X%, and for additional sale price over and above that amount the commission rate may be Y%. There may even be three or more different tiers of commission rates used for properties with very large values. The average commission rate would then be the total gross commission divided by the sale price.

Let's look at a small office property with a sale price of $950,000. The broker and seller have agreed that the commission rate will be 7% on the first $300,000 of sale price, 6% on the next $600,000 of sale price, and 5% on any sale price in excess of $900,000. If the building sells for $925,000 what will be the amount of the commission?

The solution is summarized in Equation 3.10.

Equation 3.10

Commission = ($300,000 × 0.07) + ($600,000 × 0.06) + ($25,000 × 0.05)

Commission = $21,000 + $36,000 + $1,250 = $58,250

The gross commission on the sale of the property for $925,000 with the graduated commission as stated would be $58,250. The average commission rate would be the total gross commission divided by the sale price in the transaction. The average commission rate on the transaction would be 6.3%, as is illustrated in Equation 3.11:

Average commission = Total gross commission/sale price.

This results in Equation 3.11.

Equation 3.11

Average commission = $58,250/$925,000 = 0.063 = 6.3%

Average Growth Rates

Two types of growth rates are addressed in this chapter: average growth rates and compound growth rates. Average growth rates are just that; they are the result of a simple arithmetic average. This rate does not take into consideration any compounding effect. Before looking at a multiyear growth rate, we should first address the single-period or single-year growth rate.

SINGLE-YEAR GROWTH RATES

To calculate a growth rate for a single period or single year, take the ending value minus the beginning value and divide that result by the beginning value. It may help to think in terms of prices. Let's call the beginning price P_0, meaning the price at time period 0 or the price today, and the ending price we'll call P_1, or the price at the end of the first period. The growth rate calculation is shown in Equation 3.12.

Equation 3.12

$$(P_1 - P_0)/P_0 = \text{Growth rate}$$

This is the calculation for a one-period growth rate, say a one-year rate. If you are looking for the growth rate in the value of your home and we know that last year at this time that the home was worth $185,000 and today it is worth $192,400, the calculation of the one-year growth rate would look like Equation 3.13.

Equation 3.13

($192,400 − $185,000)/$185,000 = $7,400/$185,000 = 0.04 or 4%

You see that the single-year growth rate in value for a beginning value of $185,000 and an ending value of $192,400 is 4%. Try this additional example on your own, and then come back to check your answer.

Your neighbor purchased her home one year ago for $167,500, and today it is worth $175,000. What has been her one-year growth rate in value, sometimes referred to as a one-year appreciation rate? You'll find the solution in Equation 3.14.

Equation 3.14

$$(\$175,000 - \$167,500)/\$167,500 = \$7,500/\$167,500 = 0.045 = 4.5\%$$

SHORTCUT TO ONE-YEAR GROWTH RATE

A shortcut to a one-year growth rate looks like Equation 3.15. Take the ending price, P_1, and divide it by the beginning price, P_0. The resulting answer is equal to 1 plus the growth rate. So if we subtract the 1 from the right-hand side of the equation and then convert the decimal in the resulting answer to its percentage equivalent, we have the growth rate.

Equation 3.15

$$P_1/P_0 = 1 + \text{growth rate}$$

If you plug the dollar values from the previous calculation into Equation 3.15, this results in Equation 3.16.

Equation 3.16

$$\$175,000/\$167,500 = 1.045, \text{ then}$$

$$1.045 - 1 = .045 = 4.5\%$$

By using the shortcut method, we were able to arrive at exactly the same answer that was obtained in Equation 3.14. (Additional quiz problems can be found at the end of the chapter.)

MULTIYEAR GROWTH RATES

Multiyear average growth-rate calculations start out the same as the single-year calculation. Take the ending value (P_2) divided by the beginning value (P_0) and divide the answer by the beginning value, P_0. If it is a two-year growth period, simply divide the answer by 2 to get the annual growth rate. Take a home that sold today for $205,000 and was purchased two years ago for $195,000. What is the average annual growth rate in value? Refer to Equation 3.17 for the solution.

Equation 3.17

$$(\$205,000 - \$195,000)/\$195,000 = \$10,000/\$195,000 = 0.0513, \text{ then}$$

$$0.0513/2 = 0.0257 = 2.57\%$$

Using the shortcut method from Equation 3.15, the calculation looks like Equation 3.18.

Equation 3.18

$$\$205,000/\$195,000 = 1.0513, \text{ then}$$

$$1.0513 - 1 = 0.0513, \text{ then}$$

$$0.0513/2 = 0.0257 = 2.57\%$$

Both methods indicate that the average annual growth rate was 2.57% per year. Use the method that feels most comfortable to you.

COMPOUND GROWTH RATES

Compound growth-rate calculations depend on the use of time value of money (TVM) calculations. (Since this is the case and TVM is not covered until Chapter 6, compound growth rates are addressed in Chapter 8.)

Selling Price and Required Net Proceeds

The seller of a home is interested with how much money he or she will have left after paying the broker's commission. This amount is often referred to as the *net proceeds from the sale*. In Chapter 8, you will see that another way to describe net proceeds includes the deduction of selling expenses and mortgage payoff. However, in this chapter, we define net proceeds as the amount the seller has after paying just the commission. If the seller has a specific net proceeds amount in mind, it is possible to calculate the needed sale price which will result in that specific net proceeds amount from a home sale. To arrive at this value, we make use of one of the part, percent, whole equations from Chapter 2.

Specifically, use Equation 2.7 which stated that part/percent = whole. In this case the net proceeds are equal to the part, the percent is equal to the quantity (1 minus the commission rate), and the sale price is equal to the whole. The reason that we divide by the quantity (1 minus the commission rate), rather than the commission rate itself, is that the part in this case is what is left over *after* we've paid the commission. Thus, we take the net proceeds divided by the quantity (1 minus the commission rate), and the resulting answer is equal to the sale price. This process is illustrated in Equation 3.19.

Equation 3.19

$$\text{Net proceeds}/(1 - \text{commission rate}) = \text{Sale price}$$

Let's say that a seller wants to net $150,000 from a sale, before mortgage payoff and other expenses, and that he is going to have to pay a 6% brokerage commission. If that is the case, simply plug the numbers into Equation 3.19, which results in Equation 3.20. Once again, notice that Equation 3.19 is a variation on a theme of the part, percent, whole Figure 2.1 from Chapter 2 and the accompanying Equation 2.7.

Equation 3.20

$$\$150,000/(1 - 0.06) = \$150,000/0.94 = \$159,574.47$$

In order for the seller to net at least $150,000 from the sale, the home must sell for at least $159,574.47. Intuition might tell a person that we should just take the $150,000 times 6%, and that amount added to the $150,000 should give us the necessary sale price. Let's try that and see what we get. $150,000 × 0.06 = $9,000. That added to the $150,000 gives us a projected sale price of $159,000.

Take that sale price and calculate the commission due by multiplying it by 6% ($159,000 × 0.06 = $9,540). If we subtract that commission from the sale price we get a net proceeds ($159,000 − $9,540 = $149,460) which is less than the required $150,000. However, if you take the $159,574.47 × 0.06, you get a commission of $9,574.47. If you subtract that from the $159,574.47, you do, in fact, end up with net proceeds of $150,000.

The list price of the property will depend on many market and marketing factors that the broker and seller will have to take into consideration. All we know for sure is that the property must sell for at least $159,574.47 if the seller is to net $150,000 after paying the 6% commission.

Let's try an additional problem of this type. A coworker of yours has told her broker that she needs to achieve net proceeds from the sale of her house of $110,000 before mortgage payoff and other expenses. The broker and seller decide on a 7% commission for the sale of her home. The minimum selling price that is needed for her to net at least $110,000 is illustrated in Equation 3.21.

Equation 3.21

$$\$110,000/(1 - 0.07) = \$110,000/0.93 = \$118,279.57$$

You know that the $110,000 needs to be at least 93% of the sale price because she needs the $110,000 after the 7% commission has been paid. Equation 3.21 tells us that the home must sell for at least $118,279.57 in order for your coworker to net her required amount of $110,000 before mortgage payoff and other expenses.

Quiz for Chapter 3

1. John decided to sell his condo in Honolulu and contacted a broker to determine what it might be worth in today's market and how large a commission he might have to pay. The broker did a market analysis of the condo and determined that it would probably sell for about $475,000. The broker and John agreed on a 6% commission to be paid upon a successful closing on the condo sale. How many dollars will John have to pay the broker at the closing if the condo sells for $475,000?
   a. $33,250
   b. $28,500
   c. $23,750
   d. $30,875

2. What will John's net proceeds be after the commission has been paid on the transaction in question 1?
   a. $28,500
   b. $441,750
   c. $446,500
   d. $451,250

3. Tara recently obtained her real estate salesperson's license. She sold her first house for $225,000. The seller had agreed to pay a 7% commission on the sale. The house was listed with a cooperating broker, and the custom in that market is that commissions are split 50-50 between the listing and selling brokers. Tara is on a 50-50 split with her broker. How much does Tara take home as compensation for her first real estate sale?
   a. $15,750
   b. $7,875
   c. $3,937.50
   d. $3,375

4. After Tara's first sale her broker tells her that in the future her split will be 60-40 because she is doing such a good job. Her next sale is for a sale price of $195,000, and she is both the listing agent and the selling agent. The seller paid a 6% commission. What is the amount of this pay check?
   a. $7,020
   b. $3,510
   c. $2,925
   d. $8,190

5. Tony is a commercial real estate broker. He just sold a small office build-
    ing for $1.5 million. He is told that the commission is 6% on the first
    $500,000, 4% on the next $500,000 and 2% on the last $500,000. What
    is Tony's commission in dollars if he is to receive the total amount?
    a. $90,000
    b. $30,000
    c. $50,000
    d. $60,000

6. What is the average commission rate on the transaction in question 5?
    a. 6%
    b. 5%
    c. 4%
    d. 3.3%

7. Stef bought her house exactly one year ago for $164,500. She had an
    appraisal done, and the appraiser told her that the home is currently
    worth $171,000. What was the annual growth rate in value, or the annual
    appreciation rate, rounded to the nearest percent?
    a. 3%
    b. 4%
    c. 5%
    d. 6%

8. Stef, from question 7, finds out that next year her house will be worth
    $179,700. What is the average annual appreciation rate that her home
    will experience, rounded to the nearest 1/10 of a percent?
    a. 4.0%
    b. 4.6%
    c. 4.8%
    d. 5.0%

9. Tom, a local real estate broker, goes out to a listing presentation with
    a seller and finds that the seller would like to receive net proceeds of
    $144,000 from the sale of his house after the commission has been paid.
    If Tom intends to charge the seller a 5% commission, what is the min-
    imum price the home must sell for in order for the seller to achieve the
    desired net proceeds?
    a. $151,200
    b. $144,000
    c. $153,191
    d. $151,578

10. On Tom's next listing presentation he finds that the seller needs to net $175,000 after paying a 5.5% commission. What is the minimum sale price the home must bring in order to meet the seller's needs?

a. $185,185

b. $184,625

c. $183,750

d. $184,210

Legal Descriptions and Lot Size

Does This Drawing Make My Backyard Look Big?

Land is defined as the earth's surface, everything above, and everything below (to the center of the earth), and everything put on the earth's surface by nature. (See Figure 4.1.)

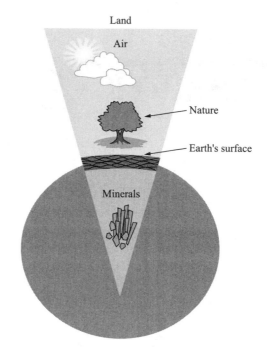

Figure 4.1 Land illustrated

Legal Descriptions

A *legal description* is a precise way of describing a parcel of land that would be upheld in a court of law. There are three basic forms of legal descriptions that are commonly used in the United States. They are metes and bounds, the government (or rectangular) survey system, and the subdivision plat system.

Metes and Bounds

The metes and bounds system is the oldest form of legal description used in the United States and was brought over by the European settlers. It makes use of a system of measurements and boundaries to describe a parcel of land. If you squint your eyes just right, it looks like "measurements and boundaries" doesn't it? (I like to think it is old English for measurements and boundaries.)

The description first measures distance and direction away from some monument. That monument may be something as precise as a surveyor's monument put in the earth's surface or something as imprecise as the old oak tree, the large block of granite, or the intersection of two roads. The nonsurveyor's monuments can be imprecise and can change over time. The old oak tree can be hit by lightening and decay away over the years. The intersection can change when roads are widened. Surveyor's monuments are of course preferred, but other monuments do indeed show up in metes and bounds descriptions.

Once you have a monument, you then measure distance and direction away from this monument to establish a beginning point. From that point of beginning you again use distance and direction to describe the perimeter of the parcel of land. When the method was created, it was described as a plan for a walk around the perimeter of the parcel. This form of legal description can be quite lengthy and occasionally inaccurate. I have seen metes and bounds descriptions that are in excess of two pages in length. The source of the inaccuracy is the nonpermanent nature of some types of monuments. If the monument in question is the old oak tree, the large block of granite, or the intersection of two roads, as mentioned previously, these monuments could change over time. As the location of these monuments change over time, so would the accuracy of the legal description.

EXAMPLE 4.1

Figure 4.1 illustrates a parcel of land that you have purchased. You have decided to place a split-rail fence around it, and the farm supply store has quoted you a cost of $4.50 per lineal foot for the materials. What is the price of the materials if you intend to enclose the entire lot in fencing? I'm thinking that the appearance of the sides may not be to scale in Figure 4.2, so focus on the linear feet as they are stated. There are two dimensions you need to fill in, but you do not have enough information to do that.

Equation 4.1

$$\text{Cost} = (60 + 30 + 20 + 30 + 80 + 60) \times \$4.50 = 280 \times \$4.50 = \$1,260$$

Beginning at the top dimension and going clockwise, the dimensions are 60 feet by 30 feet by 20 feet by 30 feet by 80 feet by 60 feet for a total perimeter lineal footage of 280 feet. If you take 280 feet times the $4.50 per lineal foot cost, you get a total cost of $1,260. Now what is the square footage of the lot in Figure 4.2? The solution is in Equation 4.2.

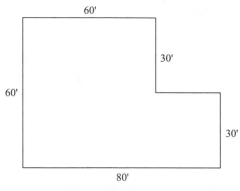

Figure 4.2   Lot size 1

Equation 4.2

$$\text{Area} = (60 \times 60) + [(80 - 60) \times 30] = 3{,}600 + (20 \times 30) = 3{,}600 + 600$$

$$= 4{,}200 \text{ square feet}$$

We have basically two shapes, a 60×60 square and a rectangle that is 20 by 30. This results in a total square footage of 4,200 square feet.

EXAMPLE 4.2

Your metes and bounds description reads like the following:

> Beginning at a point formed by the intersection of the northerly side of Georgia Avenue and the easterly side of 27th St., thence east 100 feet, thence north at a 90 degree angle for 50 feet, thence west at a 90 degree angle for 75 feet, thence back to the point of beginning in a straight line.

The parcel is illustrated in Figure 4.3. What is its square footage?

Equation 4.3

$$\text{Area} = (75 \times 50) + (50 \times 25)^{1/2} = 3{,}750 + 625 = 4{,}375$$

Once again, divide the parcel into two shapes. This time you have a rectangle and a triangle. The rectangle is 50 feet by 75 feet, and the triangle has

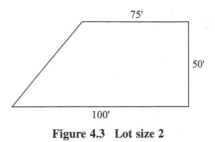

Figure 4.3   Lot size 2

a 25-foot base and a height of 50 feet. The total square footage of the parcel is 4,375 square feet.

EXAMPLE 4.3

Kate purchased the lot next to the little palace she lives in which is shown in Figure 4.4. As a favor to her husband, she decided to build a tennis court on it. If she needs to cover the entire lot with a six-inch layer of concrete, how many cubic feet of concrete will she need to complete the tennis court?

Equation 4.4

$$\text{Concrete needed} = 125 \times 95 \times 0.5 = 5{,}937.5 \text{ cubic feet}$$

If you take the depth of the lot times the width of the lot times 0.5, or one-half of a foot, you find that Kate will need 5,937.5 cubic feet of concrete. How many cubic yards will she need? (Concrete is typically sold in cubic yards.)

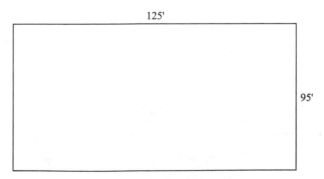

Figure 4.4   Tennis court

Government Survey System

The *government survey system* was developed by Thomas Jefferson around the time of the Louisiana Purchase. This system (also known as the *rectangular survey system* or the *township and range system*) is based on a set of imaginary lines put on the earth's surface, much like the lines of longitude and latitude, only these are referred to as principal meridians and base lines. Principal meridians run in a north-south direction, and base lines run east-west, as shown in Figure 4.5

The map in Figure 4.5 indicates the location of the principal meridians and baselines that are used for measurement in the government survey system. You will note that those states that appear without shading in the map are not covered by this system. Those include basically the original 13 colonies plus a few more, including Texas. These states were basically fully described using the metes and bounds system before the government survey system was developed.

The government survey system makes use of these lines by measuring distance and direction away from these lines to describe our property's location. The principal meridians are spaced 6 miles apart. The baselines are also spaced 6 miles apart,

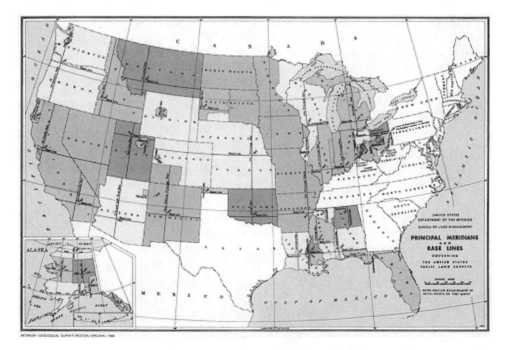

Figure 4.5 Principal meridians and baselines

Source of map: U.S. Bureau of Land Management,
http://www.blm.gov/cadastral/meridians/meridians.htm

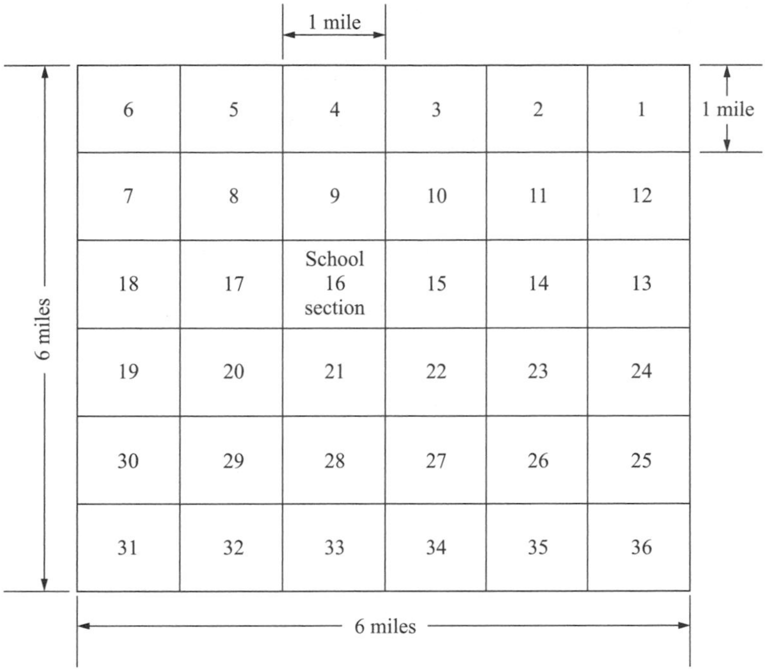

Figure 4.6 Sections in a township

thus creating parcels of land that are 6 miles by 6 miles, or 36 square miles in size. These 36-square-mile parcels are referred to as townships.

These townships are divided into 1-square-mile parcels of land referred to as sections. Thus, there are 36 sections in a township, as illustrated in Figure 4.6. The sections are always numbered in the same way with section number 1 located in the northeast corner of the township and section number 36 in the southeast corner of the township. Historically, section 16 was set aside for school purposes.

The section may be divided into quarters and halves to describe parcels of land smaller than 1 square mile. A section contains 640 acres of land, hence a quarter section contains 160 acres, and a quarter of a quarter section contains 40 acres. (Figure 4.7 contains a sample section which has been divided into quarter sections and smaller divisions.)

Relevant measures to keep in mind relative to the government survey system, as well as legal descriptions in general, include the following:

1 mile = 5,280 feet   1 section = 1 square mile = 640 acres
1 acre = 43,560 square feet   1 township = 36 sections
1 furlong = 1/8 of a mile

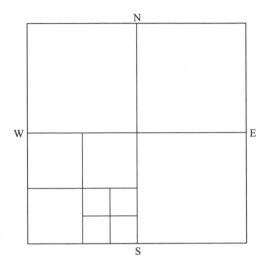

Figure 4.7 Section divided into quarters

EXAMPLE 4.4

Locate on Figure 4.7 the following tract of land—the SE $1/4$ of the SE $1/4$ of the SW $1/4$. How many acres are in the tract of land? It contains $640 \times 1/4 \times 1/4 \times 1/4 = 10$ acres of land. Locate the N $1/2$ of the SW $1/4$ in Figure 4.7. How many acres does it contain? It contains $640 \times 1/4 \times 1/2 = 80$ acres.

Subdivision Plat System

The *subdivision plat system* is also called the *lot and block system*. Within an urban area, it would become unwieldy to continue breaking the description of a 75-foot by 150-foot lot down using the SW $1/4$ of the SE $1/4$ of the SE $1/4$ and so on, until we get down to this lot size. As a result the subdivision plat system was developed. When subdividers or developers create a residential or commercial development, they must follow a series of steps to establish the subdivision. They must have the land surveyed by a licensed surveyor who provides for the creation of a subdivision plat drawing, or subdivision plan. The drawing will contain the lot dimensions, the street widths, the setbacks, and other dimensions within the subdivision.

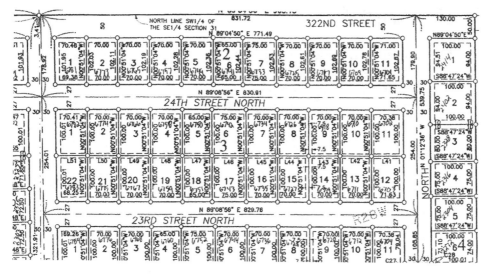

Figure 4.8 Plat drawing

Source: St. Cloud, MN, assessor's office

In order to be recorded, the plat drawing (see Figure 4.8) must be approved by the city, town, or village in which the land is located, to verify that the lot sizes, setbacks, and street widths are within the standards for the municipality. The developer must then verify that there are no outstanding real estate taxes or special assessments against any of the property in question. As a final step, the plat drawing has to be notarized. This finally allows the developer to record the subdivision plat drawing at the county recorder's office, thus informing the world that the subdivision exists. The land is divided into lots and blocks. The blocks are the larger division of land, containing approximately 8–40 different lots for residential or commercial development.

An example of a lot and block description would be: "Lot 1, Block 3, Park Manor Addition, Your County, MN, in the S 1/2 of the NW 1/4 of the SW 1/4 of section 12, Township 25 North Range 10 West of the 4th Principal Meridian." While this is the complete description, the description that is typically used would be "Lot 1, Block 3, Park Manor Addition in Your County, Your State." The county recorder is not going to allow you to record a plat with the name Park Manor Addition if there is already a Park Manor Addition recorded in the county because that would obviously cause confusion. Since that is the case, the government survey system information is no longer necessary.

Quiz for Chapter 4

1. Given the information in Figure 4.8, what is the square footage of Lot 1, Block 3?
   a. 6,500
   b. 7,000
   c. 7,500
   d. 7,041

2. If all of the lots in Block 3 sell for the same price of $35,000, which lot sells for the highest price per square foot?
   a. 1
   b. 5
   c. 6
   d. 7

3. How many lots are contained in Block 3 in Figure 4.8?
   a. 6
   b. 11
   c. 22
   d. 4

4. In Figure 4.7, locate the NE 1/4 of the SE 1/4 of the SW 1/4 of the section. How many acres does the parcel contain?
   a. 640
   b. 160
   c. 40
   d. 10

5. Again looking at Figure 4.7, how many acres are contained in the NW 1/4 of the SW 1/4 and the S 1/2 of the NW 1/4?
   a. 40
   b. 120
   c. 160
   d. 80

6. Describe the dimensions of the parcel of land detailed in question 5 above, starting with the northern side of the parcel.
   a. 2,640 feet × 1,320 feet × 1,320 feet × 1,320 feet × 2,640 feet
   b. 5,280 feet × 2,640 feet × 2,640 feet × 2,640 feet × 5,280 feet

c. 2 furlongs × 1 furlong × 1 furlong × 1 furlong × 2 furlongs

d. 80 acres × 40 acres × 40 acres × 40 acres × 80 acres

7. Li has just purchased sections 1, 2, 11, and 12 of the township illustrated in Figure 4.5. How many acres of land did she purchase?

 a. 640 acres

 b. 1,280 acres

 c. 2,560 acres

 d. 5,120 acres

8. If Li purchased the land in question 7 with a 40% cash down payment, how large was the loan she took out from the bank, if she bought the land for $2,000 per acre?

 a. Less than $1 million

 b. Between $1 million and $2 million

 c. Between $2 million and $3 million

 d. More than $3 million

9. Given the dimensions in Figure 4.9, shown below, what is the area of the lot in the diagram?

 a. 6,000 square feet

 b. 11,200 square feet

 c. 7,200 square feet

 d. 8,400 square feet

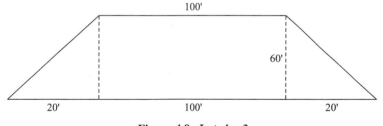

Figure 4.9 Lot size 3

10. If we were to make a bingo card out of the sections in a township in Figure 4.6 and put section 1 in the NE corner of the bingo card, which section would be the "free" space?

 a. 15

 b. 16

 c. 21

 d. 22

Real Estate Taxes

Hold On to Your Wallets!

There are basically two types of real estate taxes that are covered in this chapter. These are the property taxes and the taxes associated with real estate transactions. The taxes associated with real estate transactions are the state deed tax, sometimes called the real estate transfer tax, and the mortgage registration tax.

Property Tax

Property taxes are referred to as ad valorem taxes, that is to say they are based on value. The tax levy, or the total amount of revenue that needs to be generated, is spread over the taxpayers based on the value of their individual property. The property tax is the method that local government uses to raise revenue to pay for schools, roads, police and fire protection, parks, libraries, and other local services.

Property taxes are based on two factors. The first of these is the annual budget of the taxing authority. That budget can be made up for many different services that need funding. This budget amount is called the *property tax levy*, or the total amount of revenue to be raised from property taxes.

Table 5.1 contains the items listed on a property tax statement for taxes payable in 2007. This indicates where the tax dollars of this particular taxpayer are going. While not a taxing authority budget as such, it does give a clear picture of where the county and local government dollars are being spent. All these items do not have dollar values listed on any one statement, and they may vary from county to county; and they certainly may vary in your state. However, the table does convey the magnitude of establishing the annual budget for the taxing authority.

The second factor in estimating tax liability is the assessed value of the property within the taxing authority's assessment area. The type of value that may show up on the property tax statement may vary. The type of value may be called appraised

Table 5.1   Sample tax statement

Budget item	$ Amount
County	$562.66
City or town	$130.28
State general tax	$0.00
School district	
1. Voter-approved levies	$188.94
2. Other local levies	$190.90
Special taxing districts	
1. Metropolitan special tax	$27.56
2. Other special tax districts	$4.00
3. Tax increment	$0.00
4. Fiscal disparity	$0.00
Nonschool voter-approved levies	$0.00
Total property tax before special assessments	$1,104.34
Special assessments added	
City street curbing	$30.00
Total property tax + special assessments	$1,134.34

value, assessed value, market value, estimated market value, limited market value, or taxable market value. All these won't show up on a single tax statement but a couple of them might. I will use a Minnesota tax statement as an example in this chapter. Currently, on the Minnesota tax statement we have estimated market value and taxable market value. The two values are very often the same. If they are not the same, the estimated market value would be larger than the taxable market value, sometimes called the *limited market value*. The reason the estimated market value may be greater than the taxable market value is that value increases were capped at a certain percentage for a number of years, and there may have been increases in the estimated market value that didn't find their way into the taxable market value.

The individuals who estimate market values and assessed values for city and county government taxing authorities are called *assessors*. Assessors are simply appraisers working for a governmental entity. There are often separate parallel licensing processes for public assessors and private appraisers.

While the paragraph relating to the second factor in estimating tax liability may sound a little confusing, it is just the tip of the iceberg when it comes to understanding property taxes as a whole. Maybe property taxes in Minnesota are more confusing than taxes in your state.

TAX RATE AND MILL RATE

Let's move on to what is referred to as the *tax rate*. The tax rate can be stated a number of different ways. Some states refer to it in a percentage format, or dollars per hundred. Other states use the term *mill rate*. One mill equals $1/1,000$ of a dollar, or a tenth of a cent per dollar. Still other states use measure of dollars per thousand. In order to obtain the tax rate or mill rate, we need the aforementioned tax levy and the total assessed value within the taxing district.

Equation 5.1

Tax rate = Budgeted revenue ÷ total assessed value of all property

Let's try an example. Given a revenue budget for the city and county of $50 million and total assessed value for property in the taxing district of $400 million, what is the implied tax rate for the district?

Equation 5.2

Tax rate = $10,000,000 ÷ $400,000,000 = 0.025 = 2.5%

In many states we would then just take that tax rate times the assessed value of the individual property, and that would result in the tax liability. If we have a property that has an assessed value of $175,000, the tax liability falls out in Equation 5.3. If this example was stated in mills, we would have 25 mills times $175,000/1,000 or 25 × $175 = $4,375. The answer is the same whether your state uses the term mill rate or it uses a tax rate in percentage form.

Equation 5.3

$$\text{Tax liability} = \$175{,}000 \times 0.025 = \$4{,}375$$

If a community wanted to reduce the tax rate, it could encourage development to increase the denominator or the total assessed value. That would result in a lower tax rate. Of course more developed land will result in greater budgetary requirements, so it wouldn't be a direct reduction in the rate. As an example, if the city encouraged and received another $50 million in assessed value through additional development, the tax rate would go down to 2.2% if there was no increase in the budget.

Equation 5.4

$$\text{Tax rate} = \$10{,}000{,}000 \div \$450{,}000{,}000 = 0.022 = 2.2\%$$

This would bring the tax liability of our $175,000 house down to $3,850. That would be a decrease of 12%.

Equation 5.5

$$\text{Tax liability} = \$175{,}000 \times 0.022 = \$3{,}850$$

$$\text{Reduction} = \$4{,}375 - \$3{,}850 = \$525/\$4{,}375 = 0.12 = 12\%$$

Taxpayers often assume that if their assessed value goes up, their tax will automatically go up also. That is not the case as long as everybody's assessed value goes up. If all property values go up, then the tax rate will go down to compensate for that increase. There are only two ways for your property taxes to go up. Either your assessed value has to increase faster than everybody else's in your tax district, or your local and country governments are spending more money. So, either the numerator goes up in Equation 5.3, or your assessed value goes up and all other values stay the same so that the tax rate is virtually unchanged but it is multiplied against your higher assessed value to give you a greater tax liability.

MINNESOTA EXAMPLE

The example here is neither advocating the Minnesota property tax system nor is it an endorsement or request for you to move to Minnesota. It is just another

Table 5.2   Home tax liability

Tax inputs	Values
Taxable market value	$250,000
× Tax capacity %	×0.01
Tax capacity	$2,500
× Tax rate	×1.02268
Base tax	$2,556.70
− Homestead exemption	− $147.40
Tax liability	$2,409.30

example of how property taxes may be determined. Table 5.2 contains the relevant calculations of the tax liability for a $250,000 home.

First the assessed value is multiplied by the tax capacity percentage. In the case of this home in St. Cloud, the tax capacity percentage is 1% or 0.01. That results in a tax capacity of $2,500. That is now multiplied by the tax rate of 1.02268 which results in a base tax of $2,556.70. Minnesota has a homestead credit if you own and occupy your own personal residence. The maximum homestead credit is $304 per year on a home with a value of $76,000 and then begins to be reduced beyond that value. The calculation for the homestead credit for this home is contained in Equation 5.6.

Equation 5.6

$$\text{Homestead credit reduction} = (\$250,000 - \$76,000) \times 0.0009 = \$156.60$$

$$\text{Homestead credit} = \$304 - \$156.60 = \$147.40$$

The homestead credit is then deducted from the base tax to give the final tax liability of $2,409.30. There are several other tax credits and adjustments that apply to special interest situations but this will suffice for now.

Transaction Taxes

As mentioned at the beginning of this chapter there are taxes associated with the transfer of real estate—the state deed tax and the mortgage registration tax.

STATE DEED TAX

The state deed tax is the seller's expense in Minnesota. This tax is sometimes referred to as the state deed tax stamps because stamps are actually affixed to the deed based on the value of the transaction. The rate is currently $3.30 per $1,000 of the sale price. If you wanted to know how much a seller paid for a piece of property, you could go to the county recorder's office, look at a copy of the deed that was filed, and add up the value of the stamps.

Your brother has recently sold his home, and the closing will take place in two weeks. The house was listed for $220,000 for a five-week period, and then the price was reduced to $210,000 and was finally sold for $205,000. The buyer was taking out a $160,000 mortgage at 7% for 30 years. How much state deed tax will your brother have to pay at the closing in St. Paul?

Equation 5.7

$$\text{State deed tax} = 205 \times \$3.30 = \$676.50$$

The state deed tax on the transaction described above would be $676.50.

MORTGAGE REGISTRATION TAX

Whenever a new mortgage is recorded in Minnesota, a mortgage registration tax must be paid. The rate for the mortgage registration tax is $2.30 per $1,000 of new mortgage amount. The tax need not be paid in the case of a mortgage assumption because the tax has already been paid on that mortgage. How much mortgage registration tax has to be paid on the transaction mentioned in the paragraph directly preceding Equation 5.7? It is the buyer's expense to record the mortgage, and it is the buyer's expense to pay the mortgage registration tax.

Equation 5.8

$$\text{Mortgage registration tax} = \$2.30 \times 160 = \$368.00$$

Dave had been trying to sell his home in Minnesota for some time. His original listing price was $195,500. After three months he decided to reduce the asking price to $190,500. Three days later he had an offer for $193,700 which he accepted. The buyer was to take out an FHA mortgage for $175,500 to complete the purchase. The closing is this afternoon and Dave is wondering who pays the state deed tax and how much it will be, and who pays the mortgage registration tax and how much that will be. Punch some buttons and see what you come up with. Then look at Equations 5.9 for the solution.

Equation 5.9

$$\text{State deed tax} = 193.7 \times \$3.30 = \$639.21, \text{seller's expense}$$

$$\text{Mortgage registration tax} = 175.5 \times \$2.30 = \$403.65, \text{buyer's expense}$$

Quiz for Chapter 5

1. There are two major factors in determining the property tax rate. Which of the following items is one of those factors?
    a. Annual budget of the taxing authority
    b. State deed tax rate
    c. Mortgage registration tax rate
    d. The state annual budget

2. Which of the following is the second factor in determining property tax rates?
    a. The total limited market value of homes on your block
    b. The total assessed value of homes on your block
    c. The total assessed value of property in your taxing authority area
    d. The total assessed value of homes plus investment properties on your block

3. Budgeted revenue ÷ Total assessed value of all property is the formula for:
    a. Assessed value
    b. Tax rate
    c. Estimated market value
    d. Tax liability

4. You are buying a townhouse. The list price was $142,900, and you made an offer of $140,000 which the seller accepted. The mortgage you are taking out is for $138,000 to be amortized over 30 years at a 6.25% rate, and closing costs will come to $3,600. How much mortgage registration tax will you have to pay at the closing?
    a. $328.67
    b. $322.00
    c. $317.40
    d. $455.40

5. In the transaction described in question 4, how much state deed tax will the seller have to pay at the closing?
    a. $471.57
    b. $462.00
    c. $455.40
    d. $322.00

6. The authorized budget for your city and county for next year comes to $8.5 million. The total assessed value for the taxing authority area is $365 million. Your home has an assessed value of $163,000. What is the tax rate in your area for the coming year?
   a. 1.92%
   b. 2.33%
   c. 4.0%
   d. 2.43%

7. In question 6, what will your tax liability be?
   a. $3,129
   b. $3,797
   c. $6,520
   d. $3,960

8. Using the same criteria that are detailed above in the Minnesota example that is summarized in Table 5.2, what would the tax liability be on a home with an assessed value of $325,000? Use the same tax capacity and tax rate that you find in Table 5.2.
   a. $3,250
   b. $3,323.71
   c. $3,243.81
   d. $224.10

9. Using the same information from question 8, what is the amount of the homestead exemption?
   a. $304.00
   b. $79.90
   c. $224.10
   d. $76,000

10. Why is mortgage registration tax paid only when new mortgages are recorded and not for mortgage assumptions?
    a. Just because
    b. New mortgages are for larger dollar amounts than are mortgage assumptions
    c. It's Minnesota, for gosh sake
    d. Someone has already paid mortgage registration tax on an existing mortgage

Time Value of Money (TVM)

Six Equations That Will Change Your Life

Money has differing values over time. A dollar we receive today is not worth the same as a dollar that we receive five years from today. Since most people are thought to fit the definition of wealth-maximizing individuals, a dollar received today should have a greater value than a dollar we are to receive in five years. One explanation for this is that if we had the dollar today, we could set it aside in an interest-bearing account so that it could grow in value for that five-year period and have a much greater value at the end of the five years.

This chapter addresses the value of money over time and will enable you to calculate the value of money over time so that you can use these tools to analyze a mortgage, analyze a real estate investment opportunity, and analyze your retirement portfolio so that you can make the necessary allocations to maximize your retirement income. Stated quite simply, we look at *six equations that will change your life!* They will change your life because if you understand them, they give you command over financial calculations that banks make, that real estate brokers use, and that investors need to understand in order to adequately analyze investment opportunities.

Four Major Premises

The concept of time value of money is driven home by remembering four separate major premises. These major premises are referred to several times throughout this chapter as well as in other parts of the book; if you can master these four time value of money concepts, the financial world will be yours to work with and profit from.

1. The higher the discount rate, the lower the present value.
2. The sooner you get the money, the more its worth.
3. The principal balance at any point in time is equal to the present value of the remaining payments.
4. An investor will pay only the present value of all cash flows to be received, discounted at the required rate of return.

Future Value

The first of the six equations is the calculation of what is called the future value (FV) of a lump some, or single amount. Future value is either the amount that a sum today, which is called a present value (PV) will grow to in the future, or the value of some amount of money that is to be received in the future. Equation 6.1 is the mathematical calculation for converting a PV into a FV, or taking an amount of money today and compounding it forward to achieve its corresponding future value.

Equation 6.1

$$FV = PV (1 + r)^n$$

This equation says that we take the present value and multiply it by 1 plus the rate of interest, raised to the nth power based on the number of compounding periods. If it compounded for two periods, we square the $(1 + r)$; if it's three periods we cube it, and so on.

If raising values to a power makes you nervous, you can use Equation 6.2 because all of the values for the FVIF (future value interest factor) can be calculated using your financial calculator.

Equation 6.2

$$FV = PV (FVIF)$$

The FVIF can be calculated by putting a –1 in your financial calculator as the [PV], 5 as your [i/y], 3 [n] and then hitting [cpt] [FV]. You can use any interest rate and any number of periods. The calculator in fact renders the equations obsolete, but I have found that the students who understand the equations have a more complete understanding of the time value of money concept.

As an example, if you took $100 today and put it in a 5% account for three years and wanted to know what the value of the account would be at the end of those three years, your calculation would look like Equation 6.3.

Equation 6.3

$$FV = PV (FVIF_{3n,5\%}) = \$100(1.1576) = \$115.76$$

The future value is equal to the present value times the future value interest factor for 5% interest for 3 periods, or 3n. If you put 1 [+/−] [PV], 3 [n], 5 [i/y] in your financial calculator and [cpt] [FV], you will get a value of 1.1576; plugging that into the equation results in a future value of $115.76. Notice that the calculator operates in terms of cash inflows and cash outflows. The present value must be entered as a negative number for your future value to come out as a positive number. In order to make the present value negative, you must hit the [+/−] key after entering the amount that you want as a present value. If it doesn't bother you when you get a negative sign in your answer, then don't worry about using the [+/−] key on your input. However, when you input both the present value and the future value on a problem, you must have one positive and the other negative. Otherwise the calculator will give you an error message.

The same calculation can be made using a financial calculator. The keystrokes for the TI Business Analyst II Plus calculator would be as follows.

Solution 6.1

   100 [+/−] [PV]
   3 [n]
   5 [i/y] .>
   [cpt] [FV] 115.76

Prior to making the above calculation with your Texas Instruments financial calculator, you should make sure that the calculator is set on one compounding period per year. To do that, hit the [2nd] key followed by the [i/y] key. Your screen should look like this, P/Y = 1.00. The calculator is telling you it will use one compounding period per year. The alternative that could show up on the screen is P/Y = 12.00 which would be 12 compounding periods per year. While it seems that this setting would work well for monthly compounding problems, we work with a method that won't require us to change back and forth from 1 compounding period per year to 12 compounding periods per year, because invariably we forget to make the technical change and end up getting a bogus answer.

In order to change the calculator to one compounding period per year hit the [2nd] key again followed by the [enter] key, followed by 1, followed by the [enter] key again. Now the calculator is set to one compounding period per year. I have found it most convenient to always have the calculator set to one compounding period per year and to just make the needed adjustments when more compounding periods are required. All the calculator solutions in this book assume you have the calculator set to one compounding period per year.

If you did not get an answer of 115.76 the first time because you had the incorrect number of compounding periods set on your calculator, make the changes mentioned in the previous paragraph and try the problem again.

Let's look at my all-time favorite future problem. It may be your favorite problem too when we get done with it. Let's look at the best real estate deal ever struck in the United States. When I bring this up in class, it's usually the third one mentioned, and by "usually" I mean 95% of the time. The first one mentioned is usually the Louisiana Purchase. I say that it was a good deal, but not the best deal. Then Seward's Icebox, Alaska, is mentioned. Again, this is a good deal but not the best deal. The best real estate deal ever struck in the United States has to be the purchase of Manhattan by the Dutch. The supposed purchase price was $24 worth of beads. For those of you who doubt that it was the best deal, I worked it out on a cost per acre basis, and it was in fact the lowest purchase price. The assumption has always been that the Native Americans got robbed by the Dutch and were taken advantage of. Now, let's look at the transaction a little closer and see who got robbed. We can analyze the transaction from a time value of money standpoint and see how everyone did.

First of all, the deal took place in the year 1628, some 379 years ago. Let's take the $24 and compound it forward 379 years and see if the indicated value makes sense. The question is what rate of annual appreciation has taken place since the year 1628? Experts indicate that the average home in the United States has gone up by 4% per year over the last 50 years or so. I tend to think that Manhattan Island may appreciate faster than the average home. Let's use 8% for our calculation. The calculator keystrokes should look like this.

Solution 6.2

24 [+/−] [PV]

378 [n]

8 [i/y]

[cpt] [FV] 1.116386   14

The answer is in scientific notation. That 14 floating out to the right-hand side of the display means that we have to shift the decimal point 14 places to the right. That gives us an answer of $111,638,600,000,000. That reads about 111 trillion dollars! Does it seem reasonable that the land of Manhattan Island would be worth 111 trillion dollars? No, I don't think so either. The total U.S. land area is about 852.6 million acres. About half of that is farmed, and most of the rest is in forest, plains, and park lands.

If we use an optimistic $5,000 per acre, which is nearly twice the value of the most productive farmland, and apply that value to the entire 852.6 million acres, the total U.S. land value would only be $4.26 trillion. The logical conclusion then is that the Dutch overpaid for the property. What do you think it was worth? $11? Maybe $11.50 tops? If indeed there is anything wrong with the calculation, maybe it is the 8% appreciation rate that was used. Maybe from 1628 to 1629 it didn't go up by 8% in value. If we just reduce the appreciation rate from 8% to 4%, the ending value goes from $111 trillion down to $68.5 million!

Here is one final item in my favorite FV problem. When looking at the original answer of $111 trillion, how much of that is interest? That's right. Everything except for the $24 is interest. That's why, when someone asked Albert Einstein what the most powerful force in the world was, he didn't answer nuclear fission, he didn't answer nuclear fusion, he answered compound interest. If it's good enough for Al, it's good enough for me.

Present Value

The future value calculation tends to be the easiest for people to understand since most of us have put money into a savings account and watched it grow over time.

Somewhat less intuitive is the present value of a lump sum calculation. Rather than pushing money forward over time, as we do in the future value calculation, in the present value calculation we are bringing money back over time. While the future value calculation is called *compounding*, the present value calculation is referred to as *discounting*.

Let's say my grandmother offers me $115.76 in three years or some money today. Which should I take? Well, it depends on how much she is going to give me today. The equation for the calculation of a present value looks like Equation 6.4.

Equation 6.4

$$PV = FV/(1 = r)^n = FV \; (PVIF)$$

Hopefully you can see then that the PVIF is simply the reciprocal of the FVIF, or 1/FVIF. This means that both the compounding of FV calculations and the discounting of PV calculations are based on the same compound interest concept. In fact, all six equations that will change your life are based on the same compound interest basis.

Plugging our numbers into Equation 6.4, we get $100.00. The PVIF can be calculated by inputting a 1 [FV], 3 [n], 5 [i/y] and then hitting [cpt] [PV] which results in a value of 0.8615. To set the number of decimal places displayed, use the keystrokes [2nd] [Format] and then put in the number of decimal places you want displayed, followed by the [Enter] key. To get four decimal places, use [2nd] [Format] 4 [Enter].

Equation 6.5

$$PV = FV \; (PVIF) = \$115.76 \; (0.8639) = \$100.00$$

The calculator keystrokes for the calculation give us the same answer.

Solution 6.3

115.76 [FV]

3 [n]

5 [i/y]

[cpt] [PV] −100.00

Again we have shown that I would be indifferent to either $115.76 in three years or $100.00 today, if my required rate of return was 5%.

Let's try that same problem with one change. This time let's say that our required rate of return, or our discount rate, is 7%. In that case the calculator solution looks like this.

Solution 6.4

> 115.76 [FV]
>
> 3 [n]
>
> 7 [i/y]
>
> [cpt] [PV] −94.49

This illustrates the first major premise mentioned at the beginning of the chapter. The higher the discount rate, the lower the present value. This is important because it is just the reverse of the future value calculation. In a future value calculation a higher interest rate will get you a larger future value. Well, it's just the other way around in a present value calculation. The higher the discount rate the lower the present value. In this case increasing the discount rate from 5% to 7% reduces the present value from $100 to $94.49.

The second major premise—the sooner you get the money, the more it's worth—can also be illustrated with a slight change in Equation 6.5 using the original 5% discount rate. Let's say that instead of waiting for three years to get our money, we have to wait for five years. Solution 6.5 illustrates the new calculation.

Solution 6.5

> $115.76 [FV]
>
> 5 [n]
>
> 5 [i/y]
>
> [cpt] [PV] −90.70

Instead of the $115.76 having a present value of $100, if we have to wait five years, the present value goes down to $90.70. In other words, the sooner we get the money, the more its worth.

Let's say that an investor has an opportunity to purchase the right to receive a $10,000 cash payment, but it won't be received for 10 years. If he needs an 8% return on his investment, how much should he pay today for the right to receive the $10,000 in 10 years? As you recall from the fourth major premise at the beginning of this chapter, an investor will pay only the present value of all cash flows to be received, discounted at the required rate of return. The resulting calculator keystrokes are shown in Solution 6.6.

Solution 6.6

> 10000 [FV]
>
> 10 [n]
>
> 8 [i/y]
>
> [cpt] [PV] −4631.93

If the investor needs an 8% return on his investment, he will pay $4,631.93 today for the right to receive $10,000 at the end of 10 years. Stated in another way, if the investor pays $4,631.39 today and receives $10,000 as a result in 10 years, he will receive an 8% rate of return.

Future Value of an Annuity

Before discussing the future value of an annuity, we should address the concept of an annuity. An *annuity* is a series of equal payments that come at regular intervals. Mortgage payments are considered an annuity; they are typically paid on a monthly basis. Lease payments also follow a regular monthly pattern.

There are two types of annuities; the ordinary annuity and the annuity due. The payments in an ordinary annuity come at the end of the period as shown in Figure 6.1. Mortgage payments are ordinary annuity payments. They are considered end-of-the-month payments because they accrue interest until the end of the month. When you make that monthly payment, you are paying interest for the previous month.

Rent payments on the other hand are considered annuity due payments which come at the beginning of the period as shown in Figure 6.2. Rental payments are made at the beginning of the month to cover rent for the space during that same month. Whenever the annuity payments come at the beginning of the period, they are considered an annuity due.

Now, let's get back to the future value of an annuity. Let's say that my grandmother says she will give me $100 at the end of each year for the next three years, or an amount of money at the end of the three-year period, whichever I prefer. If I knew what the future value of that three-period annuity was going to be, I could

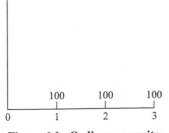

Figure 6.1 Ordinary annuity

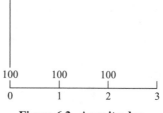

Figure 6.2   Annuity due

make an informed decision about the payment plan that I would prefer. The cash flows are diagramed in Figure 6.1, and we assume that my interest rate is 5%.

To find the future value of this annuity, we could take each payment individually and calculate its future value, that is, take the first payment and compound it forward to the end of period three, take the second payment and compound it forward, and then take the third payment with no compounding since it is already at the end of period three, and then we could add those three values to get our future value. The solution looks like the following:

100 [+/−] [PV]	100 [+/−] [PV]	100 [+/−] [PV]
2 [n]	1 [n]	0 [n]
5 [i/y]	5 [i/y]	5 [i/y]
[cpt] [FV] 110.25	[cpt] [FV] 110.00	[cpt] [FV] 100.00

When the three future values are added, $110.25 + 110.00 + 100.00 = 315.25$, the total future value of $315.25 is achieved. That is almost doable when you have only three payments. If you had a series of 300 payments to compound forward, it would take forever.

Equation 6.6 illustrates how the future value of an annuity is calculated using time value of money tables, or the mathematically calculated Future Value Interest Factor of an Annuity (FVIFA). It allows us to use a single TVM equation, or calculation, rather than the three calculations used above. The FVIFA can be calculated with these keystrokes; 1 [+/−] [pmt], 3 [n], 5 [i/y], [cpt] [FV], 3.1525.

Equation 6.6

$$FV_A = pmt\ (FVIFA) = 100\ (3.1525) = \$315.25$$

The calculator keystrokes are shown in Solution 6.7.

Solution 6.7

> 100 [+/−] [pmt]
> 3 [n]
> 5 [i/y]
> [cpt] [FV] 315.25

The future value of this three-period annuity of $100 per year is $315.25. It appears I would be indifferent between receiving the $100 payment at the end of each year for three years or a lump sum payment of $315.25 at the end of the three-year period. Both payment plans are worth the same to me, assuming my interest rate or required rate of return is 5%. Thus I would tell my grandmother that I will take either $100 at the end of each year or I would take $315.25 at the end of the three-year period. Notice that the payment value in the calculator keystrokes is entered as a negative number. Since the calculator operates in terms of cash inflows and cash outflows, we have to tell it that the payments are cash outflows, which will give us a positive number for the future value or cash inflow.

If the cash flows were to be received at the beginning of the year rather than the end of the year, the diagram of cash flows would appear as shown in Figure 6.2.

The future value of the annuity due will always be greater than the future value of an ordinary annuity of the same payment amount, number of payments, and interest rate because you are earning more interest. One way to look at it is that the final payment in the ordinary annuity has been shifted from the end of period 3 back to time period 0, or today. It will earn three periods' worth of interest by the time we want its value at the end of period three. Alternatively, you could think of it as picking up all three payments and shifting them one period to the left. In that case we are earning one more period's worth of interest on each of the three payments. Regardless of whether we earn three more period's worth of interest on one payment or one more period's worth of interest on three payments, the result is the same.

The calculation for the future value of an annuity due is to simply take the future value of the ordinary annuity times the quantity (1 plus the rate of interest), as shown in Equation 6.7. The annuity due will always have a greater value than the ordinary annuity because we will be receiving one more period's worth of interest on all of our payments. By multiplying the value of the ordinary annuity ($315.25) by the quantity (1 plus the rate of interest), we are taking that ordinary annuity value and adding on one more period of interest.

Equation 6.7

$$FV_{A\text{-Due}} = FV_A (1 + r) = \$315.25 (1 + 0.05) = \$315.25 (1.05) = \$331.01$$

If you decide to use the [beg] key on your calculator, that is what the calculator is doing, multiplying the value of the ordinary annuity by the quantity (1 plus the rate of interest).

Another future value of an annuity problem might look like this. You plan on setting $100 aside at the end of each month for the next 40 years. You plan to put this into a mutual fund which has on average earned 10% per year over the last several decades, and you expect that rate of return to continue for the next 40 years. How much will you have in your mutual fund account after those 40 years? The financial calculator keystrokes look like those presented in Solution 6.8.

Solution 6.8

100 [+/−] [pmt]

40 × 12 = [n]

10 ÷ 12 = [i/y]

[cpt] [FV] 632407.96

Setting aside $100 per month in a 10% account each month for 40 years will result in an accumulation of $632,407.96! In this case the 10% interest is an annual rate. Interest rates are typically annual rates unless stated otherwise. Since the payments are monthly, the rate of interest is converted to the monthly rate by dividing it by 12. For the same reason, the number of years is multiplied by 12 to arrive at the number of monthly payments. In all time value of money calculations the interest rate and the number of payments have to be compatible with each other. If we have monthly payments, we need the interest rate stated put in the calculator as a monthly rate. If we have quarterly payments, we need a quarterly rate of interest. If we have annual compounding, we need an annual rate of interest and we use the number of years as our "n."

Present Value of an Annuity

Similar to the present value calculation we did earlier in the chapter, the present value of an annuity calculation is a discounting process rather than a compounding one, as in the future value calculations. In other words, we bring the value of the money back to today's value, or present value.

Once again, look at the cash flows as pictured in Figure 6.1, but this time, my grandmother asks if I want the $100 payments or an amount of money today. We are really asking what the present value of this annuity is.

The Present Value Interest Factor of an Annuity (PVIFA) uses these keystrokes from our calculator; 1 [+/−] [pmt], 3 [n], 5 [i/y], [cpt] [PV] 2.7232. The present value of an annuity equation is shown in Equation 6.8.

Equation 6.8

$$PV_A = pmt\ (PVIFA) = 100\ (2.7232) = \$272.32$$

The calculation using the financial calculator will follow in Solution 6.9. Note that from this point on I will assume that you know that when I use a negative payment or negative present value, you will know to use the [+/−] key.

Solution 6.9

−100 [pmt]

3 [n]

5 [i/y]

[cpt] [pv] 272.32

The conclusion this time is that we would either take the $100 payments at the end of each year for three years or we would take the lump sum of $272.32 today. We are indifferent between the two plans because they have exactly the same value to us. Now, if Grandma says that she will either give us the annual payments or $275 today, we jump all over that. That is because the payments have a value of $272.32, and she is offering us $275, which is a higher present value.

The present value of an annuity calculation can be used to find the principal balance on a loan, such as a mortgage. If we look back to the four major premises at the beginning of the chapter, specifically premise 3, we see that the principal balance at any point in time is equal to the PV of the remaining payments. Let's work with a $175,000 mortgage amortized over 30 years at a 7% rate of interest. The keystrokes are shown in Solution 6.10.

Solution 6.10

175000 [PV]

30 × 12 = [n]

7 ÷ 12 = [i/y]

[cpt] [pmt] 1164.28

This results in a monthly payment of $1,164.28. If the question is to determine the principal balance of the mortgage after 5 years, we simply take the present value of the remaining payments as is indicated in major premise 3. This can be accomplished by first hitting the recall key, [rcl] followed by the number of payments key, [n]. The number of months, 360, will show up in the screen. Simply subtract 60 from the 360 (since 5 years, or 60 months are gone) and get an answer of 300; there are 300 payments remaining. Put the 300 in [n] without changing anything else on the calculator, and now compute the new present value, [cpt] [PV], and get $164,730.28. All of those keystrokes are shown in Solution 6.11.

Solution 6.11

175000 [PV]

360 [n]

7 ÷ 12 = [n]

[cpt] [pmt] 1164.28

[rcl] [n] −60 = [n]

[cpt] [PV] 164730.28

Note that this time I just put 360 directly into [n] without multiplying 30 × 12. It was a shortcut because I already knew that 30 × 12 is equal to 360. I didn't take a shortcut with the interest rate however. First of all I can't do that one in my head, and second if I just put in 0.58 which is the two decimal place answer to that division problem, I would be leaving off nine other decimal places worth of information that the calculator actually has "behind" the display screen. Your calculator calculates answers to 11 decimal places and displays only what you ask it to. You can change the number of decimal places you display by hitting [2nd] [Format] followed by the number of decimal places you would like displayed, say 2 or 4, followed by the [enter] key. For that same reason, if we were to put the payment of 1,164.28 directly into the calculator, with 300 [n] and the interest rate as 7 ÷ 12 and then calculated the present value, we would get a slightly different answer (164,730.37) because we put in a truncated, or chopped off, payment, with only two decimal places, as is illustrated in Solution 6.12.

When we did the calculation above, the payment had some additional decimal places hiding behind the display. If the calculator is asked to display four decimal places, the payment becomes 1,164.2794. So, by plugging a payment of 1,164.28 into the calculator we are losing some precision.

Solution 6.12

1164.28 [pmt]

300 [n]

7 ÷ 12 = [i/y]

[cpt] [PV] 164730.37

The answer is different from that in Solution 6.11 by 9 cents. The first calculation in Solution 6.11 is more precise, and that is the number the bank will come up with. The second method in Solution 6.12 is certainly acceptable in most cases, unless of course it is your money, in which case you will want to be as accurate as possible!

The present value of an annuity due works in similar fashion to the future value of an annuity due. The third payment in Figure 6.1 gets shifted to the front end, or time period 0 in Figure 6.2. This means that instead of being discounted for three periods, there is no discounting at all because it is received today. Once again, the present value of the annuity due must be greater than the present value of the ordinary annuity. The present value of the annuity due is equal to the present value of the ordinary annuity times 1 plus the rate of interest. So using the ordinary annuity in Equation 6.8, the value of the annuity due is shown in Equation 6.9.

Equation 6.9

$$PV_{A\text{-Due}} = PV_A\,(1+r) = \$272.32\,(1+0.05) = \$272.32\,(1.05) = \$285.94$$

The value of the annuity due becomes \$285.94 because the cash flows are earning one more period's worth of interest, via discounting, since the payments are all received one period sooner. Going back to the second major premise, the sooner we get the money, the more it's worth.

Sinking Fund Payment

There are two types of payments that come out of the time value of money. The first of these is called a *sinking fund payment*. For the sinking fund payment there is a target future value that an investor is shooting for. The sinking fund payment is the size of the payment needed to set aside at regular intervals that will accumulate the desired future value.

This is an example I like to use with my college students, who are typically juniors and seniors. Assume that you want to go on a vacation, say in three years, and you decide you will need \$5,000 for that vacation. If you set aside some money at the end of each year in a 5% account, how large should the payments be that you are placing in the account? The calculation in Equation 6.10 makes use of the time value of money table values, or the calculated factor.

Equation 6.10

$$Pmt = FV_A/FVIFA = \$5,000/3.1525 = \$1,586.04$$

The future value of the annuity is the amount of money we want to accumulate in the future, in this case $5,000. The FVIFA, or the future value of an annuity interest factor, is for 3n and 5% interest. The calculation tells us that the students will need to set aside $1,586.04 at the end of each year in a 5% account in order to accumulate the $5,000 needed for their vacation. The calculator keystrokes are shown in Solution 6.13.

Solution 6.13

5000 [FV]

3 [n]

5 [i/y]

[cpt] [pmt] 1586.04

Another situation that this calculation may be used in would be when your neighbor has a balloon payment due in five years on her contract for deed. The balloon payment is going to be $10,000, and she wants to set aside some money each month in her 5% account to accumulate the $10,000 in five years.

In order to do the calculator calculation, make sure to set your [i/y] key to 1 payment per period. Do that by hitting [2nd] [i/y] 1 [enter]. Now hit the [CE/C] twice, and you're set to go. See if you can come up with the answer. Your keystrokes should look like those in Solution 6.14.

Solution 6.14

10000 [FV]

5 ÷ 12 = [i/y]

5 × 12 = [n]

[cpt] [pmt] 147.05

You will note that when using the financial calculator for TVM calculations, the interest rate and the number of periods have to be compatible with each other. When the calculator is in its default setting, one compounding period per year, it is set to do annual problems. When we do something other than annual compounding, we have to tell the calculator what we plan to do. In this problem, since we have monthly payments, we tell the calculator that we need the interest rate per month, so we divide the 5% by 12 and put that in the [i/y] key. We also take the 5 years and multiply that by 12 and put that in the [n] key. Now we have payments per month and interest rate per month, so the number of periods and interest rate are compatible with each other.

The keystrokes above tell us that if we set aside $147.05 at the end of each month for 5 years, or 60 months, in a 5% account, we will accumulate $10,000.

Also note that the calculator assumes that the annuity problems are ordinary annuities, with the payments at the end of the period, unless you tell it otherwise. You can do that with the [BGN] key, but it is not necessary. Just take the PV or the FV of an ordinary annuity and multiply that answer by 1 plus the rate of interest to get the PV or the FV on an annuity due, as mentioned earlier in this chapter.

Payment to Amortize

The final equation of the six equations that will change your life (has it started to happen yet?) is the calculation of the payment to amortize. The payment to amortize is the payment needed to repay a debt over a certain period of time at a certain rate of interest. You have probably used the payment to amortize whether it was a car loan repayment, a student loan repayment, or a mortgage loan repayment. The variables in this calculation are the loan amount, or present value, the interest rate, and the repayment period, usually in numbers of months.

If you borrow $20,000 to buy a car and the credit union says that you can repay it monthly over a five-year period at 6% interest, what would your loan payment be? The calculation looks like Solution 6.15.

Solution 6.15

20000 [PV]

6 ÷ 12 = [i/y]

5 × 12 = [n]

[cpt] [pmt] 386.66

Your monthly payment would be $386.66. If you did not get this answer, there are two possible explanations. First check your number of payments per year by hitting [2nd] [p/y] key. If a 1 is not in the screen, hit 1 followed by [enter] and then [CE/C] key twice. If that was already set at 1, then you may need to clear your TVM memory registers. This can be done by hitting [2nd] [CLR TVM]. If you don't clear the memory registers between problems, the calculator will try to pick up a number from a previous problem and plug it into the new problem, thus giving a bogus answer to the new problem. So try and make it a practice to clear the memory registers after each problem.

Let's try another one, this time a mortgage loan. Your favorite mortgage lender says that you may obtain a $165,000 mortgage at 6.5% interest amortized over 30 years. What will your mortgage payment be on this loan? The keystrokes are shown in Solution 6.16.

Solution 6.16

165000 [PV]

30 × 12 = 360 [n]

6.5 ÷ 12 = [i/y]

[cpt] [pmt] 1042.91

The payment on the $165,000 mortgage amortized over 30 years at a 6.5% rate of interest comes out to be $1,042.91 per month. In the next chapter, we do some additional payment calculations in addition to calculating mortgage balances and the breakdown between principal and interest on a monthly payment.

Compound Growth Rates

A compound growth rate takes into consideration the compounding effect that results from the time value of money as opposed to an average growth rate which simply takes the total growth rate divided by the number of years. If a home experienced a 4% average growth rate over say three years, that would result in a value increase of 12% over the three-year period, or 4% × 3 = 12%.

A 4% compound growth rate would take into consideration that the 4% increase in year two is going to be on top of the 4% for year one, so in year two we would receive the appreciation not only on the beginning value but also on the 4% appreciation from year one. The 4% compound appreciation is illustrated in Solution 6.17.

Solution 6.17

−1 [PV]

3 [n]

4 [i/y]

[cpt] [FV] 1.1249

Solution 6.17 states that we start with $1 as a PV and we grow it at the 4% rate compounded over three years resulting in a total future value of $1.1249. When we subtract our initial $1 we are left with 0.1249, or an increase of 12.49%. The average growth rate that we learned about in Chapter 3 would be 12% for this problem $(3 \times 4\%) = 12\%$. The extra 0.49% in appreciation comes from the compounding effect, or the interest on interest that results from compounding.

Net Present Value

There are two more TVM concepts that are presented as they come up again in Chapter 11, "Real Estate Investment Analysis." The first of these is net present value, or NPV. The NPV of an investment is the difference between the PV of the cash inflows and the PV of the cash outflows. The cash outflow is typically the cash investment at the front end, or time period zero. If there are additional cash outflows during the holding period of the investment, those are also discounted to PV. The cash investment at time period zero does not need to be discounted because it is already at time period zero. In the NPV calculation then, the total PV of the cash inflows is net out against the PV of the cash outflows. Let's do a small example using Table 6.1.

Illustrated in Table 6.1 is a $5,000 investment that generates annual cash inflows over a three-year period of $1,000 at the end of year 1, $2,000 at the end of year 2, and $3,000 at the end of year 3. The question we are asking is, given a discount rate of 10%, what is the net present value of this set of cash flows. The first step is a simple PV calculation, 1000 [FV], 1 [n], and 10 [i/y], [cpt] [PV], and the result is $909.09. The second step is 2000 [FV], 2 [n], 10 [i/y], [cpt] [PV], and the result is $1,652.89. The third step is 3000 [FV], 3 [n], 10 [i/y], [cpt] [PV], and the answer is $2,253.94. We then sum those present values to get the total PV of $4,815.92. We then net that against the cash outflow, $4,815.92 − $5,000 = −$184.08, which is the NPV of these cash flows given a 10% discount rate.

The same calculation can be done with the financial calculator with a little more ease and fewer keystrokes. Solution 6.18 contains the keystrokes to find the NPV of the cash flows for the problem we analyzed in Table 6.1.

Table 6.1   NPV of cash flows

Time period	Cash flow	PV at 10%
0	−$5,000	−$5,000
1	$1,000	$909.09
2	$2,000	$1,652.89
3	$3,000	$2,253.94
Total PV		$4,815.92
NPV		−$184.08

Solution 6.18

[CF] 5000 [+/−] [enter]

[↓] 1000 [enter] [↓]

[↓] 2000 [enter] [↓]

[↓] 3000 [enter] [↓]

[↓] [NPV] 10 [enter]

[↓] [cpt] 184.07

Notice that the answer from the cash flows keys is $.01 different from the answer in Table 6.1. This is caused by the rounding of the answer. The calculator has 13 decimal places in its answers, but we are looking at only 2 of them. If we had stored the answers to the PV problems in the storage registers of the calculator and recalled them and summed them up, we would have gotten the same answer as the one achieved using the cash flow keys. Check your calculator manual on the storage keys.

After hitting the down arrow key following the enter key, you will notice that you receive an F01 in the screen. The calculator is asking for the frequency of C01, or the frequency of cash flow 1. In other words, how many cash flows of this same amount will there be? The default value is 1, so that is why we just hit the down arrow key again, and the worksheet goes on to the next cash flow.

While the keystrokes for the cash flow keys may appear to be daunting at first glance, once you have done a few problems using them, they become very familiar and their use can save a large amount of work. They also can bring more accuracy to your calculations because you don't have to worry about inverting numbers as you write them down.

Internal Rate of Return

The final TVM calculation of this chapter is the internal rate of return, or IRR. This is a cousin of the NPV calculation, and you will notice the resemblance in the definition. The *IRR* is the discount rate that makes the PV of the cash inflows equal to the PV of the cash outflows. Now, if these two PVs become equal to each other, what will the NPV be? Zero, you are absolutely correct. Another definition for the IRR is that it is the discount rate that makes the NPV = 0. The IRR is a compound rate of return calculation, because the IRR assumes that the cash flows can be reinvested at the same rate of return. In Chapter 11 we look at a straightforward method of estimating IRR. Right now we look at how the calculation can be made with the cash flow keys of our calculator.

The keystrokes are illustrated in Solution 6.19. Note that the only difference between Solution 6.18 and Solution 6.19 is the last line. After we have calculated the NPV, we just have to hit two additional keys, [IRR] and [cpt], and the IRR comes up on the screen.

Solution 6.19

[CF] 5000 [+/−] [enter]

[↓] 1000 [enter] [↓]

[↓] 2000 [enter] [↓]

[↓] 3000 [enter] [↓]

[↓] [NPV] 10 [enter]

[↓] [cpt] 184.07

[IRR] [cpt] 8.21

So the IRR of this investment with this set of cash flows is 8.21%.

We again discuss the NPV and IRR calculations in both the mortgage chapter and the investment chapter, later in this book.

Summary

This chapter addresses what some finance books refer to as six functions of a dollar, or what I like to call six equations that will change your life. The six equations, or calculations, allow you to calculate the future value of a lump sum, the present value of a lump sum, the future value of an annuity, the present value of an annuity, a sinking fund payment, and finally the payment to amortize.

To maximize our understanding of the six calculations, we looked at the four major premises association with time value of money. These major premises are:

1. The higher the discount rate the lower the present value.
2. The sooner we get the money the more it's worth.
3. The principal balance at any point in time is equal to the present value of the remaining payments.

4. An investor will pay only the present value of all cash flows to be received, discounted at the required rate of return.

These major premises also come up in the investment chapter later in the book. Please don't just look at these premises and say, "Oh, that's nice." Study them and remember them and you will achieve an understanding of time value of money.

Quiz for Chapter 6

1. Savings institutions in your neighborhood are advertising certificates of deposit of $10,000 that have a three-year maturity and pay 5.5% interest. What will be the value of the CD at the end of three years?
   a. $11,576
   b. $11,592
   c. $11,742
   d. $10,000

2. You are participating in a company savings plan and will be depositing $150 at the end of each month for the next 20 years. If the plan earns annual interest of 8%, how much money should you expect to be in your account at the end of the 20-year period?
   a. $6,864
   b. $88,353
   c. $61,655
   d. $65,344

3. You need to accumulate $75,000 in 12 years. How much should you put in your 10% account at the end of each year to accumulate the necessary funds?
   a. $3,507
   b. $4,273
   c. $4,705
   d. $3,107

4. You would like to provide an annual scholarship of $1,000 each year for the next 25 years. The first scholarship will be awarded one year from today. If you deposit an amount of money in an 8% account, how much should you deposit today so that there will be sufficient funds for the 25 scholarships?
   a. $73,105
   b. $3,650
   c. $10,674
   d. $3,328

5. If your starting salary is $35,000 and you receive 4% raises each year for 15 years, how much will your salary be after 15 years?
   a. $56,000
   b. $63,033

c. $85,000

d. $65.075

6. Your neighbor just took out a mortgage for $95,000 at a 6% rate for 30 years. What is her monthly payment?
   a. $569.57
   b. $6,901.65
   c. $575.14
   d. $475.00

7. Given the mortgage in question 6, what is the mortgage balance after 10 years, assuming that all payments have been made on time?
   a. $88,401
   b. $79,501
   c. $38,000
   d. $103,518

8. What is the current principal balance of a mortgage with a monthly payment of $659.00, a 7% interest rate, and 20 years remaining?
   a. $85,000
   b. $158,160
   c. $99,053
   d. $112,971

9. An investor is purchasing a note that will pay him $45,000 at the end of five years. If his required return is 8%, how much should he pay for the note today?
   a. $62,253
   b. $30,457
   c. $30,626
   d. $66,485

10. You have decided to go back to school, and you feel that you will need $5,000 for tuition for each of the four years you intend to be there. If you intend to enroll exactly one year from today, how much should you deposit in your 5% account so that you will have enough money for your four tuition payments?
    a. $21,000
    b. $18,616
    c. $19,000
    d. $17,729

CHAPTER 7

Mortgage Calculations Using TVM

I Will Gladly Give You a Dollar Tomorrow for the Dollar You Give Me Today

This chapter is an extension of Chapter 6 in that we use the tools that we learned in that chapter to make some standard mortgage calculations that will be useful to the real estate broker or salesperson, the real estate appraiser, the real estate lender, and the real estate investor. In this chapter we address calculations of mortgage payments and principal balances. We analyze the impact of discounts points on a mortgage APR and effective rate of return. Finally, loan-to-value ratios, homeowner's equity, and borrower qualifications are explored.

If you have not already read Chapter 6 and tried out the problems in that chapter, I strongly suggest that you do so before you attempt to read Chapter 7. The chapters were in fact put in this order for a reason.

Mortgage Payment

The mortgage payment on a constant payment mortgage is the payment to amortize that we refer to in Chapter 6 as one of those equations, or calculations, that would change your life. As a review of the financial calculator key strokes that are required for this calculation, the mortgage amount gets plugged in as [PV], the mortgage term in months is plugged into [n], the interest rate per month is plugged into [i/y], and then we [cpt] [pmt] to come up with the monthly payment. Remember to take the number of years the mortgage is being amortized over times 12 to get the number of months in the mortgage term, or [n]. Since the interest rate and the term have to be compatible with each other, you must now take the annual interest rate and divide that by 12 to get the monthly rate of interest, and that is what gets placed in [i/y]. If you were to compute an annual payment using the number of years for [n] and the annual interest rate for [i/y], it would be less meaningful because most mortgages today have monthly payments. What we could not do is calculate the annual payment and divide that by 12 and expect to get the correct monthly payment. That would not work because it would not allow for the principal reduction that takes place each month when we make our monthly payment.

If we borrow $142,500 in the form of a home mortgage amortized monthly over 25 years at an annual rate of 6.5%, our mortgage payment calculation would look like Solution 7.1 below.

Solution 7.1

142,500 [PV]

$25 \times 12 = $ [n]

$6.5 \div 12 = $ [i/y]

[cpt] [pmt] -962.17

Our monthly mortgage payment on that $142,500 mortgage amortized monthly over a 25-year period at 6.5% interest comes in at $962.17. This mortgage payment is made up of both principal and interest, sometimes referred to as P & I. One way to break that payment down into the principal portion of the payment and the interest portion is to multiply the principal amount of $142,500 by the decimal equivalent of the interest rate and divide that by 12 to get the monthly interest due on the mortgage, as shown in Equation 7.1.

Equation 7.1

$$\text{Monthly interest} = \$142,500 \times 0.065 = \$9,265.50 \div 12 = \$771.88$$

Since the payment is made up of principal plus interest, to get the principal portion of the payment, simply take the monthly payment minus the monthly interest and that will leave the principal portion of the payment, also referred to as the principal reduction, as shown in Equation 7.2.

Equation 7.2

$$\text{Principal portion of the payment} = \$962.17 - \$771.88 = \$190.29$$

The principal balance after the first payment has been made would then be $142,500 − $190.10 = $142,309.71.

Table 7.1 is an amortization schedule containing the payment breakdown between principal and interest for the first year of the mortgage described in Solution 7.1. It shows the payment number, the total principal plus interest payment, the principal portion of the payment as well as the interest portion of each payment, and finally the principal balance after the given payment is made. You will notice how the principal portion of each payment increases as the interest portion of each payment decreases. This takes place thanks to the principal reduction. As the outstanding principal balance goes down, the interest portion of the payment declines. This type of table can be created using an Excel spreadsheet or you could create one with your financial calculator.

The interest due in the second month would be the principal balance at the end of the first month, $142,309.71 × 0.065 = $9,250.13/12 = $770.84. The total payment of $962.17 minus the interest of $770.84 equals the principal portion of $191.33. That deducted from the previous principal balance equals the new principal balance of $142,118.38.

A 1/2% increase in the rate of interest can have a significant impact on the mortgage payment. As the interest rate goes up, keeping the mortgage amount and the term constant, our mortgage payment will go up. Try the same calculation at 7%.

Table 7.1 Amortization schedule

Mortgage amount		$142,500.00		
Mortgage term		25		
Interest rate		6.50%		

Payment number	Payment	Principal	Interest	Principal balance
				$142,500.00
1	−$962.17	$190.29	$771.88	$142,309.71
2	−$962.17	$191.33	$770.84	$142,118.38
3	−$962.17	$192.36	$769.81	$141,926.02
4	−$962.17	$193.40	$768.77	$141,732.61
5	−$962.17	$194.45	$767.72	$141,538.16
6	−$962.17	$195.51	$766.67	$141,342.66
7	−$962.17	$196.56	$765.61	$141,146.09
8	−$962.17	$197.63	$764.54	$140,948.46
9	−$962.17	$198.70	$763.47	$140,749.76
10	−$962.17	$199.78	$762.39	$140,549.99
11	−$962.17	$200.86	$761.31	$140,349.13
12	−$962.17	$201.95	$760.22	$140,147.18

Solution 7.2

142500 [PV]

25 × 12 = [n]

7 ÷ 12 = [i/y]

[cpt] [pmt] −1007.06

As the interest rate goes from 6.5% to 7% the monthly mortgage payment goes from $962.17 to $1,007.06. Thus an increase in the rate of interest will result in an increase in the monthly payment. Why don't you fill in the first five months worth of payments on the amortization schedule in Table 7.2 using the $142,500

Table 7.2 Amortization schedule

Mortgage amount		$142,500.00		
Mortgage term		25		
Interest rate		7.00%		

Payment number	Payment	Principal	Interest	Principal balance
1				
2				
3				
4				
5				

principal amount, the 25-year term, and the 7% rate of interest. Once you have completed the table, you can check the solution table (Table 7.3) at the end of this chapter.

We can find another interesting calculation by looking at the original mortgage of $142,500 at 6.5% interest amortized over 25 years. This time let's keep the mortgage payment constant when we change the interest rate. By doing this, the principal balance, or the PV of the mortgage, will change when the interest rate goes up, as in the scenario that follows. If you are a home buyer and, while you are searching for a home, market rates of interest go up from 6.5% to 7% and you wanted to keep your anticipated mortgage payment constant at $962.17, you would find that you couldn't borrow the same amount of money. Solution 7.3 illustrates the calculation starting from the initial mortgage payment calculation at 6.5% interest followed by changing the interest rate to 7% and then calculating the new PV, or mortgage amount.

Solution 7.3

142500 [PV]
25 × 12 = [n]
6.5 ÷ 12 = [i/y]
[cpt] [pmt] −962.17
7.0 ÷ 12 = [i/y]
[cpt] [PV] 136134.45

As you see, if rather than keeping the [PV] constant, as we did in Solution 7.2, we keep the [pmt] constant, the [PV], or the mortgage amount, decreases from $142,500 to $136,134.45. In order to keep the payment constant, we couldn't borrow as much money at the higher rate of interest. This is a reflection of major premise 1 from Chapter 6 which states that the higher the discount rate, the lower the present value. It also gives you a hint about why housing price bubbles take place in times of increasing interest rates. When interest rates go up, people can't afford to pay as much for a home because they can't afford to borrow as much mortgage money.

Let's try another of these problems. Your brother goes to the bank and is told that he can borrow $175,000 at 6% interest amortized over 30 years. From that he calculates that his monthly payment will be $1,049.21.

Solution 7.4

175000 [PV]
30 × 12 = [n]

$6 \div 12 = [i/y]$

[cpt] [pmt] -1049.21

One week later he calls the bank and is told that rates have gone up to 6.75% on 30-year loans. If he still borrows $175,000, what will his mortgage payment be?

Solution 7.5

175000 [PV]

$30 \times 12 = [n]$

$7 \div 12 = [i/y]$

[cpt] [pmt] -1164.28

Thus the monthly payment increases from $1,049.21 to $1,164.28 when the interest rate increases from 6% to 6.75% on a $175,000 mortgage. If your brother told the bank that he couldn't afford the new payment and wanted to keep the payments constant at $1,049.21 how much mortgage money could the lender give him at the 6.75% interest rate?

Solution 7.6

175000

$30 \times 12 = [n]$

$6 \div 12 = [i/y]$

[cpt] [pmt] -1049.21

$7 \div 12 = [i/y]$

[cpt] [PV] 157704.72

Biweekly Mortgages

As the name implies, in a biweekly mortgage the payments are made every two weeks rather than once a month. When calculating the size of the payment in a biweekly mortgage rather than multiplying the number of years by 12 to get the level of [n], we would multiply the number of years by 26, since there are 26 biweekly periods in a year. We would then divide the annual interest rate by 26 to get the biweekly interest rate. Let's calculate the biweekly payment on the problem we analyzed in Solution 7.1. The calculations are shown in Solution 7.7.

Solution 7.7

    142500 [PV]
    25 × 26 = [n]
    6.5 ÷ 26 = [i/y]
    [cpt] [pmt] −443.82

This biweekly payment would pay off the loan in 25 years, just as the monthly payment from Solution 7.1 would pay off the loan in 25 years. What lenders will sometimes do is take the monthly payment and divide it by 2 and make that the biweekly payment. The monthly payment divided by 2 in this case would be $481.09. You will notice it is larger than the calculated biweekly payment by $37.27. That additional money would go to pay off the principal balance faster than the biweekly amortized payment in Solution 7.4. That results in a shorter payoff term for the loan, and this is sometimes attractive to the borrower. In this case, the $481.09 payment would pay off the $142,500 mortgage at 6.5% annual interest in 20.81 years, as shown in Solution 7.8.

Solution 7.8

    142500 [PV]
    6.5 ÷ 26 = [i/y]
    −481.09 [pmt]
    [cpt] [n] 541
    541 ÷ 26 = 20.81

Principal Balance

As stated in major premise 3 in Chapter 6, the principal balance at any point in time is equal to the present value of the remaining payments. Just as the principal balance at the beginning of the loan is equal to the present value of the total number of payments, at any point along the timeline the principal balance is equal to the present value of the number of payments left on the loan. This is true whether there are 300 payments left or 3 payments left.

If five years ago you took out a mortgage for $150,000 to be amortized over 30 years at an interest rate of 7% and you wanted to know the current mortgage balance, or principal balance, you would follow the steps shown in Solution 7.9. First you calculate the monthly payment, and then you tell the calculator that your [n] is no longer 360, but it is now 300, because 60 months (or 5 years) are gone.

Then you ask the calculator what the new present value of the payments is. You do that because the principal balance at any point in time is equal to the present value of the remaining payments.

Solution 7.9

150000 [PV]

30 × 12 = 360 [n]

7 ÷ 12 = [i/y]

[cpt] [pmt] 997.95

[rcl] [n] −60 = 300 [n]

[cpt] [PV] 141197.38

Thus the principal balance after five years on the mortgage would have decreased from the original $150,000 down to $141,197.38.

Your parents have decided to sell their home, and they ask you what their current mortgage balance is. They took out a $125,000 mortgage 15 years ago. The mortgage had an original term of 25 years and carried an interest rate of 8%. Following the same steps you used in the previous problem, (1) first calculate the monthly payment, (2) next change the [n] to the number of remaining payments, and (3) finally calculate the new present value, as shown in Solution 7.10.

Solution 7.10

125000 [PV]

25 × 12 = 300 [n]

8 ÷ 12 = [i/y]

[cpt] [pmt] −964.77

[rcl] [n] −180 = 120 [n]

[cpt] [PV] 79517.79

The monthly payment comes in at $964.77 per month. Since the mortgage was originally amortized over 25 years and 15 years have passed, there are 10 years of payments remaining. By hitting [rcl] [n], the original 300 appears in the screen and then we can subtract 180 (or 15 × 12) from that original 300 and find there are 120 [n] remaining. After plugging the new 120 [n] into the calculator, we can now solve for the new [PV] and find that the principal balance is $79,517.79.

Interest Paid

Calculating the amount of interest paid on a loan is quite straightforward once we have learned how to calculate principal balance. One key to keep in mind is that the payment is made up of principal plus interest, or P + I.

Let's take the mortgage analyzed in Solution 7.10 and ask the question, how much interest would have been paid on that mortgage had your parents let the mortgage run for it's full course of 25 years? Assuming that all payments were made in a timely manner, we would first take the monthly payment and multiply it by 300. That would give us the total principal plus interest paid over the life of the loan, or 300 × $964.77 = $289,431.08. We know that $125,000 of that amount is principal because that is the original amount that was borrowed. The final calculation is simply to take the total (P + I) − P = I, so $289,431.08 − $125,000 = $164,431.08 is the total interest paid over the life of the loan as shown in Equation 7.3.

Equation 7.3

$$300 \times \$964.77 = \$289,431.08 = P + I$$

$$(P + I) - P = I$$

$$\$289,431.08 - \$125,000 = \$164,431.08$$

To calculate the amount of interest paid over a term shorter than the entire mortgage term, the calculation is similar to the one in Equation 7.3. If we wanted the interest paid for the same mortgage, but just during the 15 years that your parents were making payments on the mortgage, we again would need to multiply the monthly payment by the number of payments that were made. In this case the number would be 180, because they made payments over 15 years. So the total P+I paid over the 15 years would be 180 × $964.77 = $173,658.65. From that amount we have to subtract the principal reduction that took place over the 15-year period. That principal reduction is equal to the beginning principal amount minus the principal balance at the end of year 15. This comes to $125, 000 − $79,517.79 = $45,482.21.

You will recall that the $79,517.79 was the principal balance that we calculated in Solution 7.10 above. The difference between the original principal amount and the principal balance at the end of year 15 is $45,482.21. So once again we take the total P + I and subtract the P (or principal reduction) to get the amount of interest paid over the first 15 years of the mortgage. A summary of this calculation is shown in Solution 7.11.

Solution 7.11

125000 [PV]

25 × 12 = 300 [n]

8 ÷ 12 = [i/y]

[cpt] [pmt] 964.77

[rcl] [n] − 180 = 120 [n]

[cpt] [PV] 79517.79

125,000 − 79,517.79 = 45,482.21 = P

$964.77 × 180 = $173658.65 = P + I

(P + I) − P = I

$173658.65 − $45482.21 = $128176.44

Thus the total interest paid over the first 15 year of the loan is $128,176.44.

Annual Percentage Rate

The annual percentage rate, or APR, is the effective cost of mortgage money that the borrower is paying once all (in fact, most) of the up-front costs associated with the loan are factored into the calculation. It is considered a yield to maturity, which assumes the loan will run the full term and not be prepaid. The APR is the discount rate that makes the present value of the mortgage payments equal to the net proceeds that the borrower receives at the time of closing after deducting the additional finance charges, such as points paid by the borrower, origination fees, and mortgage insurance if there is any. Lenders will typically round off the APR to the nearest 1/8 of a percent.

Let's say you have recently applied for a mortgage of $212,000 at a 6.75% rate of interest to be amortized over 30 years. The lender says that in addition to the rate of interest you will have to pay a 2% origination fee. What is your APR on the loan if you expect the mortgage to be in place for the full 30 years? First you would calculate the monthly payment on the mortgage, as shown in Solution 7.12.

Solution 7.12

212000 [PV]

30 × 12 = 360 [n]

6.75/12 = [i/y]

[cpt] [pmt] 1375.03

Next we have to reduce the net proceeds that the borrower is actually receiving from the loan. The borrower receives $212,000 from the bank but then turns right around and pays the bank the 2% origination fee, so the net proceeds the borrow gets from the loan is actually $212,000 × 0.98 = $207,760. Leaving the previous calculation in the calculator, this amount now gets placed in the [PV], and we solve for the new rate of interest, as shown in Solution 7.13.

Solution 7.13

207760 [PV]

[cpt] [i/y] 0.58 × 12 = 6.95

The APR is rounded to the nearest 1/8% which would make that 7.0%.

Effective Rate of Return

The effective rate of return or the effective rate of interest is to the lender as the APR is to the borrower. It is the total rate of return on a loan taking interest and additional financing charges into consideration. The effective rate is calculated by first calculating the payment on the mortgage at the stated interest rate over the stated term. The points and/or other prepaid items are then deducted from the mortgage amount. That new value is then input as the new present value, and then the new [i/y] is calculated. The result is the effective rate of return or the effective rate of interest the lender is receiving. If the points and other prepaid items are being paid by the borrower to the lender, the effective rate of return to the lender will be the same as the annual percentage rate paid by the borrower. If a third party is paying the points, such as the seller, the APR and the effective rate will not be the same.

Discount Points and Prepaid Items

Discount points and prepaid items have an effect on the annual percentage rate that the borrower is paying and on the effective interest rate that the lender is receiving. Discount points, or just points, function like prepaid interest. It is an amount of up-front money paid at the time of closing, and the impact of the points is to increase the yield to the lender. If they are paid by the buyer, they also increase the annual percentage rate that the buyer is paying on the loan. It is possible that the points could be paid by the seller, usually in a buyer's market, and in that case they would again increase the yield to the lender, but they would have no impact on the annual percentage rate that the borrower would be paying.

To determine how much the buyer or seller would have to pay in points, 1 point is equal to 1 percent of the mortgage amount. If the buyer was taking out a $170,000 mortgage and the lender said that the loan would be at a 7% interest rate plus 1 1/2 points, the buyer would have to pay $170,000 × 0.015 = $2,550 cash at the closing to cover the points. Given a mortgage of $200,000 with 3 points, the buyer would have to pay $200,000 × 0.03 = $6,000 in order to get the mortgage.

A rough estimate, or rule of thumb, of the impact that points have on the yield of the mortgage to the lender is that 1 point will increase the yield to the lender by approximately 1/8 of a percent. The accuracy of that estimate will vary depending on the general level of interest rates.

EFFECTIVE RATE ON A FULLY AMORTIZED MORTGAGE

Let's analyze the mortgage mentioned above. If that $200,000 mortgage was at a stated rate of interest of 7% and was to be amortized over 30 years, the payment calculation would look like Solution 7.14.

Solution 7.14

> 200000 [PV]
> 30 × 12 = [n]
> 7 ÷ 12 = [i/y]
> [cpt] [pmt] −1330.60

In other words, the net proceeds to the borrower would be $200,000 and would result in monthly payments of $1,330.60. If the borrower had to pay 3 points in order to get the loan, the net proceeds from the loan would not be $200,000. Rather, the net proceeds from the loan would be the $200,000 minus the $6,000 they would have to pay in points, or a net of $194,000. The borrower would, however, still be making payments on the mortgage amount of $200,000. Thus, the payment calculation would still look like Solution 7.14; however, the yield to the lender and the annual percentage rate to the borrower would be calculated as shown in Solution 7.15.

Solution 7.15

$$200000 - 6000 = 194000 \ [PV]$$

$$30 \times 12 = [n]$$

$$-1330.60 \ [pmt]$$

$$[cpt] \ [i/y] \ 0.61 \times 12 = 7.3$$

If the borrower had to pay 3 points to get this $200,000 mortgage, the yield to the lender would be 7.3%. If the borrower paid the points, the annual percentage rate that the borrower would be paying would also be that same 7.3%. You can think of the mortgage amount in terms of money the borrower borrows or the amount of money the lender invests in the transaction. When the points are paid by the borrower, it reduces the net proceeds from the loan thus increasing the cost of borrowing. From the lender's perspective the points decrease the amount of money invested in the transaction by $6,000, but since the payments are based on the mortgage amount of $200,000, it increases the yield, or effective rate of return, to 7.3%.

You will notice that the increase in yield is less than predicted by the rule of thumb. The rule of thumb indicated approximately a 3/8% increase in yield, and the actual increase is only 3/10%. Still, that is not a bad estimate.

Let's try another problem of this type from beginning to end. We have a mortgage amount of $154,000 at an 8% interest rate amortized over 25 years. If the borrower has to pay 2 points to get the loan, what is the effective interest rate on the loan? The entire solution is contained in Solution 7.16 below.

Solution 7.16

$$154000 \ [PV]$$

$$25 \times 12 = [n]$$

$$8 \div 12 = [i/y]$$

$$[cpt] \ [pmt] \ -1188.60$$

$$154000 \times 0.02 = 3080$$

$$154000 - 3080 = 150920 \ [PV] \ \text{or} \ 154000 \times 0.98 = 150920$$

$$[cpt] \ [i/y] \ 0.69 \times 12 = 8.24\%$$

To summarize Solution 7.16, first the monthly payment on the mortgage is calculated. The $154,000 mortgage amount, 25-year term, and 8% interest rate result in a monthly payment of $1,188.60. To calculate the value of the points, multiply the mortgage amount by 0.02, or 2% of the mortgage amount. This results in the cash value of the points being equal to $3,080. The cash amount of the points is then deducted from the mortgage amount to result in net proceeds of the loan of $150,920. That net proceeds are then keyed into the present value key, and then we solve for [i/y] and get 0.69 (plus the unseen decimal values inside the calculator). That value is a monthly effective rate so we take that times 12 and get the annual effective rate of 8.24%.

Other prepaid charges or expenses can have a similar impact on the effective rate of interest that a borrower is paying. If the charge is linked to the mortgage, then the annual percentage rate being paid will increase. Let's say a borrower is obtaining a $100,000 mortgage at 7% interest amortized over 30 years. As part of the mortgage costs, the borrower has to pay an origination fee of $500 associated with obtaining the mortgage. The monthly payment would be calculated, and then the prepaid charges would be deducted from the mortgage amount. The resulting net proceeds would be put into present value, and the [i/y] would then be calculated as shown in Solution 7.17.

Solution 7.17

100000 [PV]

30 × 12 = [n]

7 ÷ 12 = [i/y]

[cpt] [pmt] −665.30

100000 − 500 = 99500 [PV]

[cpt] [i/y] 0.59 × 12 = 7.05%

The impact on the cost of the mortgage money to the borrower is that the rate goes from 7% to 7.05%. Keep in mind that while your calculator is showing 0.59 when you compute your [i/y], that value is rounded and your calculator actually has 11 more decimal places that are unseen. That means you can't just take the truncated, or chopped off, value of 0.59 times 12 and get the same answer. In fact, the four decimal place value in the [i/y] key is 0.5875, and your calculator is just showing you 0.59 when you have your decimal places set to two places. Whenever possible, keep the value in your calculator and don't truncate it.

EFFECTIVE RATE ON A PARTIALLY AMORTIZED LOAN

The impact of points and other prepaid costs will be much greater on a partially amortized mortgage than they are on a fully amortized mortgage. If you pay off your mortgage after five years, which is what we mean by a partially amortized mortgage, and you pay points as an example, you will be paying a disproportionately greater portion of your interest on the loan at the front end. As an example, if you were to pay $2,000 in points and your loan ran the full 30 years, you would be spreading the cost of the points over 30 years when you calculate your effective rate. If you pay your loan off after five years, you would be spreading the $2,000 cost over only 5 years so your annual percentage rate would be affected much more because of the shorter term.

Let's take a look at the problem from Solution 7.15. This time we assume that the loan will be paid off after five years. The first thing we have to do is calculate what the cash flows from the mortgage are going to be. First of all there will be five years of monthly payments, and those will be followed with the cash flow from the principal balance that will be paid off. Thus we need to calculate the monthly mortgage payment, or the payment to amortize. That step is identical to Solution 7.15, and we get a payment of $1,330.60. The second step to the problem is to calculate the principal balance at the end of five years. Recall that the principal balance at any point in time is equal to the present value of the remaining payments. The payment and principal balance calculations are found in Solution 7.18.

Solution 7.18

200000 [PV]
$30 \times 12 = $ [n]
$7 \div 12 = $ [i/y]
[cpt] [pmt] -1330.60
[rcl] [n] $- 60 = $ [n]
[cpt] [PV] 188263.18

We now have all the cash flows associated with the mortgage. We do not have the net proceeds to the borrower however. You will recall that the borrower had to pay 3 points in order to get the mortgage, which means that the borrower had to pay $6,000 at the closing. This results in a net proceeds to the borrower of $200,000 - $6,000 = $194,000. Now we can plug the cash flows into the calculator and solve for the new [i/y] which will be the effective rate the borrower is paying and the lender is receiving.

Solution 7.19

194000 [PV]
-1330.60 [pmt]
-188263.18 [FV]
60 [n]
[cpt] [i/y] $0.65 \times 12 = 7.74\%$

The answer you get when you compute [i/y] is a monthly rate of 0.65% which you then must multiply by 12 to get the annual rate of 7.74%. You will notice that I have the cash flows set up from the borrower's perspective. The $196,000 is a cash inflow to the borrower so it has a positive sign. The monthly payment is a cash outflow to the borrower so it has a negative sign. The mortgage payoff, or future value, is a cash outflow to the borrower so it also has a negative sign. The signs must be correct to obtain the correct answer because your calculator operates in terms of cash inflows and cash outflows.

Had we wanted to look at the loan from the lender's perspective, we would just change each of the signs around and get the same answer. The net proceeds for the borrower would be a cash outflow to the lender so it would have a negative sign, the monthly payment would be a cash inflow to the lender so it would have a positive sign, and the principal payoff would be a cash inflow to the lender with a positive sign. The resulting effective rate to the lender would still be 7.74%. The only time the effective rate to the lender would be different from the effective cost to the borrower is when the prepaid costs are not paid to the lender, but to a third party, such as an appraiser. An appraisal fee would affect the effective cost to the borrower because the borrower pays the cost of the appraisal. The appraisal fee would not affect the effective rate to the lender because the lender does not get to keep the appraisal fee so it has no impact on the lender's return. While the appraisal fee would increase the effective cost of the mortgage, technically it does not go into the APR calculation for the borrower according to current disclosure regulations.

As Solution 7.19 indicates, the annual percentage rate that the borrower is paying because of the 3 points and the expected five-year payoff of the loan is 7.74% as opposed to the 7.3% if the loan were to go full term. So, shortening the term with the same number of points increases the effective cost of the mortgage money because of a disproportionate share of the interest being paid up front. If you expect to stay in a home for a short period of time, you would prefer not to pay any points and you may in fact be better off with a slightly higher rate of interest and no points than with a lower rate of interest with points. You now know how to do the analysis and the calculations that will show you which is the better deal or lower effective rate.

Let's try one more problem with a partially amortized mortgage. Your brother-in-law is taking out a new mortgage of $215,000 amortized over 30 years at a 7.25% interest rate with 2 points being charged, and he believes he will sell the house and pay off the mortgage in seven years. He asks you, since you have read this book and now fully understand effective rates, what the effective cost of his mortgage will be. You state, "That will be no problem," and you start by coming up with the cash flows found in Solution 7.20.

Solution 7.20

   215000 [PV]

   30 × 12 = [n]

   7.25 ÷ 12 = [i/y]

   [cpt] [pmt] −1466.68

   [rcl] [n] − 84 = 276 [n]

   [cpt] [PV] 196716.86

Now that you have your cash flows, you just need to calculate the net proceeds that your brother-in-law will receive from the mortgage. So you multiply the $215,000 mortgage amount by 0.02, and you find that the points will come to $4,300 which you then deduct from the $215,000 to get the net proceeds of $210,700. Now the cash flows can be analyzed just as they were in Solution 7.19. Verify your calculations by comparing them to Solution 7.21.

Solution 7.21

   210700 [PV]

   −196716.86 [FV]

   −1466.68 [pmt]

   84 [n]

   [cpt] [i/y] 0.64 × 12 = 7.63%

As the solution indicates, the annual percentage rate to the borrower, or the effective rate of return earned by the lender, in this case increases from the stated rate of interest of 7.25% to 7.63% when the up-front cost of the points is factored into the calculation.

Adjustable Rate Mortgage

An *adjustable rate mortgage* (ARM) is a mortgage that shifts the interest rate risk from the lender to the borrower (see Chapter 12). Suffice it to say that when a lender makes fixed interest rate mortgage loans and the market rate of interest goes up, the value of the lender's mortgage portfolio goes down. This reflects perfectly the TVM major premise—the higher the discount rate, the lower the present value. To protect the lender from this loss in value, the ARM was developed, so that when the market rate of interest goes up, the interest rate on the mortgage

goes up. This protects the lender from an erosion in the value of the mortgage portfolio resulting from increases in market interest rates. There are certain key terms associated with an ARM, and they are listed here:

- Margin
- Index
- Initial mortgage interest rate
- Composite rate
- Adjustment interval
- Caps/floors
- Negative amortization

In an ARM the mortgage will start with an initial mortgage interest rate. This initial interest rate is typically set slightly below the rate on a fixed-rate mortgage so that it looks attractive to a borrower. Hence, this initial rate is sometimes called a *teaser rate*. After the adjustment interval or adjustment period the rate will be adjusted based on the interest rate movement of the index. The index may be the index of one-year treasury securities, five-year treasuries, the average of conventional mortgage interest rates for the previous thirty days, or some other similar interest rate benchmark index. As the index moves, so would the interest rate on our ARM. At the adjustment time the new index rate plus the margin would be the new mortgage interest rate, or composite rate, on the ARM.

If there are no payment caps, or limitation on the payment increase that can be passed on to the borrower, then the new mortgage payment would be calculated using the new composite rate, the number of payments remaining, and the principal balance at the time the interest rate changes. There could also be payment floors which are limitations on the amount of payment decrease that could be passed on to the borrower. Let's try an example. Your neighbor took out an adjustable rate mortgage with an initial rate of 5.5% for $130,000. After one year, which was the adjustment interval, the index rate is at 5%, and there is a 2% margin. Those values are added together to give a composite rate of 7%. What happens to your neighbor's monthly payment if the original term was 30 years?

Solution 7.22

130000 [PV]

360 [n]

5.5/12 = [i/y]

[cpt] [pmt] −738.13

[rcl] [n] − 12 = [n]

[cpt] [PV] 128248.78

$7/12 = [i/y]$

[cpt] [pmt] -862.00

The payment increases over \$123 per month to \$862 per month from \$738.13 per month. That is what is sometimes called payment shock when discussing adjustable rate mortgages. If the borrower is not expecting that, it can have tremendous negative impact on the household budget. It can also lead to foreclosure if the borrower is not prepared.

If there is a payment cap associated with the ARM, that means that the entire payment increase might not be able to be passed on to the borrower. In the case when all the interest due per month cannot be passed on, the amount that is not passed on to the borrower gets added to the principal balance. This phenomenon is referred to as *negative amortization*. Instead of a decreasing principal balance, the loan can result in an increasing principal balance. This is another characteristic that the borrower should not be thrilled with. In order to get the low teaser rate and some degree of payment protection, this is one of the risks that the borrower may have to take on.

The Shared Appreciation Mortgage

The *shared appreciation mortgage* (SAM) is one of the alternative mortgage instruments developed in the late 1970s–early 1980s time period. Many of these alternative mortgages were developed to help borrowers cope with the high market rates of interest that were in effect at that time. The shared appreciation mortgage allowed the borrower a lower rate of interest in exchange for a piece of the appreciation that the borrower was expected to gain as a result of home ownership. The lender would say, "I'll give you an X% reduction in your mortgage interest rate in exchange for X% of the appreciation you experience in the first five years of home ownership."

Let's try an example with a SAM. The bank says that the interest rate on the \$150,000 30-year fixed-rate mortgage is 14% on the home you expect to purchase for \$175,000. You can't qualify for a fixed-rate loan at 14%, so the lender says it will reduce your interest rate by 25% in exchange for 25% of the appreciation (see Chapter 8) you receive in your first five years of ownership. What is the mortgage payment you would have had at 14%? What is your new interest rate? What is your new payment? What is the effective interest rate you end up paying over the first five years if your home goes up in value by 4% per year compounded annually?

First we look at what the payment would have been at 14% interest.

Solution 7.23

> 150000 [PV]
> 360 [n]
> 14/12 = [i/y]
> [cpt] [pmt] −$1777.31

The monthly payment would have been a very healthy $1,777.31 per month. The second question is, what is the new interest rate on the SAM?

Equation 7.4

$$\text{New interest rate} = 14\% \, (1 - 0.25) = 14\% \, (0.75) = 10.5\%$$

So the new interest rate on the SAM would be 10.5% or a 25% reduction from the previously quoted 14%. What is the new payment on the SAM?

Solution 7.24

> 150000 [PV]
> 360 [n]
> 10.5/12 = [i/y]
> [cpt] [pmt] −1372.11

The final question, what is the effective rate on the loan if your home goes up in value by 4% per year compounded annually, is a little more challenging. We first must establish what the cash flows are that the lender is receiving. We have already established that the lender will receive $1,372.11 per month for 60 months. The lender will also receive the principal balance at the end of five years. Finally, the lender will receive 25% of the appreciation that takes place in the first five years. The principal balance is found in Solution 7.25.

Solution 7.25

> 150000 [PV]
> 360 [n]
> 10.5/12 = [i/y]
> [cpt] [pmt] −1372.11
> [rcl] [n] −60 = [n]
> [cpt] [PV] −145322.55

To estimate the appreciation, we need to know what the value of the property is after five years. That is found by taking the purchase price of $175,000 and calling that a PV, compounding it forward five periods, at a 4% growth rate. We find that future value by executing the keystrokes in Solution 7.26.

Solution 7.26

    −175000 [PV]
    5 [n]
    4 [i/y]
    [cpt] [FV] −212914.26

   Thus the appreciation would be $212,914.26 − $175,000 = $37,914.26. Now the agreement says that 25% of that amount will go to the lender in exchange for the interest rate reduction. The amount of the appreciation going to the lender is $37,914.26 × 0.25 = $9,478.56. The cash flows going to the lender along with the effective rate calculation are indicated in Solution 7.27.

Solution 7.27

    −150000 [PV]
    1372.11 [pmt]
    60 [n]
    145322.55 + 9478.56 = 154801.11 [FV]
    [cpt] [i/y] 0.95 × 12 = 11.45%

   The effective return to the lender, which happens to be the same as the effective cost to the borrower, for this loan is 11.45%. Now many borrowers were terribly upset with the prospect of sharing their appreciation with the lender. However, when the choices were to share the appreciation or not get the mortgage because the interest rate was too high, this was in fact a viable option for the borrower. In this example the total cost of the loan turned out to be only 11.45% versus the market rate of 14%, so it was a good deal for the borrower. The catch is, if market rates were 14%, then the appreciation rate probably would have exceeded the 4% per year used in the example.

Reverse Annuity Mortgage

The *reverse annuity mortgage* (RAM) was developed around the time of the SAM, but it appears to have greater staying power in the marketplace because it is still used today. Its use is limited to specific situations. The mortgage is designed to allow senior citizens to stay in their homes longer by turning their equity into a cash flow stream. Seniors are often on a fixed income and get caught in a squeeze. When the real estate taxes and the maintenance costs continue to escalate, they are often forced from their homes. The RAM allows them to get some of their equity out of their home on a monthly basis so that they can afford to stay in the house for a prolonged period of time.

Let's say that a senior couple owns their home and that it is currently worth $170,000. The bank says it will enter into a RAM at 7% interest for 15 years up to 80% of the home's current value. In other words, the most the loan balance could grow to over 15 years would be $170,000 \times 0.80 = $136,000. The payments that the couple could receive over the next 15 years are indicated in Solution 7.28.

Solution 7.28

136000 [FV]

15 × 12 = 180 [n]

7/12 = [i/y]

[cpt] [pmt] −429.07

So the couple could receive monthly payments over the next 15 years of $429.07. At the end of the 15 years the couple would either have to refinance into a standard mortgage and start repaying the $136,000 debt, or they would have to sell their home. In either case they were able to stay in the house an extra 15 years beyond the time they thought they would.

Loan-to-Value Ratio

The *loan-to-value ratio* is the ratio of mortgage amount divided by the property value. If you are dealing with a property that has a market value of $200,000 and you are taking out a $160,000 mortgage to purchase the property, your loan to value ratio is as indicated in Equation 7.5.

Equation 7.5

$$\text{Loan-to-value ratio} = \$160,000/\$200,000 = 0.80 = 80\%$$

The equity-to-value ratio is 1 minus the loan-to-value ratio, which for the above situation, would be Equation 7.6.

Equation 7.6

$$\text{Equity-to-value ratio} = 1 - 0.80 = 0.20 = 20\% = \$40,000/\$200,000$$

As you can see in Equation 7.6, this value may also be determined by dividing the equity investment, or down payment, by the property value. The lesson to be learned here is that the total property value is made up of equity plus debt, or equity plus the mortgage amount. This is summarized in Equation 7.7.

Equation 7.7

$$\text{Property value} = \text{Equity} + \text{mortgage amount}$$

Homeowner's Equity

One of the glorious features of real estate is that the equity that homeowners have in their property tends to increase over time. This equity increase comes from two different sources. If we take Equation 7.7 and manipulate it a little by subtracting mortgage amount from both sides of the equation, we end up with Equation 7.8.

Equation 7.8

$$\text{Property value} - \text{mortgage amount} = \text{Equity} + \text{mortgage amount}$$

$$-\text{mortgage amount}$$

$$\text{Equity} = \text{Property value} - \text{mortgage amount}$$

Once the mortgage amount has been subtracted from both sides, Equation 7.8 states that the equity is equal to the property value minus the mortgage amount. You will notice that Equation 7.8 is identical to Equation 2.5 from Chapter 2. The terms used are slightly different, but synonymous. In Equation 2.5 we use the terms *market value* instead of *property value* and *mortgage balance* instead of *mortgage amount*. The terms *market value* and *mortgage balance* are actually preferable because they refer to the changes that can take place over time. Over time the property value can change, and the term that we use to refer to that new value is market value. In addition, as payments are made on the mortgage, the principal gets paid down, and we refer to the new mortgage amount as the principal balance. See Table 7.3.

These two actions then, the appreciation in the home's market value and the principal reduction on the mortgage can both result in an increase in the home-owner's equity. This is reflected in Equation 2.6, which is replicated below in Equation 7.9.

Table 7.3 Amortization schedule solution

Mortgage amount	$142,500.00
Mortgage term	25
Interest rate	7.00%

Payment number	Payment	Principal	Interest	Principal balance
				$142,500.00
1	−$1,007.16	$175.91	$831.25	$142,324.09
2	−$1,007.16	$176.94	$830.22	$142,147.15
3	−$1,007.16	$177.97	$829.19	$141,969.18
4	−$1,007.16	$179.01	$828.15	$141,790.18
5	−$1,007.16	$180.05	$827.11	$141,610.13

Equation 7.9

$$\uparrow \text{Equity} = \uparrow \text{Market value} - \downarrow \text{mortgage balance}$$

Equation 7.9 says that an increase in equity can result from two sources. If market value increases, then the homeowner's equity will increase. Second, if the mortgage balance decreases, the homeowner's equity will increase. This is indeed one of the major benefits of home ownership. It is the primary source of wealth for the average individual in the United States.

Quiz for Chapter 7

1. Sara recently purchased a house for $187,500 and took out a mortgage for $150,000 at a 6.5% annual interest rate amortized over 30 years to finance the purchase. What is the monthly payment on her mortgage?
   a. $11,486.62
   b. $957.22
   c. $948.10
   d. $812.50

2. Five years later Sara (from problem 1) is considering refinancing her mortgage. What is the mortgage balance, or principal balance, on Sara's original mortgage?
   a. $93,114.00
   b. $140,416.47
   c. $150,000.00
   d. $140,112.33

3. Your cousin Michael is purchasing a home in a new subdivision. The purchase price of the home is $225,000, and he is taking out a $170,000 mortgage at 7% interest amortized over 25 years. One of the requirements of the mortgage is that he pay 3 discount points and a 1% origination fee to the lender in order to get the loan. What annual percentage rate (rounded to two decimal places) is Michael paying on the loan if it is expected to run the full 25 years? (Use your financial calculator.)
   a. 7.00%
   b. 7.20%
   c. 7.37%
   d. 7.46%

4. If Michael (in problem 3) knows he is going to stay in this house for only five years and then plans to sell the house, what will his APR be rounded to two decimal places?
   a. 8.01%
   b. 7.46%
   c. 7.00%
   d. 7.37%

5. XYZ Federal Savings Bank is considering making a mortgage loan to Jennifer to assist her with her new home purchase. She is asking for a

loan of $145,000 to be amortized over 30 years at a 7.5% rate of interest. If the lending officer tells Jennifer she will have to pay 2 points to get the loan, what is the effective rate of interest that XYZ Federal will be earning on the loan, assuming the loan will run for the full 30-year term?

a. 7.5%

b. 7.71%

c. 7.81%

d. 8.01%

6. Aaron is buying a new house with a purchase price of $162,500. The bank has told him it will give him a mortgage of $130,000 at 7% interest amortized over 30 years. What is the loan-to-value ratio for this particular mortgage?

a. 125%

b. 80%

c. 75%

d. 7%

7. Using the information in question 6, if Aaron's house goes up by 2% in value each year for the next three years and he makes all his mortgage payments on time, how much equity will he have in his home at the end of three years? In order to get this answer, you will need to answer four questions in total. They are: (a) What is the monthly mortgage payment? (b) What is the principal balance at the end of year 3? (c) What is the market value of the home after three years? (d) How much equity does Aaron have at the end of year 3? Check the quiz solutions for the answers.

a.

b.

c.

d.

8. Ashley is taking out a $215,000 mortgage to purchase a new home. The mortgage will have a 30-year term and a stated rate of interest of 6%. The lender is charging Ashley 1.5 discount points for her to get the loan. If Ashley believes that she will pay off the loan within five years, either because she will move or refinance, what is the annual percentage rate she will be paying on the loan?

a. 6%

b. 6.36%

c. 6.5%

    d. 6.76%

9. Chase is buying a new home with a purchase price of $195,000. He is taking out a 75% loan-to-value mortgage amortized over 25 years with a 6.25% rate of interest. What is Chase's principal balance at the end of three years if he makes all his payments on time?

    a. $146,250

    b. $140,770

    c. $111,518

    d. $138,232

10. Ashley's grandparents are considering a reverse annuity mortgage to generate some extra cash flow during their retirement since their original mortgage was paid off eight years ago. The lender says they can accumulate debt to a maximum of 75% of their home's current value of $220,000. Given a 15-year term and an interest rate of 7.25%, how large a monthly payment can they expect to receive?

    a. $679.13

    b. $1,506.22

    c. $2,008.30

    d. $509.35

8

CHAPTER

Appreciation and Depreciation

You Win Some and You Lose Some

Value Increase Caused by Appreciation

Real estate tends to go up in value over time, which is a phenomenon referred to as *appreciation*. A prime cause of this is general inflation in the economy, but it is also the result of other market-driven factors such as amount of competing property on the market, number of buyers in the market, demographics of those buyers, and other factors. A historic average of single-family home appreciation over the last 50 years in the United States is about 4% per year. This value can vary dramatically however.

It is important to note the difference between average, or nominal rate of appreciation, and the compound rate of appreciation. The methods of calculating these two different types of appreciation are spelled out a little later in the chapter. Suffice it to say at this point that the compound rate takes into consideration the phenomenon of compounding and the average rate does not. The result is that the average rate will sound greater than the compound rate.

According to the U.S. Census Bureau, the median value of a home in the United States from 2002–2005 averaged a compound annual increase of 6.9%. Appreciation rates can vary by time and by market area. Over the same time period listed above the median home values in New Mexico increased by only 2.6% per year while the median home value in California increased at a compound rate of 20.1% per year. Appreciation rates are much more volatile over shorter time periods, and the rates tend to be much smoother over longer time periods. Home buyers and investors are interested in the rate of appreciation the properties in their market area have experienced. It gives them a clue about the sort of appreciation they might earn on their property in the future, even though past appreciation rates are no guarantee of what future rates of appreciation may be earned.

DOLLAR AMOUNT OF APPRECIATION

If that 4% rate over the last 50 years is accurate and a homeowner purchased a home four years ago for $175,000, then that home may be worth $204,725 today if the rate of appreciation over the past four years has been at the average rate. There are two ways to get to that answer. Multiplying the purchase price by 1 plus the growth rate four times will get us there as shown in Equation 8.1. Each multiplication means that the homeowner will end up with the beginning value plus the additional 4%. After year one that means the homeowner will be earning appreciation on the previous appreciation in addition to appreciation on the initial home value. This is the compounding process at work.

Equation 8.1

$$\$175{,}000 \times (1.04) \times (1.04) \times (1.04) \times (1.04) = \$204{,}725$$

The reason we can't just multiply the $175,000 by 1.16, which is four years of 4% growth, is because we must capture the compounding effect of the 4% growth each year. As you can see in Equation 8.2, multiplying the purchase price by

1 plus 16%, or 1.16, yields a future value of only $203,000. This method misses the additional $1,725 in value growth from the compounding.

Equation 8.2

$$\$175,000 \times (1.16) = \$203,000$$

The second method of finding the value after four years of 4% annual growth involves the following financial calculator keystrokes which also yield the answer of $204,725.

Solution 8.1

−175000 [PV]

4 [n]

4 [i/y]

[cpt] [FV] 204725

Using the financial calculator to determine our future value takes into consideration the compounding effect of our 4% growth rate and gives us the correct answer.

Given the purchase price of $175,000 and the current value of $204,725, you have experienced appreciation of $204,725 − $175,000 = $29,725. Another way this appreciation can be exhibited is by looking at the equity that the homeowner has in the property. As mentioned in other chapters, equity is defined as shown in Equation 8.3.

Equation 8.3

$$Equity = Market\ value - mortgage\ balance$$

As you can see, if market value goes up, so does the equity that we have in the property. So if we saw the market value go from $175,000 to $204,725, we have seen our equity increase by $29,725 regardless of what happened to our mortgage balance. Fortunately, if we have been making our mortgage payments on time, the mortgage balance has also gone down. That decrease in mortgage balance has only added to our equity, because as mortgage balance goes down, our equity also goes up. An increase in our equity results in an increase in our net worth, but that's a topic for another day.

Let's look at another example. If you purchased your home two years ago for $189,000 and have been told that your market experienced appreciation two years ago of 4% and 6% last year, what is your home currently worth? See Equation 8.4.

Equation 8.4

$$\text{Home value} = \$189,000 \times 1.04 \times 1.06 = \$208,353.60$$

Based on the appreciation rates of 4% the first year you owned the home and 6% the second year you owned the home, the current value should be approximately $208,353. The answer can be found using the financial calculator as well. However, this time it will take two separate calculations because of the two different growth rates. The keystrokes are contained in Solution 8.2.

Solution 8.2

−189000 [PV]

1 [n]

4 [i/y]

[pt] [FV] 196560

And then,

−196560 [PV]

1 [n]

6 [i/y]

[cpt] [FV] 208353.60

In this case, it is almost easier to use Equation 8.4 rather than the financial calculator because of the requirement of entering two separate future value calculations at two different growth rates.

COMPOUND ANNUAL GROWTH RATE

Some situations require you to figure out what growth rate caused the value to move from an initial value to a greater value. In that case we are trying to solve for the rate of interest, or the growth rate. In this type of calculation the financial calculator is a tremendous asset.

Look at a case where a homeowner purchased her home for $125,000 five years ago, and she has it appraised and finds that the current value is $153,000. She would like to know what annual rate of appreciation she has earned over the five-year period. Using the following financial calculator keystrokes will get her the answer.

Solution 8.3

−125000 [PV]

5 [n]

153000 [FV]

[cpt] [i/y] 4.13%

Her annual compound rate of appreciation has been 4.13%. This means that it went up in value by 4.13% the first year, then by 4.13% the second year, and so on. It is a compound growth rate.

Let's assume that you are selling a piece of investment property that you purchased 10 years ago for $275,000. One of the tenants would like to purchase the building and has made an offer of $435,000. You have told the tenant that you wouldn't sell unless you have earned a compounded annual rate of appreciation of at least 4.5%. Should you sell the property? Go ahead and push some buttons. If you were paying attention when we went through the last problem, you probably went back to check Equation 8.3 and did something similar to what is shown in Solution 8.4.

Solution 8.4

−275000 [PV]

435000 [FV]

10 [n]

[cpt] [i/y] 4.69%

Your decision, of course, would be to sell the property because you are earning in excess of your required appreciation rate of 4.5%. In fact you are earning a compound rate of 4.69%.

AVERAGE OR NOMINAL APPRECIATION

The owner's average, or nominal, noncompounded annual rate of appreciation is calculated using $(P_1 - P_0)/P_0$ as follows. The total change in value over the five-year period is $28,000, and that figure divided by the initial value results in 22.4% of the initial value. That 22.4% divided by five years gives us an average growth rate of 4.5% per year as shown in Equation 8.5.

Equation 8.5

$$(\$153{,}000 - \$125{,}000)/\$125{,}000 = \$28{,}000/\$125{,}000 = 0.224/5 = 0.045 = 4.5\%$$

This average rate is not compounded, which is why it is higher than the compounded rate. The compounded rate takes into consideration that the owner is receiving interest on interest in the compounding process. The average growth rate has the advantage of being much easier to calculate. We don't need a financial calculator to find the average growth rate. We can solve Equation 8.5 with a standard four-function calculator.

While the average growth rate is much easier to calculate, it also gives us a somewhat distorted picture of the actual growth rate because it tends to overstate the rate of growth. The compound growth rate requires the use of a financial calculator, but it gives us a truer picture of how the growth rate works. Each year we go up in value, that value increase is based on the value of what has happened in the past. Property values truly do increase at a compounded rate of growth.

TOTAL APPRECIATION OVER A NUMBER OF YEARS

If the total amount of appreciation is the percentage that is desired, it can also be determined in a couple of different ways. Let's say that a homeowner purchased a home for $120,000 and it is currently worth $150,000. The total amount of appreciation can be determined in a few different ways. The first of these is by dividing the current value by the purchase price, subtract 1 and convert the decimal to a percentage.

Equation 8.6

$$\$150,000/\$120,000 = 1.25 - 1 = 0.25 \text{ or } 25.0\%$$

In Equation 8.6 we have taken the current, or ending, value and divided it by the purchase price, or beginning value. Then we took the answer of 1.25 and subtracted the 1 so we are left with 0.25 or 25%. Over the holding period, however long it was, this property increased in value by 25%.

Alternatively the calculation can be made again using the $(P_1 - P_0)/P_0$ format, and the same value is achieved as follows.

Equation 8.7

$$(\$150,000 - \$120,000)/\$120,000 = 0.25 \text{ or } 25.0\%$$

What we have done in Equation 8.7 is taken P_1, or $150,000, and subtracted P_0, or $120,000, and divided that quantity by P_0, which again is $120,000. The result of the calculation is once again 0.25 or 25%. This illustrates that the home has experienced appreciation of 25%.

A third way to get the total amount of appreciation is by using the financial calculator. This time the (n) value will not be a number of years; it will simply represent the entire holding period, so it is given a value of 1.

Solution 8.5

> −120000 [PV]
>
> 150000 [FV]
>
> 1 [n]
>
> [cpt] [i/y] 0.25 = 25%

All three calculations result in the same answer for total appreciation, which is 25%.

If an investor purchased a building for $375,000 and has been told that the building has appreciated by 25% in value, what would that building be worth today?

Equation 8.8

$$\$375,000 \times (1 + 0.25) = \$375,000 \times (1.25) = \$468,750$$

The ending value based on a total appreciation rate could also be found using the financial calculator. Solution 8.6 shows the required keystrokes. Make note that since we are using a total amount of appreciation rather than an annual amount, the [n] we use is simply 1. It is not 25% per year; it is 25% over the total holding period. Think of it as one holding period.

Solution 8.6

> −375000 [PV]
>
> 1 [n]
>
> 25 [i/y]
>
> [cpt] [FV] 465750

Today that building would be worth $468,750 if it had indeed appreciated 25% in value. Equation 8.8 and Solution 8.6 take us to the same place.

If the question went a step further and asked, what was the compound annual rate of appreciation that took the value from $375,000 to $468,750 over the five-year period, the solution on the financial calculator would look like this.

Solution 8.7

> −375000 [PV]
>
> 468750 [FV]
>
> 5 [n]
>
> [cpt] [i/y] 4.56% per year

The compound annual rate of appreciation is 4.56%. This rate is again lower than the average rate of appreciation of 5%, or 25%/5 = 5%. The lower compound rate is lower because of the compounding effect.

Depreciation in Appraisal

According to the *Dictionary of Real Estate Appraisal*, published by the Appraisal Institute, *depreciation* is a loss in value due to any cause. This depreciation is applied to the replacement cost of the improvements in the cost approach as you will see in Chapter 10 on real estate appraisal.

The depreciation can come in three forms: physical deterioration, functional obsolescence, and economic or locational obsolescence. The first of these, physical deterioration, is probably what comes to mind when most people think of depreciation. This is the physical wearing out of the improvements. It is the chipped paint, the cracked plaster, or the missing roof shingles. When this form of depreciation is valued separately, it is usually based on the cost to cure. How much would it cost to repaint the rooms? How much would it cost to repair the plaster? Or how much would it cost to replace the roof?

The second form of depreciation may escape casual observers. They may not recognize it as depreciation, but they may respond that, "There is something funny about that house." That something funny is functional obsolescence. This is either something that doesn't function the way it should or something that is no longer desirable in the marketplace. It may be a dysfunctional floor plan, such as a bedroom off of the living room. It may be a stairway coming directly into a room rather than into a hallway. I think of my grandmother's kitchen when I think of functional obsolescence. She had these very large cupboard doors that were about four feet tall, reaching up to the high ceiling. Nobody could ever get anything down from the top two shelves. There were linoleum countertops in the kitchen, in a red swirl pattern as I recall, with a little aluminum band around the edge where all of the "gunk" got caught. Other examples of functional obsolescence would include shag carpet, avocado colored appliances, a gravity furnace, or a single-car garage.

A dollar value is a little more difficult to establish for this type of depreciation. The concept of curable versus incurable depreciation comes into play with functional obsolescence as well as for physical deterioration. The basic test is economic viability. If the change is not economically viable, the depreciation is incurable; if it makes economic sense, it's curable. It is pretty difficult to change a floor plan deficiency, which makes that incurable. Replacing shag carpeting makes economic sense.

The third form of depreciation is locational, or economic, obsolescence. Let's say you own a house in Hibbing, Minnesota, and the taconite plants are closed down. Suddenly there are scores of unemployed workers who decide they have to move to another town for employment. They all put their houses on the market at the same time. This tremendous increase in the supply of housing without a corresponding increase in demand will cause values to go down. This loss in value is simply the result of where the home is located—in Hibbing. This value loss, or depreciation, is pretty much incurable.

An appraiser will be asked to determine the loss in value that has resulted from these three forms of depreciation on the property. Some of the valuation service companies such as Marshall & Swift publish tables that have combined the different forms of depreciation into depreciation tables. Depreciation tables give a percentage of depreciation that should be taken based on the age of the structure and the original quality of construction. If a house has a construction cost of $200,000 new, and the depreciation tables recommend taking depreciation of 20%, then the house would have a depreciated cost as stated in Equation 8.9.

Equation 8.9

$$\$200,000 \times 0.20 = \$40,000 \text{ and then } \$200,000 - \$40,000 = \$160,000$$

The depreciated cost of the improvements is equal to the cost times 1 minus the depreciation rate. This is the same calculation as shown in Equation 8.10.

Equation 8.10

$$\$200,000 \times (1 - 0.20) = \$200,000 \times (0.80) = \$160,000$$

The question may be worded in reverse fashion. A house is currently worth $140,000 and has depreciated by 15% since it was purchased. What was its original value? The calculation then becomes Equation 8.11.

Equation 8.11

$$\$140,000/(1 - 0.15) = \$140,000/0.85 = \$164,705.88$$

Rather than multiplying by 1 minus the rate as we did in Equation 8.9, you simply divide by 1 minus the rate of depreciation. Dividing the $140,000 by 0.85 gives us the value of $164,705.88. To check your answer, now multiply the $164,705.88 by 1 minus the rate, or $164,705.88 \times (1 - 0.15)$, which is the same as $164,705.88 \times 0.85$, and get the correct value of $140,000.

Depreciation in Investment Property

Depreciation in an investment property scenario is quite a different thing from depreciation in appraisal. In the previous section it was stated that depreciation is a loss in value due to any cause. For investment property, depreciation is a theoretical wearing out of the property that is deducted from income for taxation purposes. Uncle Sam, the IRS, says that investors can deduct the value of this depreciation from their income so that the investors' tax liability will be reduced. Uncle Sam is saying that investors can have a larger cash flow from operations because of this depreciation. The purpose of depreciation is to allow investors to recapture this wearing out of the asset so that they could theoretically replace it once it wears out. In effect, depreciation is another expense that can be deducted from investors' operating income. However, it is called a noncash expense since the investor doesn't actually write out a check to depreciation.

Current tax law states that real property wears out in one of two ways. It either wears out over 27.5 years in the case of residential property, or it wears out over 39 years in the case of nonresidential property. *Residential property* is defined as someplace where you can live. This depreciation may be taken over what is referred to as a straight line. That means that the same amount of depreciation expense is taken each year until the asset is fully depreciated, when the basis equals zero. Adjusted basis is equal to the acquisition cost minus depreciation that has been taken. To calculate the amount of depreciation expense that can be taken, subtract the land value from the acquisition cost to obtain the value of the improvements. Then divide the value of the improvements by either 27.5 for residential property or by 39 for nonresidential property.

Equation 8.12

Depreciation expense = (Acquisition cost − land value)/27.5 (or 39)

THE IMPACT OF DEPRECIATION ON TAXABLE INCOME

The impact of depreciation on taxable income is illustrated in Table 8.1. The top portion of the table, calculating net operating income (NOI) and before-tax cash flow (BTCF), is addressed in Chapter 10, "Real Estate Appraisal." The bottom portion of the table, calculating after-tax cash flow (ATCF) is covered in Chapter 11, "Real Estate Investment Analysis."

By looking at depreciation in the left-hand column of Table 8.1, one can see that interest expense and depreciation are deducted from net operating income. The result of this deduction is called taxable income if the number is positive and taxable loss if the number is negative. As we will see in Chapter 11, the investor

Table 8.1   After-tax cash flow

Potential gross income	
− Vacancy and rent loss	
Effective gross income	
− Operating expenses	
Net operating income	
− Debt service	
Before-tax cash flow	
Net operating income	$32,490
− Interest	−$26,129
− Depreciation	−$14,545
Tax income (loss)	−$8,185
× − Marginal tax rate	× − 0.28
Tax liability (savings)	$2,292
Before-tax cash flow	
−/+ Tax liability or savings	
After-tax cash flow	

does not mind if this number is negative, or a tax loss. In any event, you can see that more depreciation expense means we end up with either a lower taxable income or a larger tax loss. When the taxable income is lower, this means that we will have a lower tax liability. When we have a larger tax loss, this means that we will have a larger tax savings. Both of these possibilities are good things as far as the investor is concerned.

If the marginal tax rate (MTR) is plugged into the table as a negative number, the product of the tax rate times the taxable income or loss has the correct sign, from a cash flow standpoint. Note in Table 8.1, that the tax loss of −$8,185 is multiplied by the −28% tax rate to get a +$2,292 tax savings. This tax savings of $2,292 increases the after-tax cash flow by that same amount. These calculations are expanded upon in Chapter 11.

As an example of how depreciation is calculated, consider an investor who purchases an apartment building for $500,000 which includes land value of $100,000. Her annual depreciation calculation is shown in Equation 8.13.

Equation 8.13

$$(\$500,000 - \$100,000)/27.5 = \$14,545.45$$

The investor could deduct $14,545.45 in depreciation expense from the net income on her building for tax purposes. See Chapter 11 to see how this tax benefit can result in greater cash flow to the investor. Additional IRS regulations, Accelerated Cost Recovery System, or ACRS, state that the entire $14,545.45 cannot be taken the first year the property is put in service, but that is another story entirely. It is referred to as the half-year convention. Please consult your tax accountant to determine how much depreciation expense you may deduct from the income of your own investment property.

If the investor purchases a warehouse to rent out to a tenant, the calculation follows the same process. The only difference is that a 39-year life is used for nonresidential property. If the purchase price is $750,000 and the land value represents 20% of the value, or $150,000, the depreciation calculation would look like Equation 8.14.

Equation 8.14

$$(\$750,000 - \$150,000)/39 = \$15,384.62$$

ACCELERATED DEPRECIATION

In past years depreciation other than straight line was allowed for real property. As recently as 1986 the IRS permitted the use of 175% declining balance depreciation. At the time a 19-year life was used. This means that the investor could take much more depreciation expense under those provisions. Equation 8.15 illustrates that calculation for depreciation using a 19-year life and a 175% declining balance.

Equation 8.15

$$175\%/19 = 0.0921 = 9.21\% \text{ per year}$$

The investor could take 9.21% of the value of the improvement per year as depreciation. Let's say we had a piece of property with an improvement value of $100,000. We would take that times the 0.0921 and get depreciation expense in the first year of $9,210. The declining balance tells us to take $100,000 − $9,210 and get an adjusted basis of $90,079. In year 2 we would take $90,079 × 0.0921 and get a depreciation expense of $8,361.76. This would again be deducted from the previous adjusted basis, and so on until the basis is down to zero, hence the term declining balance. Under current IRS regulations, that same property would receive a depreciation deduction of only $2,560. We can get that by taking 100%/39 = 2.56% and then taking 2.56% of the $100,000 improvement value. Hopefully you can see the magnitude of this change that took place under the 1986 Tax Reform Act. Using this small piece of property as an example, the difference in taxable income between these two different tax regulations would be $6,650 per year. This is not a small change in income. You can see why property values did not increase significantly directly after the 1986 Tax Reform Act took effect.

Quiz for Chapter 8

1. A seller signs a purchase agreement to sell her home for $225,000. She purchased the home several years ago for $162,900. What was the total appreciation percentage that she experienced?

   a. 23.4%

   b. 17.9%

   c. 38.1%

   d. 27.6%

2. An appraiser estimates that the current construction costs for a subject property are $185,000. The appropriate depreciation rate for the age of the building is 15%. What is the depreciated cost of the building?

   a. $185,000

   b. $212,750

   c. $160,869

   d. $157,250

3. You purchased your home six years ago for $194,500, and you have been told that homes have been appreciating at the rate of 3% per year in your neighborhood. What is your home worth today based on annual compounding?

   a. $229,510

   b. $232,243

   c. $217,842

   d. $231,652

4. An investor just purchased a warehouse for $345,000 to be rented out at market rental rates. The assessor's office tells him that the land value is $70,000. How much depreciation expense can he take using straight line depreciation?

   a. $7,051

   b. $1,794

   c. $10,000

   d. $2,545

5. Your brother finds out that you are a real estate math wiz and asks you how much depreciation expense he can take on his newly acquired rental house in Florida. The home was purchased for $220,000, of

which $44,000 was the value of the land. What amount of straight line depreciation can your brother take per year to offset income?

a. $8,000

b. $5,641

c. $6,400

d. $4,512

6. Your boss tells you that he purchased his home 19 years ago for $120,000. He goes to the bank and is told that his home is currently worth $455,000. What has been his annual compound rate of appreciation?

a. 7.3%

b. 4.5%

c. 20%

d. 3.9%

7. A homeowner purchased her home four years ago for $137,900 and sold it today for $163,500. What was her average annual rate of appreciation (not compounded)?

a. 4.6%

b. 18.6%

c. 3.6%

d. 9.7%

8. A house recently sold for $133,000. It had depreciated by 15% since it was originally purchased. What was the original purchase price?

a. $19,950

b. $152,950

c. $145,000

d. $156,470

9. Your parents are selling their home, and they ask you how much total appreciation they have experienced since they bought their home. The sale price is $175,000, and they purchased the home for $123,900. Their total appreciation rate is:

a. 8.5%

b. 29.2%

c. 41.2%

d. 43.1%

10. The purchase price of your home was $245,000 five years ago, and homes in your market have been appreciating by 4% per year. Given the compound rate of appreciation, what is the current value of your home?

    a. $298,080
    b. $254,800
    c. $294,000
    d. $294,080

CHAPTER 9

The Closing and Closing Statements

In Summation, Your Honor

The *closing* can be defined as a gathering of interested parties at which the promises made in the purchase agreement are executed. Who are the interested parties? First of all, the two parties associated with the purchase agreement, the vendor and the vendee, or the seller and the buyer. Other interested parties may include the salesperson(s), the broker(s), an attorney, a representative of the title insurance company, a representative of the mortgage lender, other lien holders (i.e., contract for deed holders), and the person referred to as the closing agent. The closing agent is the person who will calculate and create the closing statements. The closing agent may be a real estate broker, a representative of the title insurance company or mortgage lender, or an attorney. The closing agent may be someone who is licensed solely to act as a closing agent.

The closing statement is used to sort out the expenses and prepayments associated with a real estate closing. In other words, the debits and the credits of the transaction are accounted for in the closing statements. There are two separate closing statements that appear at the closing—the buyer's closing statement and the seller's closing statement. The bottom line of the buyer's closing statement tells the buyer how much additional cash must be brought to the closing. The seller's closing statement tells the seller what the net proceeds will be from the transaction, or how much cash he or she will have when they go home.

The debits on the closing statement are a charge to the debited party, or an amount of money this person owes. When you cover up the i in the word debit, you are left with the word *debt*, which is another nice explanation of a debit. The credits on the closing statement are either an amount of money the credited party has coming in or an amount of money this person has already paid and wants to get credit for having paid it.

Expenses

The types of expenses that may show up on the closing statement include sales commissions, title opinions, title insurance fees, appraisal fees, origination fees, recording fees, mortgage registration tax, state deed tax, real estate taxes, insurance premiums, discount points, credit report, document preparation, abstract extension, home warranty fee, and others. Some of these expenses typically fall under the buyer's responsibility to pay, and some typically fall under the seller's responsibility. There are by no means hard-and-fast rules and could vary depending upon the state in which the closing is taking place.

Expenses that are typically paid by the buyer would include those costs associated with the buyer's new mortgage. This would include the origination fee, the appraisal fee, the discount points, the mortgage registration tax, the recording fee associated with the new mortgage and the deed, and in some states the title insurance premium. This is not to imply that the seller might not pick up these expenses in a buyer's market, but they are most often paid by the buyer.

Those expenses that are typically paid by the seller include the sales commission to the broker, title clearing costs including recording fees for any documents needed in clearing the title, abstract extension, attorney's fees, recording of the mortgage satisfaction, and in some states the title insurance premium. The title insurance cost is kind of a variable. In some states the title insurance cost falls on the buyer since it is protecting the buyer's interest. In other states however, the title insurance cost falls on the seller, since that is the way the seller can assure the buyer that the seller is providing clear title to the property. It turns out to be whatever is the customary practice in an individual market.

PREPAID EXPENSES

Expenses can be classified as either prepaid or accrued. Expenses that are prepaid have been paid for, but not fully used up. Let's look at real estate taxes that can be prepaid in certain instances. In Minnesota real estate taxes are paid twice a year. The first half of the real estate taxes is due on May 15 of the year. This payment covers the taxes for the first half of the year, from January 1 through June 30. If the closing is to take place on May 30 of the year, the first half of the real estate taxes will already have been paid by the seller on May 15. In this situation the real estate taxes will be prepaid as far as the seller is concerned. This means that the seller will have already paid the taxes for the use of the property from January 1 through June 30, but the seller is not going to be on the property for the month of June; the buyer will be using the property then. As a result, the buyer will have to pay the seller for the real estate taxes for the month of June at the closing. The seller is said to own the property up to and including the day of closing and pays the expenses for the day of closing, so the buyer starts paying the real estate taxes as of June 1.

The real estate tax payment would show up on the seller's closing statement as a credit for the month of June. The same amount would show up on the buyer's closing statement as a debit. These expenses that are split between the seller and the buyer are referred to as *prorated items*. They are the only items that appear on both the seller's statement and the buyer's statement as the same amount.

ACCRUED EXPENSES

Accrued expenses are those expenses that have been earned but not yet paid. An example of an accrued expense can again be real estate taxes. If in the previous example the closing was to take place on March 30, the taxes would indeed be an accrued expense to the seller. The seller would have been in the property for all of January, February, and March and would not have paid any taxes for that time period. It would be the buyer that is in the property on May 15 when the check would have to be written for the taxes. The result is that the seller would have to pay the buyer at the closing for the taxes that he or she had earned, or used up, during the months of January–March. That amount would appear as a debit on the seller's closing statement, and the same amount would appear as a credit on the buyer's statement.

Prorated Items

As mentioned previously, prorated items are expenses that are split between the buyer and the seller. Real estate taxes are one area in which we see the prorating process used. Another area would be in the interest due on an assumed mortgage.

INTEREST ON AN ASSUMED MORTGAGE

Let's say that we are having a closing and the buyer is assuming the seller's mortgage. The mortgage will have a principal balance of $95,500 on March 12, the day of closing. The mortgage carries a 7% rate of interest. Mortgage payments are due on the first of the month, and they require interest to be paid in arrears. This means that we don't have to pay for using the money until we have already used it. As a result the March 1 mortgage payment contained the interest paid for the use of the money during the month of February. The next payment will be due on April 1, and that will contain the interest for the use of the money during the month of March. The seller will be using the mortgage money for twelve days, from March 1 through March 12. The buyer will be making the mortgage payment on April 1, so the buyer needs to collect from the seller the interest that the seller has accrued from the first through the twelfth. Equation 9.1 contains the calculation for the annual interest on the mortgage.

Equation 9.1

Annual interest = Principal amount × interest rate = $95,500 × 0.07 = $6,685

That amount is now divided by twelve to get the monthly amount of interest as shown in Equation 9.2.

Equation 9.2

Monthly interest = Annual interest ÷ 12 = $6,685 ÷ 12 = $557.08

To get the daily amount of interest, we divide the monthly interest by the number of days in the month of closing, in this case 31. The result is shown in Equation 9.3.

Equation 9.3

Daily interest = Monthly interest ÷ 31 = $557.08 ÷ 31 = $17.97

Now we can calculate the amount of interest that the seller owes to the buyer by multiplying the daily amount of interest due on the mortgage by 12, as shown in Equation 9.4.

Equation 9.4

Interest due from March 1 through March 12 = $17.97 × 12 = $215.64

Thus the amount of interest due from the seller to the buyer at the closing would be $215.64, which would appear as a debit on the seller's statement and a credit on the buyer's statement. Now when the buyer makes the mortgage payment on April 1, he or she will have the total amount of interest that is owed on the mortgage for the use of the money during the month of March. The buyer will have the amount of interest for the use of the money from the first through the twelfth that the seller has paid and the amount of interest from the thirteenth through the thirty-first that is owed as a result of being in the property during that time period.

REAL ESTATE TAXES

Real estate taxes can also be prorated between the seller and the buyer. Assume we are having a closing on April 14 and the real estate taxes are to be prorated between the seller and the buyer. Annual real estate taxes are $1,000, and the first half of those taxes are due and payable on May 15. In other words someone has to pay $500 for those taxes on May 15. In order to calculate the prorated amount, start by taking the $500 and divide it by 6 to get the monthly amount, as shown in Equation 9.5. The same value could be obtained by taking the annual amount of $1,000 and dividing it by 12.

Equation 9.5

Monthly amount = $500 ÷ 6 = $83.33 or $1,000 ÷ 12 = $83.33

Next, to get the daily amount, divide the monthly amount by 30, since there are 30 days in April. Occasionally closing agents and banks will use a statutory year, which has 360 days and 30 days per month. At other times they will use a calendar year that has 365 days and the actual number of days per month.

Equation 9.6

$$\text{Daily amount} = \$83.33 \div 30 = \$2.78$$

To get the amount to be prorated, multiply the daily amount by 14. Since we are closing on the fourteenth and the seller owns the property up to and including the day of closing, the seller will be accruing taxes for the first through the fourteenth.

Equation 9.7

$$\text{Prorated amount} = (\$2.78 \times 14) + (3 \times \$83.33)$$

$$= \$38.89 + \$249.99 = \$288.88$$

The total amount to be prorated would be 14 times the daily rate for the April value plus 3 times the monthly rate for January, February, and March. That total amount comes to $288.88, which would be the amount debited to the seller and credited to the buyer.

Buyer's Statement

The buyer's closing statement is designed to inform the buyer, or buyers, how much additional cash they need to bring to the closing. A typical blank buyer's closing statement is illustrated in Table 9.1 below. Before moving on to the next paragraph, look at the blank statement and try and determine which line items would show up as debits on the buyer's statement and which items would show up as credits on the buyer's statement. A little later in the chapter we use Table 9.1 in a closing statement case problem.

It is important that we have an understanding of the terminology used in the buyer's closing statement. The *purchase price* is in fact the price paid for the property. This same amount will appear as the *sale price* on the seller's closing statement. *Earnest money* is the amount of money that the buyer puts down at the time the offer is made. Earnest money serves two purposes. First it indicates that the buyer is sincere, or earnest, in his or her desire to purchase the property and should discourage the buyer from defaulting prior to the closing. Second it serves as compensation to the seller in the event a default takes place. The earnest money was put down at the time the purchase agreement was signed and thus would show up as a credit on the buyer's statement. The buyer wants to receive credit for already having paid it.

Table 9.1 Buyer's closing statement

	Debits	Credits
Purchase price		
Earnest money		
Mortgage		
– Principal		
– Interest		
Real estate taxes		
Insurance		
Title insurance		
Origination fee		
Appraisal fee		
Credit report		
Recording		
– New mortgage		
– Deed		
– Mortgage satisfaction		
Mortgage registration tax		
Subtotals		
Due from buyer		
Totals		

The *mortgage principal and interest* that show up on the buyer's statement are the new mortgage being used to finance the purchase of the property. The mortgage principal is the amount being borrowed, and it will appear as a credit on the buyer's statement. It appears as a credit because it is an amount of money the buyer has coming from the bank, and it is a part of the purchase price that the buyer won't have to bring in cash to the closing. The interest referred to is the amount of interest that would accrue from the day of closing through the end of the month of closing.

Since the first mortgage payment will not made until one full calendar month's worth of interest has accrued, the interest for the month of closing has to be paid at the closing. It was stated earlier that the seller owns the property on the day of closing, and this is true. However, the buyer receives the mortgage money from the lender on the day of closing, and as a result starts paying interest from the day of closing. If the closing is on April 14, the first mortgage payment will not be made until June 1. That is because one full calendar month's worth of interest will not accrue until then. That being the case, the buyer will have to pay for the use of the mortgage money during the month of April on the day of closing. In this case the buyer would have to pay for 17 days' worth of interest at the closing for the fourteenth through the thirtieth.

If the buyer is not taking out a new mortgage but is assuming the seller's old mortgage, then the principal amount is the principal amount of the old mortgage being assumed. This principal amount also would show up as a credit on the buyer's statement, just as the principal amount of the new mortgage shows up as a credit. It is a part of the purchase price that the buyer does not have to bring to closing in the form of cash. The interest shows up as the amount of interest that the seller has accrued from the first of the month through the date of closing, and that amount appears as a credit on the buyer's statement. It appears as a credit because the seller has to pay it to the buyer so the buyer can afford to make the next mortgage payment which is due on the first of the following month.

The *real estate taxes* show up on the buyer's closing statement because they are commonly prorated between the buyer and the seller. Depending on the common practice in a given market and the time of year that the taxes are due in that market, those taxes may appear as either a debit or a credit on the buyer's statement. Insurance may show up on the buyer's statement in regard to a homeowner's insurance policy. That amount may show up as a debit if the buyer has yet to order a homeowner's policy, or it may show up as a credit if the buyer has already prepaid a one-year policy. The mortgage lender is going to require that a one-year policy be in place to protect the lender's interest in the event of a protected catastrophe occurring during the term of the mortgage. The *title insurance* item may appear on the buyer's statement, as it does here, or it may show up on the seller's statement depending on local market practices. As mentioned earlier, in Minnesota it will appear on the buyer's statement, and in Texas it will appear on the seller's statement. In both cases it would appear as a debit on the closing statement.

The *origination fee*, the *appraisal fee*, and the *credit report* costs are all associated with the new mortgage and as a result will all appear as debits on the buyer's closing statement. Any other fees associated with the new mortgage would be the buyer's expense and thus show up as debits on the buyer's statement.

The *recording fees* appear as debits for the person who is responsible for paying them. The person paying the fees is the person whose interest is being protected by the recording of the document. The recording of the new mortgage is the buyer's expense since the new mortgage is associated with the buyer and not the seller and because recording that document protects the buyer's, as well as the lender's, interest. The recording of the deed also protects the buyer's interest. Since the recording of these two documents protects the buyer's interest, the buyer pays to record them, and they show up as debits on the buyer's closing statement. The *mortgage satisfaction* is a document issued by the mortgage lender of the seller's mortgage which tells the world the seller has paid off the mortgage. Recording this document protects the seller's interest so it is the seller's expense to record it.

This means that it will show up as a debit on the seller's closing statement and will not appear on the buyer's closing statement.

The final item on the statement in Table 9.1 is the *mortgage registration tax*. This is a tax paid by the buyer at the time the mortgage is recorded in the county courthouse and shows up on the buyer's statement as a debit.

Once all values are recorded on the buyer's closing statement, both the debit column and the credit column are summed and the resulting values are recorded in the subtotals row. The debits will no doubt exceed the credits on the buyer's statement. I tell my students that if they are reluctant to purchase a property where the credits exceed the debits, they should give me a call and I will buy that property! The next step is to subtract the subtotal of the credits from the subtotal of the debits, and that difference is the amount still due from the buyer. It gets recorded in the line below the subtotal of the credits. Now that value is added to the subtotal of the credits and gets recorded on the totals line in the credits column. The subtotal of the debits column is now brought down to the totals line in the debits column, and the buyer's closing statement is complete.

Seller's Statement

The seller's closing statement is designed to tell the seller how much cash he or she will end with after the closing. A seller's closing statement is illustrated in Table 9.2. Before moving to the next paragraph, take a look at each item on the seller's closing statement and try to determine which items will appear as debits and which items will appear as credits. This table is used a little later in the chapter in a case study.

Table 9.2   Seller's closing statement

	Debit	Credit
Sale price		
Mortgage		
– Principal		
– Interest		
Real estate taxes		
Insurance		
Recording fee		
Commission		
State deed tax		
Subtotals		
Amount due seller		
Totals		

The *sale price* that is mentioned in the seller's statement is the same amount as the purchase price that appears in the buyer's closing statement. The *mortgage principal and interest* that appear in the seller's statement are the amounts associated with the seller's old mortgage that is either being paid off or assumed. The principal amount is the mortgage balance that is either being paid off by the seller from the proceeds of the sale, or it is the amount being assumed by the buyer in the case of a mortgage assumption. In either case the principal amount will appear as a debit on the seller's statement. The interest amount that appears on the seller's statement is the amount of interest accrued from the first of the month until the day of closing, as was described previously when addressing the mortgage assumption for the buyer's statement. It is the interest expense that the seller is accruing during the month of closing while the seller is in the property. This time the amount will appear as a debit on the seller's statement. The seller has to pay the buyer for the interest accrued so that the buyer will be able to make the mortgage payment on the first of the following month.

The *real estate taxes* appear on the seller's statement because they are often prorated. If they are prorated, the amount that appears on the seller's statement will be the same amount that appears on the buyer's statement, only in the opposite column. If they are a debit on the buyer's statement, they will be a credit on the seller's statement, and vice versa. If it is a buyer's market, the parties may agree that the seller will pay all the taxes due in the year of sale. In that case they would not appear on the buyer's statement, but only on the seller's. On the other hand if it is a seller's market, the buyer may pay the full year's taxes. In that case they would not appear on the seller's statement, but only on the buyer's. Real estate taxes are very often a negotiable item. Insurance is typically an item that does not appear on the seller's statement because it is usually the buyer's expense. In certain strange circumstances the annual insurance premium may be prorated and would then appear on both statements.

The *recording fee* that appears on the seller's statement is for recording the mortgage satisfaction. Recording this document tells the world that the seller no longer owes money against this property. Since it protects the seller's interest, it is the seller's expense to record it, and thus it appears as a debit on the seller's statement.

The selling commission is typically paid by the seller and thus shows up as a debit on the seller's closing statement. Finally, the state deed tax, or a tax of similar name and purpose, is paid by the seller and shows up as a debit on the seller's statement.

Once again the subtotals of the columns are calculated and recorded. In the seller's case the credit column will usually exceed the debit column, although it is not quite as cut and dried as the buyer's statement. If the seller is in a market that has experienced price reductions resulting from rising interest rates or some other market shock, the debits may in fact exceed the credits. It is in these markets that we tend to see a dramatic increase in the number of mortgage foreclosures. If we are in a normal market under normal conditions, the total credits will typically exceed the total debits. Taking the difference between those two values, we find the amount that is due the seller. That amount is then added to the total debits, and the resulting figures balance in the totals row.

The following case study can be completed by using the blank statements in Table 9.1 and 9.2 which appeared earlier in this chapter. Using those tables, and the information provided in this chapter, complete the case study that follows. The completed closing statements will be found on the following pages, but don't look at them until you have completed Table 9.1 and Table 9.2 on your own. Helpful hint: You may want to use pencil on this.

Case Study

Given the following information, calculate both the buyer's closing statement and the seller's closing statement for the transaction described with a closing date of September 15, 20—.

- Sale price—$123,000
- New mortgage of $90,000, 7% interest rate, 30 years
- Old mortgage with $45,000 balance, 10% interest rate
- Earnest money—$3,000
- Insurance premium—$400 payable at closing
- Real estate taxes $1,680 per year, payable May 15 and October 15
- Sales commission of 6%
- State deed tax—$3.30 per $1,000 of the sales price
- Mortgage registration tax—$2.30 per $1,000 of new mortgage amount
- Recording fees of $15 per document; new mortgage, mortgage satisfaction, deed
- Title insurance—$500
- Origination fee for the new mortgage of 1% of the mortgage amount
- Credit report—$75
- Appraisal fee—$350

CASE STUDY SOLUTION

As is indicated in the completed buyer's closing statement (Table 9.3), the buyer would be required to bring another $32,392 to the closing. That amount of $32,392 represents the balance of the down payment plus the net of the expenses and prorations. The balance of the down payment, $33,000 − $3,000 = $30,000, would

Table 9.3 Buyer's closing statement

	Debits	Credits
Purchase price	$123,000	
Earnest money		$3,000
Mortgage		
– Principal		$90,000
– Interest 9/15 – 9/30	$280	
Real estate taxes		$350
Insurance	$400	
Title Insurance	$500	
Origination fee	$900	
Appraisal fee	$350	
Credit report	$75	
Recording		
– New mortgage	$15	
– Deed	$15	
– Mortgage satisfaction		
Mortgage registration tax	$207	
Subtotals	$125,742	$93,350
Amount due from buyer		$32,392
Totals	$125,742	$125,472

have to be in cash or certified funds. A personal check could be used for the difference.

CALCULATIONS

Mortgage interest:

$$\$90,000 \times 0.07 = 6,300 \div 12 = 525 \div 30 = 17.50$$

$$\$17.50 \times 16 = \$280$$

Sixteen days' worth of interest due at closing:

$$9/15 - 9/30 = 16 \text{ days}$$

which includes the fifteenth, the first day we get the money.

Real estate taxes: $1,680 ÷ 2 = $840 for six months, first six months already paid on May 15.

$$\$840 \div 6 = \$140 \times 2.5 = \$350$$

Taxes of $140 per month for 2.5 months, which is a credit to the buyer.

Origination fee:

$$\$90,000 \times 0.01 = \$900$$

Mortgage registration tax:

$$\$90,000 \div 1,000 = 90 \times \$2.30 = \$207$$

Amount due from buyer:

$$\$125,742 - \$93,350 = \$32,392$$

As stated previously, the seller's closing statement will inform the seller of the net proceeds to expect as a result of the sale. In Table 9.4 that figure is represented by the amount due to the seller.

CALCULATIONS

Interest:

$$\$45,000 \times .10 = \$4,500 \div 12 = \$375 \div 30 = \$12.50 \times 15 = \$187.50$$

Twelve days of interest at $12.50 per day. Real estate taxes: The same amount that is a credit to the buyer is a debit to the seller. See the calculation under the buyer's statement.

Table 9.4 Seller's closing statement

	Debit	Credit
Sale price		$123,000
Mortgage		
– Principal	$45,000.00	
– Interest 9/1 – 9/15	$187.50	
Real estate taxes	$350.00	
Insurance		
Recording	$15.00	
Commission	$7,380.00	
State deed tax	$405.90	
Subtotals	$53,338.40	$123,000
Amount due seller	$69,661.60	
Totals	$123,000.00	$123,000

Commission:

$$\$123,000 - 0.06 = \$7,380$$

State deed tax:

$$\$123,000 \div \$1,000 = 123 - \$3.30 = \$405.90$$

Amount due seller:

$$\$123,000 - \$53,338.40 = \$69,661.60$$

Quiz for Chapter 9

1. Which of the following is true of real estate closings?
    a. Closings are generally conducted by real estate salespeople.

    b. The buyer usually receives rent for the day of closing.

    c. The buyer must reimburse the seller for any title evidence provided by the seller.

    d. The seller usually pays the expenses for the day of closing.

2. The earnest money deposited in the broker's trust account would show up on the closing statements as:
    a. A debit to the seller.

    b. A debit to the buyer.

    c. A credit to the seller.

    d. A credit to the buyer.

3. The buyer's new mortgage amount shows up on the closing statements as:
    a. A debit to the seller.

    b. A debit to the buyer.

    c. A credit to the seller.

    d. A credit to the buyer.

4. The subtotals on the buyer's closing statement look like this: subtotal of debits = $175,000, and subtotal of credits = $54,700. What amount will appear in both the total of the debits column and the total of the credits column?
    a. $175,000

    b. $54,700

    c. $120,300

    d. None of the above

5. In the scenario stated in Question 4, how much additional cash is due from the buyer at the closing?
    a. $175,000

    b. $54,700

    c. $120,300

    d. None of the above

6. When an expense has accrued to a seller, it appears on the seller's closing statement as:

    a. A debit to the seller.

    b. A debit to the buyer.

    c. A credit to the seller.

    d. It doesn't appear on the seller's statement.

7. The interest due for the month of closing on the new mortgage appears as what on the seller's closing statement?

    a. A debit to the buyer.

    b. A credit to the buyer.

    c. A debit to the seller.

    d. It doesn't appear on the seller's statement.

8. When the seller's old mortgage is being assumed,

    a. The principal balance appears as a debit on the seller's statement.

    b. The principal balance appears as a credit on the seller's statement.

    c. The principal balance appears as a debit on the buyer's statement.

    d. The principal balance appears on neither statement.

9. If the buyer's new mortgage is $115,000 at a 7% interest rate and the closing in on the May 13, how much interest expense will be debited to the buyer at the closing?

    a. $380.10

    b. $357.80

    c. $402.50

    d. $670.80

10. If the mortgage registration tax is calculated at the rate of $3.30 per $1,000 of new mortgage amount and the buyer purchased the house for $225,000 with a new mortgage of $180,000 at 6.5% interest, what is the amount of mortgage registration tax due at the closing?

    a. $594.00

    b. $742.50

    c. $975.00

    d. $3,300.00

CHAPTER 10

Real Estate Appraisal

We Value Your Opinion

Introduction

An *appraisal* is an informed estimate or opinion of value. It can also be referred to as the process of estimating the value of real property. The type of value that the appraiser is called on to determine is most often the fair market value of a piece of property. A fair market value definition can be summarized as the most probable price a property could bring if exposed to the market for a reasonable period of time. It is assumed that the buyer and seller are under no duress and are well informed, the property is exposed to the market for a reasonable period of time, and payment is made in cash or its equivalent.

Another type of value that a property may have is called *investment value*. Investment value is the value that a property may have for a specific individual investor. One investor may have a different investment objective than the typical

investor in the marketplace. The investor may require a 12% return on equity rather than a 14% return that may be typical in the market. Obviously these returns will vary by property type and individual market characteristics.

The Three Approaches

The appraisal process incorporates three different approaches for estimating property value. These are the cost approach, the sales comparison approach, and the income approach. Each of the three approaches makes use of different mathematical calculations. These three approaches are described in some detail, and typical calculations for each approach are reviewed and practiced.

THE COST APPROACH

The first of the three approaches is the *cost approach* which is based on an appraisal principle called the *principle of substitution*. This principle states that nobody will pay more for a property than it would reasonably cost to construct a new substitute for that property. As a result the value of existing housing tends to be tied to the cost of new construction. If the two types of property were not relatively similar in value, one type of property would sell and the other would not.

The cost approach can be broken down into five steps. They are:

1. Estimate the value of the land (site) the building is sitting on.
2. Estimate the current construction costs.

   - They may be reproduction costs, replacing everything exactly as it is today, brick for brick.
   - They may be replacement costs, replacing the building with one of similar size and similar utility.
   - Replacement costs are generally used unless reproduction costs are specified.

3. Estimate the accrued depreciation that has taken place since the building was constructed. The depreciation may be one of three types: physical deterioration, functional obsolescence, or economic/locational obsolescence.
4. Deduct the accrued depreciation from the construction costs to get the depreciated construction costs.
5. Add the depreciated construction costs to the value of the land to get the value estimate using the cost approach.

The equation for the value of a property using the cost approach would look like Equation 10.1, which is in fact a summary of steps 1–5 above.

Equation 10.1

$$\text{Value} = (\text{Construction costs} - \text{depreciation}) + \text{land value}$$

In summarizing the tasks involved in the five steps listed above, the land value estimate, which is the fourth step in the appraisal process, usually shows up in the cost approach portion of the appraisal report. The land value is typically estimated by comparing the subject site with similar sites that have recently been sold. I like to refer to this as a mini sales comparison approach. The complete explanation of a sales comparison appears in the next section of this chapter.

The second step of estimating current construction costs is accomplished by researching a reference such as the *Marshall and Swift Current Construction Cost Guide*. This, and other similar publications, contains square-foot construction cost estimates for different sized houses of five different construction and material qualities. There are also multipliers used for materials in different parts of the country. Using these costs produces very reasonable construction cost estimates.

If we had a subject property of 1,550 square feet and the construction cost manual suggested a replacement cost per square foot of $67.50 per square foot and based on the home's age the appropriate depreciation was 20% of the construction costs, what would the depreciated cost of the improvements be? We would simply follow the steps in Equation 10.1 and Equation 10.2.

Equation 10.2

Depreciated cost of the improvements

$$= (1{,}550 \times \$67.50) - 0.20(1{,}550 \times \$67.50) = \$104{,}625 - \$20{,}925$$

$$= \$83{,}700$$

Thus the depreciated cost of the improvements would be equal to $83,700. The same value could have been obtained by taking the construction costs times $(1 - 0.20)$ or $\$104{,}625 \times 0.80 = \$83{,}700$.

The third step in the cost approach involves the estimation of the depreciation that the subject property has experienced since the home was constructed. *Depreciation* is defined as a loss in value due to any cause. The depreciation can take one of three different forms: physical deterioration, functional obsolescence, and economic (or locational) obsolescence. Calculating the value of the depreciation can be the most challenging part of the cost approach, particularly in older properties. There is a table used for estimating depreciation in the Marshall and Swift cost guide based on the remaining economic life of a property.

Step 4 is a straightforward subtraction problem, and step 5 is an addition problem; they are both self-explanatory.

The cost approach should establish the upper limit of value since nobody should pay more for a home than it would cost them to rebuild that home. This approach works best on new construction and special purpose type properties. It works well on new construction because there hasn't been much depreciation when the property is new or nearly new. The depreciation estimate is the most difficult part of the cost approach, so by reducing the magnitude of that calculation, the appraiser can be more confident in the value estimate that results from the cost approach. The cost approach is useful for appraising special purpose properties because they don't sell very often, making the sales comparison approach difficult to use, and they don't generate any income so the income approach is not very useful.

THE SALES COMPARISON APPROACH

The second of the three approaches is the *sales comparison approach*. The sales comparison is the best approach to use in valuing single-family residential property. The approach is based on the principle of substitution. Someone will not pay substantially more for a house today than a similar house sold for yesterday. The subject property is compared to a number of houses that sold recently, which are referred to as comparable sales, or comps. The houses are compared based on a number of different factors, called *elements of comparison*. These elements of comparison include;

- Lot size
- Square footage of the improvements
- Conditions of sale
- Architectural style
- Type of heating
- Air-conditioning
- Fireplaces
- Garages
- Outbuildings
- Quality of materials
- Condition of the improvements
- Age of improvements
- Location
- Date of sale
- Financing used

- Number of bedrooms
- Number of baths

Every time there is a difference between the subject and the comparable, an adjustment must be made. The adjustments are made to the sale price of the comparable as follows:

- Deduct the value of the features that are in the comparable but not in the subject.
- Add the value of those features that are in the subject but not in the comparable.
- Adjust the comparable to make it equal to the subject property.

To come up with an adjusted sale price for the comparable, simply net out the adjustments against the sale price. Those comparables that require the fewest adjustments are in fact the best comparables. The adjusted sale price of the comparable would be the sale price minus the net value of the total adjustments.

Problem 10.1

Your subject property is a three-bedroom rambler with 1,000 square feet of improved living area with a single bathroom and a two-car garage. You found a comparable sale of similar type house with three bedrooms, 1,000 square feet of space, a single bathroom and a two-car garage. The only difference between the subject property and the comparable is that the comparable has a fireplace and the subject property does not. The comparable sold for $150,000. You have determined that the fireplace has a market value of $5,000. This may have been done by analyzing market sales, or it may be some depreciated cost calculation. If this is the one and only difference between the two properties, then the first bullet above says that we deduct the value of those features that are in the comparable but not in the subject. Thus, Equation 10.3 contains the appropriate calculation.

Equation 10.3

Value of subject = Sale price of the comparable − value of the fireplace

$145,000 = $150,000 − $5,000

The sale price of the comparable in this problem would reflect the value of a home with a fireplace. Since our subject does not have a fireplace, we would have to deduct the value of the fireplace from the sale price of the comparable to reflect the value of a home without a fireplace. Thus the value of our subject property in this example would be $145,000 if the fireplace was the only difference between the subject and the comparable.

Problem 10.2

If the subject property used in the previous problem had the fireplace and the comparable did not have one, the calculation of the subject's value would look like Equation 10.4. The value of the subject would be equal to the value of the comparable plus the value of the fireplace. This is because in this case the sale price of the comparable would reflect the value of a home without a fireplace, so we would have to add its value into the sale price to reflect the value of a home with a fireplace.

Equation 10.4

Value of the subject = Sale price of the comparable + value of the fireplace

$$\$155,000 = \$150,000 + \$5,000$$

THE INCOME APPROACH

There are several forms of the income approach. These include the gross rent multiplier (GRM), income capitalization, and discounted cash flow. The gross rent multiplier is the most effective form of the income approach for valuing single-family residences. The gross rent multiplier is calculated, or extracted, from a comparable sale. The comparable should have been rented at the time of the sale to be the best comparable. The GRM is equal to the sale price of the comp divided by the gross monthly rent of the comp, as shown in Equation 10.5.

Equation 10.5

$$\text{GRM} = \text{Sale price}_c / \text{gross monthly rent}_c$$

The GRM is then applied to the market rent of the subject as shown in Equation 10.6.

Equation 10.6

$$\text{GRM} \times \text{market rent}_s = \text{Value}_s$$

The value of the subject is equal to the GRM times the market rent of the subject. The market rent is the monthly rent that could be generated by the subject property if it were exposed to the rental market. You should notice that there are no adjustments made to the comparables as there were in the sales comparison approach. This is because the market should have already factored in property difference through the rental rates. Renters know the value of additional square footage or a fireplace since they have looked at other units in the marketplace.

As a result we don't see the adjustments made in the income approach like those that appeared in the sales comparison approach.

Problem 10.3

You are called on to appraise a single-family home in your neighborhood that is a 1,000 square foot rambler (ranch) that has three bedrooms. You find a number of comparables in the neighborhood that have recently sold. The best comparable sold for $165,000 and was generating rent of $1,450 per month. In conducting your market research, you have determined that the market rent of your subject property would be $1,275 per month. What is the value of your subject property using the GRM form of the income approach using your best comparable? First you would make use of Equation 10.5 to estimate your GRM, as shown in Equation 10.7.

Equation 10.7

$$GRM = \$165,000 \div \$1,450 = 113.79$$

You would then use Equation 10.6 to estimate the value of the subject property by taking the product of the GRM that you have just calculated times the market rent of the subject property, getting a value of just over $145,000. This calculation is illustrated in Equation 10.8.

Equation 10.8

$$\text{Value of subject} = 113.79 \times \$1,275 = \$145,082$$

The income capitalization form of the income approach is an effective valuation technique when applied to income-producing properties. These may be residential properties, such as apartment buildings, or commercial buildings like office buildings, warehouses, or retail centers. This form of the income approach can be broken down to five steps.

1. Estimate the potential gross income (PGI) the building could generate in a 12-month period, assuming tenants always paid their rent and the building were occupied 100% of the time. For an apartment building this would be the number of units times the rent per unit, plus any garage income that may be generated during the year, plus any extraneous income such as laundry income. The PGI for a four-unit apartment building with each unit renting for $950 per month would be $4 \times \$950 \times 12 = \$45,600$. The PGI for an office building would be the number of rentable square feet in the building times the rent per square foot per year. The PGI for

a 5,000 square foot office building renting for $14 per square foot would be $5,000 \times \$14 = \$70,000$.

2. Deduct a vacancy and rent loss allowance from the potential gross income to get the effective gross income (EGI) for the property. Effectively this is the amount of income the owner will actually see.

3. Then deduct the annual operating expenses for the property from the effective gross income to get the net operating income (NOI). These expenses will include snow removal, accounting expenses, management fees, real estate taxes, and any other operating expenses for the year. This will not include financing charges. This NOI is the income that the investor is buying and the income that the appraiser is valuing.

4. Next a capitalization rate, or cap rate, is estimated. Two methods of estimating a cap rate are market extraction and band of investment. To estimate the cap rate using market extraction, you need a comparable sale. Take the NOI of the comparable and divide it by the sale price of the comparable using the IRV (income rate value) formula in Equation 10.9.

Equation 10.9

$$IRV: I_c/V_c = R$$

where $I = NOI$, $R = $ cap rate, and $V = $ value. So IRV tells us to take the NOI of the comparable for the coming period and divide it by the value, or the sale price, of the comparable, and that will give us our cap rate.

5. The final step in the income capitalization form of the income approach is to again use IRV, this time dividing the subject property's NOI for the coming period by the cap rate just extracted from the comparable sale, and that will result in the value estimate, as is illustrated in Equation 10.10.

Equation 10.10

$$I_s/R = V_s$$

The five steps mentioned above are summarized in Table 10.1.

Table 10.1   NOI estimation

PGI
– Vacancies
EGI
– Operating expenses
NOI

Note that IRV is simply a variation on the part, percent, whole format that is mentioned in Chapter 1 of this book. The income, or NOI, is a part, the R, or capitalization rate, is a percent, and the value is the whole.

Problem 10.4

You are called on to appraise a six-unit apartment building in which all apartments are rented for $1,100 per month. The building and local market for similar buildings are both experiencing a 6% vacancy rate. Operating expenses for the coming year are expected to be $27,000. A similar building in the subject property's neighborhood sold recently for $650,000 and was generating $52,000 in NOI at the time it was sold.

The PGI calculation is contained in Equation 10.11. Since this is an apartment building, we multiply the rent per unit by the number of units by 12 months to get the potential gross income. In this instance there is no income other than that received for the apartment rent.

Equation 10.11

$$PGI = \$1,100 \times 6 \times 12 = \$79,200$$

The EGI calculation follows in Equation 10.12, with the PGI minus the vacancy allowance. In this case the PGI is multiplied by 1 minus the vacancy rate which accomplishes the same goal. The vacancy allowance in this problem is equal to 6% of the PGI.

Equation 10.12

$$EGI = PGI - \text{vacancy allowance} = \$79,200 - \$4,752 = \$77,448$$

An algebraic shortcut to this calculation appears in Equation 10.13. Algebraically what is happening is that by extending the equation, we are multiplying the PGI by 1 and the PGI by the negative of the vacancy rate which yields the answer of the PGI minus the vacancy rate. Whichever method is more comfortable to you is the one you should use. Both methods lead to the same answer.

Equation 10.13

$$EGI = PGI\,(1 - \text{vacancy rate}) = \$79,200\,(1 - 0.06) = \$79,200 \times 0.94 = \$77,448$$

By plugging the numbers into the equation, we can obtain the resulting EGI of $77,448.

Table 10.2   NOI estimation solution

PGI	$79,200
– Vacancies	–$4,752
EGI	$77,448
– Operating expenses	–$27,000
NOI	$47,448

The NOI of the building for the coming year is obtained by deducting the annual operating expenses from the EGI and is summarized in Equation 10.14.

Equation 10.14

$$NOI = EGI - \text{operating expenses} = \$77{,}448 - \$27{,}000 = \$47{,}448$$

The NOI estimation is also summarized in Table 10.2.

Now that the NOI is in place, we need to estimate the capitalization rate (R), which is simply the NOI/value, or sale price, of the comparable. The cap rate estimate is illustrated in Equation 10.15.

Equation 10.15

$$R = NOI/Value = \$52{,}000/\$650{,}000 = 0.08$$

The final step is the value estimate itself. This again depends on the IRV formula which indicates that the value is equal to the NOI divided by the cap rate, as found in Equation 10.16.

Equation 10.16

$$Value = NOI/R = \$47{,}448/0.08 = \$593{,}100$$

Thus the value of our six-unit building with each unit renting for $1,100 per month is $593,100.

Referring back to step 4 of the income capitalization form of the income approach mentioned previously, the second method of estimating the cap rate is called the band of investment method. The band of investment provides a method of estimating a cap rate, such that the resulting value estimate ensures that the property will generate sufficient NOI to provide an adequate return to the debt holder and an adequate return to the equity holder. Stated another way, the lenders will achieve their required rate of return and the investors will achieve their rate of return.

The equation for estimating the cap rate using the band of investment is contained in Equation 10.17. The equation says that the cap rate is equal to the loan-to-value ratio (L/V) times the annual mortgage constant (MC), plus the equity to value ratio (E/V) times the investor's required return on equity (ROE).

Equation 10.17

$$R = (L/V \times MC) + (E/V \times ROE)$$

The L/V ratio, or loan-to-value ratio, is the mortgage amount divided by the value of the property, typically stated as a percentage or its decimal equivalent. The annual mortgage constant is taken from the payment to amortize time value of money calculation. It is actually the payment necessary to amortize the debt of one dollar per month multiplied by 12 to annualize it. If we wanted to calculate the annual mortgage constant for a 75% L/V mortgage amortized over 30 years at 7% interest, we would use the calculator keystrokes shown in Solution 10.1. Computing the monthly payment to amortize results in a value of 0.006653, which we multiply by 12 to get a rounded annual mortgage constant of 0.0798.

Solution 10.1

1 [PV]

360 [n]

7/12 = [i/y]

[cpt] [pmt] 0.006653 × 12 = −0.0798

The third variable in Equation 10.17 is the equity-to-value ratio, or E/V. This is simply 1 minus the loan-to-value ratio. At the time of purchase the E/V ratio is the percentage of the purchase price represented by the down payment. The final variable in Equation 10.17 is the investor's required return on equity. This return is stated by the investor and is based on his or her risk tolerance, investment goals, and so on.

Problem 10.5

You are called on to estimate a capitalization rate to value a property, and you are told it should be derived using the band of investment technique. The parameters you are given include an 80% L/V mortgage amortized over 30 years at 6.5% interest and an investor's required rate on equity of 12%. What is the implied cap rate?

First of all, refer to Solutions 10.1 and 10.2 to estimate the annual mortgage constant. Next, plug your values into Equation 10.17, and you will end up with Equation 10.18.

Solution 10.2

1 [PV]

360 [n]

6.5/12 = [i/y]

[cpt] [pmt] $0.0063 \times 12 = -0.0758$

Equation 10.18

$$R = (0.80 \times 0.0758) + (0.20 \times 0.12) = 0.0607 + 0.024 = 0.0847$$

Notice that the 12% required return on equity has been converted to the decimal equivalent in order to be consistent with the format of the mortgage constant. Thus the cap rate indicated by the band of investment technique is equal to 0.0847 or 8.47% given the information provided.

Problem 10.6

Let's try a more comprehensive problem. An investor has called on you to estimate the value of a 10-unit apartment building. All of the units are the same size and are currently renting for $1,200 per month. There is a 5% vacancy rate for this property and others like it, and operating expenses for the coming year are expected to be $54,720. The investor is contemplating a 75% L/V mortgage amortized over 25 years at a 7% rate of interest. Her required return on equity is 14%. Given this information, what is the building's value using income capitalization and the band of investment technique for estimating the cap rate?

First we need to estimate the expected NOI, and then we need to estimate the appropriate capitalization rate. Potential gross income is found in Equation 10.19.

Equation 10.19

$$PGI = \$1,200 \times 10 \times 12 = \$144,000$$

The effective gross income is equal to the PGI minus the vacancy allowance, as shown in Equation 10.20.

Equation 10.20

$$EGI = \$144,000 \ (1 - 0.05) = \$144,000 \times 0.95 = \$136,800$$

Finally, the NOI is equal to the EGI minus the annual operating expenses, as shown in Equation 10.21.

Table 10.3 NOI estimation

PGI	$144,000
– Vacancies	–$7,200
EGI	$136,800
– Operating expenses	–$54,720
NOI	$82,080

Equation 10.21

$$NOI = \$136,800 - \$54,720 = \$82,080$$

The NOI calculation is also summarized in Table 10.3.

In order to estimate our cap rate, we again refer to Equation 10.17 and plug in the needed numbers to get Equation 10.22. First we need to get our annual mortgage constant using the TVM keys of our financial calculator as shown in Solution 10.3.

Solution 10.3

1 [PV]

$25 \times 12 = 300$ [n]

$7/12 =$ [i/y]

[cpt] [pmt] $0.0071 \times 12 = -0.0848$

Equation 10.22

$$R = (0.75 \times 0.0848) + (0.25 \times 0.14) = 0.0636 + 0.035 = 0.0986 = 9.86\%$$

The cap rate of 0.0986 can now be applied to the NOI of $82,080 using IRV as can be seen in Equation 10.23.

Equation 10.23

$$Value = I/R = \$82,080/0.0986 = \$832,454$$

So the value of our 10-unit building is the NOI of $82,080 divided by the cap rate of 0.0986 which is $832,454 given the financing and investment assumptions that were stated above. An interesting exercise, and when I make this statement to my students, they hear the words, "This is going to be hard to do." Now check to see if this value *estimate results in there being adequate NOI to satisfy both the debt holder and the equity holder* as we said it would at the beginning of this band of investment section, just two paragraphs prior to Equation 10.17. It really won't be that hard to do, and it usually results in a "wow" moment.

First we will need to examine the return on equity (ROE) calculation. The general equation is Equation 10.24.

Equation 10.24

$$ROE = BTCF/equity$$

The BTCF is the before-tax cash flow, and it is calculated by deducting the annual debt service, which is the sum of the year's monthly mortgage payments, from the net operating income. Thus we multiply the monthly mortgage payment by 12, and that is the annual debt service. When we deduct that amount from the NOI, we are left with before-tax cash flow. Equity at the time of purchase is equal to the investor's down payment. Calculating equity at any time during the holding period is shown in Equation 10.25.

Equation 10.25

$$Equity = Market\ value - mortgage\ balance$$

Now that we know how to come up with ROE, let's see if we did Problem 10.6 correctly.

The value estimate that we arrived at is $832,454. Our financing plans called for a 75% L/V mortgage amortized over 25 years at a 7% rate of interest. The mortgage amount is $832,454 × 0.75 which is equal to $624,340.50. The monthly payment for that mortgage is found in Solution 10.4 below.

Solution 10.4

624340.50 (PV)

25 × 12 = 300 [n]

7/12 = [i/y]

[cpt] [pmt] −4412.37

The annual debt service is equal to 12 × $4,412.37 or $52,952.51. That amount is deducted from the NOI as illustrated in Table 10.4 to get the before-tax cash flow.

Now, to determine whether there is sufficient NOI to satisfy both the debt holder and the equity holder, we can first look at the debt holder. The lender is earning the required rate of return because the payment was calculated using the 7% return needed by the lender. As we see in Table 10.4, the lender will receive the debt service of $52,952 and be happy with that 7% return. That will leave another $29,127 of the NOI that will go to the investor in the form of BTCF. In order to see whether that satisfies the investor's requirement, we calculate the return on

Table 10.4   Before-tax cash flow

PGI	$144,000
– Vacancies	–$7,200
EGI	$136,800
– Operating expenses	–$54,720
NOI	$82,080
– Debt service	–$52,952
BTCF	$29,127

equity, or ROE. In Equation 10.26 we divide the BTCF by the investor's equity investment, which in this case is the 25% of the purchase price, or value. We are doing that because the E/V ratio is equal to 1 – L/V, and 1 – 0.75 = 0.25. Thus, equity is equal to $832,454 × 0.25 or $208,113.50.

Equation 10.26

$$\text{ROE} = \text{BTCF}/\text{Equity} = \$29{,}127/\$208{,}113.50 = 0.14 = 14\%$$

As you can see in Equation 10.26, the ROE received by this investor will in fact be 14%, which is exactly the same value we indicated that the investor needed to receive at the beginning of this problem. What we have done then is, we have *created a cap rate such that the resulting value estimate ensured sufficient NOI to satisfy both the debt holder and the equity holder.* Wow!

DISCOUNTED CASH FLOW

The final form of the income approach to be addressed is called *discounted cash flow*. One of the potential drawbacks of the income capitalization form of the income approach is the result of the mathematical form that it takes. The IRV formula for the value calculation is I/R = V. This is in fact a present value calculation. It is the present value of a particular annuity. You will recall that an annuity is a series of equal payments that come at regular intervals. This type of an annuity is called a *perpetuity*, because it is a perpetual annuity. The payments are assumed to come forever, or in perpetuity. Some people say, and with some degree of validity, that this is an unreasonable expectation for a depreciating asset. As a result, another form of valuing income property has been developed that eliminates the perpetual concept, and we look at a property over a finite holding period. In the discounted cash flow (DCF) analysis we take the present value of a finite number of NOIs generated by the property and add to that the present value of a future sale price, or reversion. As you may recall from Chapter 6, on the time value of money, an investor will only pay the present value of all cash flows to be received, discounted at the required rate of return. The process follows financial theory that states that the value of a share of stock is equal to the present value of the expected dividends over a projected holding period plus the present value of the future sale price of that share of stock.

Not only does DCF overcome the problem of valuing one single year's NOI and the implicit assumption of that income being constant forever, but it allows the inputting of new assumptions regarding variability of rent levels, changes in vacancy rates, and changes in operating expenses in addition to assumptions about market conditions affecting property values during the projected holding period.

Problem 10.7

To get a feeling for how DCF works, let's take a look at a sample problem. An investor is considering the purchase of a 12-unit apartment building where each unit is currently renting for $1,250 per month. Rents are expected to increase by 3% per year. The building has a vacancy rate of 5%, and that is expected to remain constant over the near future. The operating expenses for the coming year are expected to be $68,400, and they are expected to increase at the rate of 2% per year. In five years the anticipated going out cap rate, which is the cap rate expected in the market in five years when the building is expected to be sold, will be 8.5%. The investor's required rate of return on investment is 12%. Given this information and using DCF, what is the value of this building?

Given the assumptions stated in the paragraph above, the NOI calculations for a six-year period are as stated in Table 10.5.

A sixth year of NOI is included in Table 10.5 for the calculation of the reversion, or sale price at the end of the five-year holding period. You may recall that in the initial discussion of IRV we said that we take the coming year's NOI and divide it by the cap rate. In other words, to get the value at time period 0, which is today, we divide the cap rate into the NOI for time period 1, or the coming period.

Table 10.5   Six years of NOI

	Year 1	Year 2	Year 3	Year 4	Year 5	Year 6
GPI	$180,000	$185,400	$190,962	$196,691	$202,592	$208,669
−Vacancies	9,000	9,270	9,548	9,835	10,130	10,433
EGI	171,000	176,130	181,414	186,856	192,462	198,236
−Operating expenses	68,400	69,768	71,163	72,587	74,038	75,518
NOI	$102,600	$106,362	$110,251	$114,270	$118,424	$122,718

Table 10.6   Total present value

Year	NOI (+rev in year 5)	Present value @ 12%
1	$102,600	$91,607
2	106,362	84,791
3	110,251	78,474
4	114,270	72,620
5	118,424 + 1,443,741	886,414
Total value		$1,213,906

So, if $V_0 = I_1/R$ that should tell us that for calculating V_5 we will need the NOI for period 6, since $V_5 = I_6/R$. Armed with this information, the reversion value calculation in Equation 10.27 should make sense. We divide the NOI for year 6 by the going out cap rate of 8.5%, or 0.085, and get the reversion value of $1,443,741.

Equation 10.27

$$V_6 = \$122,718/0.085 = \$1,443,741 = \text{Reversion value}$$

Now, using the values from Table 10.5 and the reversion value from Equation 10.27, we can calculate the value of the subject property using the DCF method. The calculation is summarized in Table 10.6. For the first four years' worth of NOI, we simply take the PV of that amount discounted at the 12% required rate of return. In year 5 we take the PV of the sum of the final NOI + the reversion value (rev), since both those cash flows are assumed to come at the end of year 5. We then add the present values and get the final value estimate of $1,213,906. Please be advised that most appraisers and investors do not think they can estimate the value of a $1 million plus building down to the nearest dollar, so an appraiser would probably state the value as about $1,214,000 rather than $1,213,906.

The value may also be calculated using the cash flow keys of your calculator. See Solution 10.5 for the keystrokes.

Solution 10.5

[CF] 0 [enter]
[↓] 102600 [enter][↓]
[↓] 106362 [enter][↓]
[↓] 110251 [enter][↓]
[↓] 114270 [enter][↓]

[↓] 1562165 [enter][↓]

[↓][NPV] I = 12 [enter] [↓]

NPV = [cpt] 1213907.79

The calculator display is indicated where there are no [ ] (brackets) around the letters. You will notice a slight difference between the value in Table 10.6 and the value in Solution 10.5. This is the result of the rounding that was done in the table. You will notice that we don't use cents in the present value calculation and that the calculator is accurate to 13 decimal places. The cash flow key solution is the more accurate.

By using the DCF method of the income approach, we are able to input some market assumptions that we could not have used in the income capitalization method. We are able to use a growth rate in the rents, we use a growth rate in the operating expenses that was different from the growth rate in rents, and we are able to make an assumption about the property value increase during the holding period. These are some of the benefits of using the DCF method. Keep in mind, however, that the benefit of the method can also be its downfall if one makes wild unsupportable assumptions.

CASH EQUIVALENCY

When a seller is willing to finance the sale of his or her property with a below-market rate of interest contract for deed or when the buyer assumes the seller's below-market rate of interest mortgage, the buyer is getting an advantage. Whenever property is bought using a below-market interest rate, the buyer is getting the property as well as the benefit of the below-market financing. That sale price will represent the value of the property plus the value of the financing. The technique used to separate the value of the financing from the value of the property is called *cash equivalency*. Let's take a look at the process of finding the value of below-market financing.

The first step involves calculating the monthly payment at the contract rate of interest. Second, discount those payments at the market rate of interest. The resulting value will be the present value of the financing. That discounted present value of the financing plus the cash down payment will result in the cash equivalent value, or the adjusted sale price. The difference between the cash equivalent value and the actual sale price would be the value of the beneficial financing.

Let's take a look at an example. Eileen is appraising a house, and she found a comparable sale that went for $175,000. The purchase price was made up of a $50,000 cash down payment and $125,000 in the form of a contract for deed at 6% interest amortized over 25 years. The market rate of interest at the time of the sale was 7.25%. What was the cash equivalent value, and what was the value of the beneficial financing?

First Eileen must find the payment at the contract rate. See Solution 10.6 for the calculation of the payment.

Solution 10.6

125000 [PV]

25 × 12 = 300 [n]

6/12 = [i/y]

[cpt] [pmt] −805.38

Now that monthly payment has to be discounted at the market rate, in this case 7.25%. Simply change the discount rate to 7.25/12 and solve for the new present value, as shown in Solution 10.7.

Solution 10.7

125000 [PV]

300 [n]

6/12 = [i/y]

[cpt] [pmt] −805.38

7.25/12 = [i/y]

[cpt] [PV] 111423.51

The value of the financing has dropped from $125,000 to $111,423.51. What the appraiser has done is first ask what the payment would be in a 6% market. Once Eileen had the payment, she asked how much money that payment of $805.38 would buy in a 7.25% market? The answer is $111,423.51, which is the present value of the financing. Now Eileen adds the cash down payment of $50,000 to the present value of the financing and finds the cash equivalent value, $111,423.51 + $50,000 = $161,423.51. That would make the value of the beneficial financing $175,000 − $161,423.51 = $13,576.49. So the buyer paid $161,423.51 for the real estate and $13,576.49 for the financing.

This calculation assumes that the buyer would pay for the full 25 years' worth of beneficial financing. In reality buyers won't pay for the full 25 years' worth of financing. They will probably pay for something less than that since they will either sell the property and pay off the loan before the end of the term, or they will refinance and pay off the loan. Appraisers will usually choose some shorter time period, say between five and nine years, and find the value of the financing over that time period. Let's use the same example as above, only this time we'll

say that the market is only paying for five years' worth of beneficial financing. Again, what is the cash equivalent value of the real estate, and what is the value of the beneficial financing?

The steps in the process given a truncated, chopped off, holding period are as follows.

- Calculate the monthly payment at the contract rate.
- Find the principal balance after five years at the contract rate.
- Find the present value of the five years' worth of payments at the market rate.
- Find the present value of the principal balance at the market rate.
- Add the PV of the payments to the PV of the principal balance and to the cash down payment. This equals the cash equivalent value or adjusted sale price.
- The contract sale price minus the cash equivalent value equals the value of the beneficial financing.

Just as the appraiser did in the previous example, we must first find the monthly payment at the contract rate. See the first four steps of Solution 10.8 for that calculation. Next we have to find the principal balance after five years since the market is paying for only five years of beneficial financing. That calculation is found in the final two steps of Solution 10.8. Keep in mind that the principal balance at any point in time is equal to the PV of the remaining payments.

Solution 10.8

125000 [PV]

25 × 12 = 300 [n]

6/12 = [i/y]

[cpt] [pmt] −805.38

[rcl] [n] −60 = [n]

[cpt] [PV] 112415.11

The principal balance at the end of five years is equal to $112,415.11. The third step listed above is to find the present value of the monthly payments discounted at the market rate, as shown in Solution 10.9.

Solution 10.9

−805.38 [pmt]

60 [n]

7.25/12 = [i/y]

[cpt] [PV] 40432.02

The fourth step is to find the present value of the principal balance discounted at the market rate, and we find that calculation in Solution 10.10.

Solution 10.10

112415.11 [FV]

60 [n]

7.25/12 = [i/y]

[cpt] [PV] −78318.91

Those two previous steps could be reduced to one calculation by calling the principal balance the future value, using your payment of 805.38 and the market rate of interest as the discount rate, and solving for present value as shown in Solution 10.11.

Solution 10.11

112415.11 [FV]

805.38 [pmt]

60 [n]

7.25/12 = [i/y]

[cpt] [PV] −118750.92

Notice that the answer in Solution 10.11 is the sum of the answers in Solutions 10.9 and 10.10, $78,318.91+$40,432.02 = $118,750.93 with one penny difference resulting from rounding. We take that value and add it to the cash down payment and get the cash equivalent value, or the adjusted sale price of $118,750.93 + $50,000 = $168,750.93. The value of the beneficial financing is $175,000 − $168,750.93 = $6,249.07. The financing is worth less because we are only valuing five years' worth of beneficial financing versus the entire 25 years in the previous calculation.

As you can see, cash equivalency gives us a method of finding the value of beneficial, or below-market rate, financing used in a transaction. This beneficial financing may result from a below-market rate contract for a deed being used or by the assumption of a below-market rate mortgage.

Problem 10.8

Joe is appraising a single-family house and has come up with an excellent comparable sale. The sale price of the comp is $235,000, and the sale was financed with a mortgage assumption of $185,000 at 6% interest and 20 years remaining on the loan. The balance of $50,000 was in the form of a cash down payment.

The market rate of interest at the time of the sale was 7%. What is the cash equivalent value or adjusted sale price if the market is currently paying for seven years of below-market financing? What is the value of the beneficial financing?

The steps in the process that appeared above just prior to Solution 10.8 suggest that the first thing to do is to calculate the payment at the contract rate of interest as in Solution 10.12.

Solution 10.12

185000 [PV]

20 × 12 = 24 = [n]

6/12 = [i/y]

[cpt] [pmt] −1325.40

The next step is to find the principal balance at the end of seven years, again at the contract rate of interest.

Solution 10.13

185000 [PV]

20 × 12 = 24 = [n]

6/12 = [i/y]

[cpt] [pmt] −1325.40

[rcl] [n] − 84 = [n]

[cpt] [PV] 143329.06

Next we will use the combined method of finding the present value of the payments and the present value of the principal balance which is found in Solution 10.11. Both of these sets of cash flows are discounted back 84 periods at the market rate of interest of 7%. This calculation is illustrated in Solution 10.14.

Solution 10.14

143329.06 [FV]

1325.40 [pmt]

84 [n]

7/12 = [i/y]

[cpt] [PV] −175749.67

The financing has a present value of $175,749.61, which, when added to the cash down payment, results in the cash equivalent value of $225,749.67. When the cash equivalent value of $225,749.67 is deducted from the sale price of $235,000, we find that the value of the beneficial financing is $9,250.33.

RECONCILIATION

Several times throughout the appraisal, the appraiser will be called on to take three different value estimates and convert them into a single value estimate. The most obvious situation comes about as a result of the three approaches to value. The appraiser will come up with one value estimate from the cost approach, one from the sales comparison approach, and yet another one from the income approach. At the end of the appraisal, the appraiser will have to take those three different values and convert them into a single value. The uninitiated would suggest adding them and dividing by three to get the final value estimate. An appraiser would take offense at that idea since even a third-grader can calculate an average. The reconciliation process allows appraisers to input their knowledge of the appraisal process as well as their knowledge of the quality of the data used in the appraisal into the final value estimate.

The appraiser will first consider the type of property being appraised and which of the three approaches is the more valid approach for the subject property being appraised. If the property is a single-family residence, the sales comparison approach would be the most appropriate approach. If the subject is an income-producing piece of commercial property, the most valid approach is probably the income approach. Finally, if the subject is a special-purpose property, then the best approach is probably going to be the cost approach. Once the best approach has been determined, the appraiser will analyze the quality of the data that went into each approach. Given these inputs, the appraiser will assign weights to each of the value estimates, and these weights will be applied to each of the three approaches, with the general equation in Equation 10.28. The weights assigned to the three approaches must add up to 1.

Equation 10.28

$$\text{Value} = (\text{wt}_1 \times \text{approach}_1) + (\text{wt}_2 \times \text{approach}_2) + (\text{wt}_3 \times \text{approach}_3)$$

The reconciled value is in fact a weighted average calculation. This results in a value estimate that contains information from each of the three approaches, but in fact it contains more information from the most valid approach and more information from the data that were deemed to be of the highest quality by the appraiser. Because of this process, appraisers are allowed to input their understanding of the appraisal process and their understanding of the market data into the final value estimate.

Problem 10.9

You are working on an appraisal of a one-year-old three-bedroom rambler on a half-acre lot in a neighborhood with very few rental properties. Let's say your cost approach indicates a value of $175,000. Your sales comparison approach gives you a value estimate of $168,500. Finally, your income approach indicates a value for the subject property of $159,000. Given this information, you need to come up with a single value estimate for the subject property.

The weights that you assign to the approaches in the reconciliation may be determined like this. First, you know that the subject is a single-family house and that the sales comparison approach is the best approach for this type of property if we have an adequate number of comparables to draw from. You feel that you had some pretty good comparables and, given these kinds of data, you decide to assign a weight of 0.50 to the sales comparison approach. Next, looking at the cost approach, you know that this approach works well on newly constructed property because the depreciation calculation can be relatively accurate for these new properties. Since the subject is only one year old, you decide to weight the cost approach the second most heavily, and you assign a weight of 0.40 to it. Since the income approach is going to be least reliable for this type of property and with the data quality present, you assign this approach a weighting of 0.10. Your weights sum up to 1, so you have not made an error in the weighting process: $0.50 + 0.40 + 0.10 = 1$.

The reconciled value estimate is illustrated in Equation 10.29.

Equation 10.29

$$\text{Reconciled value} = (0.50 \times \$168,500) + (0.40 \times \$175,000) + (0.10 \times \$159,000)$$

$$= \$84,250 + \$70,000 + \$15,900 = \$170,150$$

The reconciled value in Equation 10.29, which is based on the value estimates from our cost, sales comparison, and income approaches, is $170,150.

This final reconciliation is really only one of four reconciliations that is required throughout the whole appraisal. The first reconciliation to be done is in the cost approach, specifically in the land or site valuation. In this section of the appraisal the appraiser will do a mini sales comparison approach to estimate the land value. Three comparable sales will be analyzed and adjusted to find out what the subject's land value is. Those three comps will most likely yield three different adjusted sale prices that the appraiser will need to reconcile down into a single value estimate.

The sales comparison approach itself will result in three different adjusted sale prices which will also have to be reconciled to a single value estimate. Finally, the income approach will include three comparables used to determine the gross rent multiplier that is to be used. These three gross rent multipliers will be reconciled into a single gross rent multiplier, or the three GRMs will be multiplied by the market rent of the subject, and then those three values will be reconciled into a single value estimate. Thus, there may well be four different reconciliations in a single appraisal.

Summary

The appraisal chapter is filled with challenging mathematical concepts based on number of previous chapters. The simplest of the three approaches to determining value is the cost approach. In this approach the appraiser performs a mini sales comparison approach to determine land value and then adds the depreciated current construction costs to that to obtain the value estimate. In the sales comparison approach the appraiser finds sales of comparable properties that are similar to the subject property. Adjustments are made to the comparables for any differences between the comparable and the subject. Those dollar value adjustments result in an adjusted sale price for the comparable which will be an indication of the value of the subject property. The income approach establishes a value estimate for the subject property based on the amount of income the subject property could generate. For single-family residential property this is accomplished through the use of a gross rent multiplier. In the case of income-producing commercial property this will more likely be done through the use of income capitalization. Finally, the results of these three approaches to value are reconciled down from three value estimates to a single value estimate based on the quality of the data used in the three approaches and the appraisers understanding of the appraisal process.

Quiz for Chapter 10

1. An appraiser is working on the cost approach for Tom's house. The house is a 1,200-square-foot rambler that was built in 1979. The cost manual suggests that a home of this quality should have a replacement cost of $65.75 per square foot. The manual also suggests a depreciation of 19% of the construction costs. What is the depreciated cost of the house?
    a. $78,900
    b. $14,991
    c. $63,909
    d. $93,891

2. In conducting the sales comparison approach portion of the appraisal of Tom's house from question 1 above, a comparable was found in the same neighborhood that sold for $145,000. This comparable has 1,450 square feet of improved area, or about 250 square feet more than the subject property. If the appraiser concludes that the market is paying an additional $55 for each additional square foot of space over 1,200 square feet, what is the adjusted sale price of the comparable?
    a. $79,750
    b. $131,250
    c. $66,000
    d. $158,750

3. You have been called on to estimate the value of a single-family home using the gross rent multiplier (GRM) form of the income approach. The subject property you are appraising is a 1,300-square-foot home with three bedrooms, a living room, a family room, two bathrooms, and a two-car garage. You feel if it were put on the rental market, it would draw $1,400 per month in rent. A comparable that was recently sold for $162,500 was renting for $1,500 per month when it was sold. Using the GRM, what is the indicated value of the subject property?
    a. $151,600
    b. $174,100
    c. $162,500
    d. $175,000

4. In appraising a single-family home, you have found the following comparables and you have assigned the corresponding weights to these

comps based on their degree of comparability to the subject property. What is the reconciled GRM given the following information?

Sale price	Monthly rent	Weight	GRM
$179,000	$1,650	50%	
$149,750	$1,300	15%	
$187,500	$1,700	35%	

a. 112.10

b. 101.32

c. 102.10

d. 110.12

5. A 12-unit apartment building, with half the units renting for $1,050 per month and the other half of the units renting for $1,100 per month, is being appraised. The building is experiencing a 7% vacancy rate, and the operating expenses are expected to be $57,600 for the coming year. Using the table provided, calculate the building's net operating income (NOI).

```
PGI
-Vacancies
EGI
-Operating expenses
NOI
```

6. You are appraising a 4,000-square-foot office building which is currently renting for $12.50 per square foot. Given a 9% vacancy rate and operating expenses of $17,300 for the coming year, what is the expected NOI for next year?

a. $50,000

b. $45,500

c. $28,200

d. $32,700

7. Given the sales of office buildings listed in the table below and their associated NOIs and weights, what is the reconciled cap rate that you should use in estimating the value of the building in question 6?

Sale price	NOI	R	Weight
$370,000	$33,300		45%
$300,000	$24,000		35%
$280,000	$23,100		20%

a. 8.6%

b. 8.25%

c. 8.9%

d. 8.0%

8. You have decided to refinance your eight-unit apartment building, and the appraiser has decided to use the band of investment method to estimate the cap rate in her income approach. You have applied for an 80% L/V mortgage to be amortized over 30 years at a 6.5% rate of interest. Investors in today's market are expecting a return on equity of 16%. What is the cap rate the appraiser should be using in her appraisal given this information and the band of investment method?

a. 6.5%

b. 7.58%

c. 10%

d. 9.27%

9. The apartments in the eight-unit building mentioned in question 8 are each renting for $1,300 per month. The vacancy rate is running at 8%. Operating expenses for the coming year are expected to be $44,800. If the value of the building turns out to be $755,300, what is the building's before-tax cash flow (BTCF)? Use the information in both questions 8 and 9, and use the table provided.

PGI
−Vacancies
EGI
−Operating expenses
NOI
−DS
BTCF

10. If a building is generating NOI as listed below and is expected to sell after five years for the amount listed and if the appropriate discount rate is 11%, what is the indicated value of the property using the discounted cash flow (DCF) form of the income approach?

Year	NOI	Reversion
1	$5,000	
2	$5,500	
3	$5,575	
4	$6,120	
5	$6,150	$95,000

a. $45,454

b. $56,377

c. $77,103

d. $95,000

11

CHAPTER

Real Estate Investment Analysis

The PV of All Cash Flows to be Received

Cash Flow Estimation

When investors purchase investment property, they do so for reasons that are different from those of homeowners who purchase single-family homes. Home-owners purchase in order to house their families over the coming years. They spend a great deal of time in their homes raising families, playing with pets, and generally living life. As a result, buying a house is a very emotional decision for

many people. They often take a great deal of time looking at potential homes, both new and existing.

Investment property on the other hand is not an emotional decision typically. An investor is making a financial decision. The investor is buying a series of cash flows, and the largest question is how much to pay for those cash flows. Before that purchase price can be addressed, however, the make up of the cash flows must be determined. In the Chapter 10, "Real Estate Appraisal," we look at the net operating income (NOI) calculation. Chapter 8 on depreciation looks at the taxable income calculation. In this chapter we put all the cash flow calculations together and see how each of the elements is dependent on the others. The investor is interested in cash flows on a before-tax basis and an after-tax basis; the investor is also interested in both cash flows from operations and cash flows from the sale of the property.

Potential Gross Income

The cash flow analysis begins with the cash flows from operations. Investors will typically analyze the cash flows over their projected holding period for the property. That may be three years, five years, ten years, or more. (Later in the chapter we look at cash flow from the sale of the property.) The cash flow from operations estimate begins with the potential gross income (PGI) of a piece of investment property. This is the amount of income that the property could generate in one year, given two hypothetical situations. These hypotheticals are that the building is occupied 100% of the time and that all tenants always pay their rent—two things that don't always happen. This is the optimal amount of income the building could generate.

In the case of an apartment building, this would be the number of apartment units times the rent per unit plus any garage income that may be generated plus an estimate of the laundry income if there are laundry facilities. If the property is an office building or a warehouse facility, we would multiply the number of rentable square feet by the rent per square foot. This rent is typically stated as rent per square foot per year.

Effective Gross Income

We next deduct a vacancy and credit loss allowance from the PGI to obtain the effective gross income, because this is effectively the amount of money we are going to have to work with. It could also be called the "realistic" gross income because it is a more realistic number than is the potential gross income. This vacancy allowance should reflect what is going on in the investor's market for this type of property. If the market vacancy rate for this type of property is 8% and the seller says that the vacancy for the building is only 2% and that is what should be used, the seller may be indicating that rents are well below the market. The market should indicate what the appropriate vacancy rate to use is. Investors function in the market, and they should pay attention to what the market is telling them.

Net Operating Income

The net operating income (NOI) is equal to the effective gross income (EGI) minus the annual operating expenses. These operating expenses could include lawn service, snow removal, garbage pickup, accounting services, legal services, real estate taxes, and so on—whatever it costs to operate the building for one year. Operating expenses will not include finance charges. They are a completely different category, and they will be addressed shortly.

Before-Tax Cash Flow

The before-tax cash flow is where financing charges come into play. The annual debt service is the monthly mortgage payment times 12 plus any other financing payments such as contract for deed (land contract) payments. This annual debt service is deducted from the property's NOI resulting in the before-tax cash flow (BTCF). This is, in effect, the amount of money that is left in the checkbook after all the rents have been deposited and after all the expenses and the lender have been paid.

EXAMPLE 11.1

Let's use a single example to illustrate the cash flow analysis in the chapter. I refer to this single example, or problem, throughout the entire chapter. Our ultimate goal in this analysis is to calculate the after-tax cash flow from operations. Let's take a nine-unit apartment building with each unit renting for $1,175 per month. The building and the market are both experiencing a 7% vacancy rate. Operating expenses are expected to be $47,000 next year. The building can be purchased for $835,500 with an 80% L/V mortgage amortized over 20 years at a 7% interest rate mortgage. The land value of the property is $165,000. We expect rents to grow at a rate of 3% per year, operating expenses are to grow at 2% per year, and property values are expected to grow at a 3% rate per year. The investor expects to pay a 5% commission when he sells the building at the end of the holding period. The potential gross income from operations calculation is contained in the Equation 11.1.

Equation 11.1

$$PGI = \$1{,}175 \times 9 \times 12 = \$126{,}900$$

The effective gross income is illustrated in Equation 11.2.

Equation 11.2

$$EGI = \$126{,}900\,(1 - 0.07) = \$126{,}900\,(0.93) = \$118{,}017$$

The net operating income is the EGI minus the annual operating expenses as is shown in Equation 11.3. So the NOI of the building is $71,017.

Equation 11.3

$$NOI = \$118{,}017 - \$47{,}000 = \$71{,}017$$

Next we have to calculate the monthly mortgage payment, and then we'll multiply that by 12 to get the annual debt service. The mortgage amount is $835,500 × 0.80 = $668,400.

Solution 11.1

668400 [PV]
20 × 12 = 240 [n]
7/12 = [i/y]
[cpt] [pmt] 5182.10

The annual debt service is then $5,182.10 × 12 = $62,185.18. The before-tax cash flow from operations becomes Equation 11.4.

Equation 11.4

$$BTCF = \$71{,}017 - \$62{,}185.18 = \$8{,}831.82$$

The BTCF calculation is summarized in Table 11.1. You will notice in this table that the dollar values are rounded. These amounts are just fine for type B people. Type A people will, of course, want to use cents.

Table 11.1   Before-tax cash flow

PGI	$126,900
–Vacancies	8,883
EGI	118,017
–Operating expenses	47,000
NOI	71,017
–DS	62,185
BTCF	$8,832

Taxable Income or Loss

We next have to assess the impact of the IRS, or Uncle Sam, on the cash flows generated by the property. The first thing we do is look once again at the net operating income the building is generating. The question that needs to be answered is, how much of that NOI is the IRS going to want to take? Uncle Sam says that we don't have to pay taxes on the interest we pay on our financing. So we deduct our annual interest expense from the NOI.

The interest expense calculation requires us to go back to Solution 11.1. Reenter the Solution 11.1 keystrokes in your calculator. We now have our monthly payment of $5,182.10. Now calculate the principal balance at the end of year 1. Those keystrokes are in Solution 11.2.

Solution 11.2

668400 [PV]

20 × 12 = 240 [n]

7/12 = [i/y]

[cpt] [pmt] 5182.10

[rcl] [n] − 12 = [n]

[cpt] [PV] 652499.10

Given this information, we can determine the interest paid in the first year of the mortgage. The total principal plus interest paid in year 1 is $5,182.10 × 12 = $62,185.20. Principal reduction in year 1 is $668,400 − $652,499.10 = $15,900.90. That means that the total interest paid is equal to $62,185.20 − $15,900.90 = $46,284.30. These calculations are summarized in Equation 11.5.

Equation 11.5

$$\text{Total principal} + \text{interest} = \$5{,}182.10 \times 12 = \$62{,}182.20$$

$$\text{Principal reduction} = \$668{,}400 - \$652{,}499.10 = \$15{,}900.90$$

$$\text{Interest paid} = \$62{,}182.20 - 15{,}900.90 = \$46{,}284.30$$

$$(P + I) - P = I$$

The payment to amortize is made up of principal plus interest. The total principal plus interest for the year minus the principal reduction for the year is equal to the interest paid for the year.

In addition to not paying tax on our interest expense, we also do not need to pay taxes on the depreciation expense that we are allowed to take. Since that is the case, we also deduct depreciation expense from the NOI. As is discussed in Chapter 8 on appreciation and depreciation, current IRS code allows real property to be depreciated over one of two lifetimes. If the property is residential in nature, meaning you can live in it, it can then be depreciated over a 27.5-year life. If the property is commercial, it requires a 39-year life. In either case the depreciation is to be straight line, which means that exactly the same amount of depreciation is taken each year over the life of the improvement.

Equation 11.6 contains the calculation for depreciation expense. The only portion of the property's value that can be depreciated is the value of the improvements. The land cannot be depreciated, land is forever. The building and other improvements do wear out over time and can be depreciated. In effect, Uncle Sam is letting us recoup the cost of the improvements so that they can be replaced when they have worn out completely.

Equation 11.6

$$\text{Depreciation expense} = (\text{Acquisition cost} - \text{land value})/27.5 \ (\text{or } 39)$$

$$\text{Depreciation expense} = (\$835{,}500 - \$165{,}000)/27.5 = \$24{,}381$$

So what we are doing in Equation 11.6 is taking the acquisition cost and deducting the land value, leaving the value of the improvements. They are then divided by the useful life to get the depreciation expense that can be used per year. Tax code says you cannot use one full year of depreciation expense the year you put the building in service, but that is treading very close to an accountant's territory, and I don't want to go there.

Prior to the 1986 Tax Reform Act, investment property could be depreciated over a 19-year life using a 175% declining balance. What this means is that the investor could take 175% and divide it by 19 to see what percentage of the improvements could be deducted as depreciation expense each year. Today by using straight-line depreciation, we are taking 100% of the value of the improvements and dividing by 27.5, in the case of residential property, to get that percentage. Prior to 1986 the percentage would have been $175\% \div 19 = 9.21\%$ of the value of the undepreciated value each year. So the depreciation in year 1 for the problem we are working on would be equal to ($835,500 − $165,000) = $670,500 × 0.0921 = $61,753 rather than the $24,381 calculated in Equation 11.6. In year 2 the depreciation expense would have been ($670,500 − $61,753) × 0.0921 = $608,747 × 0.0921 = $56,065. That is why the method is called *declining balance*, because each year the depreciation expense was calculated on a balance that was reduced by the previous year's depreciation expense.

By deducting the interest expense and the depreciation expense from the NOI, we end up with the taxable income or taxable loss. It is considered taxable income if the result is a positive number, and it is considered a taxable loss if the result is a negative number.

Tax Liability or Tax Savings

Tax liability (or savings) is found by multiplying the taxable income or loss by the marginal tax rate (MTR) of the investor. If the property earned a positive taxable income, the result of multiplying that by the MTR will be a tax liability for the investor. If the property earned a tax loss, the result of the multiplication will be a tax savings. I find that if I make the MTR a negative number, I get the correct sign on my tax. If it is a positive taxable income multiplied by a negative tax rate, the answer is a tax liability with a negative sign. That tells me it is a cash outflow. If it is a taxable loss multiplied by the negative MTR (the product of two negative numbers) the resulting tax savings has a positive sign, a cash inflow. This is just a hint that might help you. The tax liability or tax savings calculation is summarized in Table 11.2.

Table 11.2   Tax liability

NOI	71,017
−Interest	46,284
−Depreciation	24,382
Tax income	351
−MTR	−0.28
Tax liability	−98

For this property we have a tax liability of $98 in the first year of operation. We could just as easily have had a tax savings if we would have had a negative taxable income, sometimes referred to as a *tax loss*.

In order to take advantage of any tax savings, investors must be considered small investors. That is, their annual income must be $100,000 or less. In that case they can use up to $25,000 in tax savings to offset ordinary income. For each dollar they make over $100,000, they lose $1 in tax savings benefit so that by the time they earn $150,000 in income, they have lost all deductibility of tax savings. Second, they must be considered actively involved in the management of the property. That is to say, they must be actively making some of the decisions about the property, such as when to increase rents, and so forth.

After-Tax Cash Flow

The final calculation in the cash flows from operations is the calculation of the after-tax cash flow (ATCF). We already have both the elements that go into this calculation. The BTCF minus the tax liability (or plus the tax savings) will give us the ATCF. This is illustrated in Table 11.3.

Ratio Analysis

The cash flows from operations for year one have now been estimated, but what do we do with them? Just looking at the raw numbers of $71,017 for NOI, $8,832 for BTCF, and $8,734 for the ATCF doesn't really give us an indication of whether this is a good investment or not. What we do next is exactly what financial analysts do when they analyze the stock of a company. We are going to calculate some financial ratios that we can then compare with other similar buildings to determine if this particular investment is one that we want to undertake or one that we should pass on.

Table 11.3   After-tax cash flow

BTCF	8,832
+/− Tax liability	−98
ATCF	8,734

Debt Coverage Ratio

The first of these ratios is called the *debt coverage ratio* (DCR). This ratio is of great concern to the lender who is providing the mortgage money for the transaction. This ratio tells the investor and the lender whether the NOI is adequate to cover the annual debt service. The ratio is the NOI divided by the annual debt service. The lender will typically want this ratio to be at least 1.2. In the case of riskier investments, such as new construction, the lender may want the DCR to be at least 1.25. You may ask why new construction would be riskier than an existing building. It is considered riskier because we start out with no tenants, and we don't know for sure when it will be fully occupied. The lender will want a larger cushion to cover any shortfalls in rent that may occur.

Equation 11.7

$$DCR = NOI/debt\ service = \$71,017/\$62,185 = 1.14$$

When we present this investment plan to a financial institution, it would probably decline our mortgage application given the low DCR in this example. We can look closely at Table 11.1 and try to determine how we could modify our analysis to increase our DCR. It is apparent there are only two ways we can increase this ratio. We either have to increase the NOI, or we have to decrease the debt service (DS). There are three possible changes we can make to increase NOI. We can increase rents, decrease vacancies, or decrease operating expenses. Any one of these changes will increase our NOI if everything else is held constant. The problem is that everything else will not remain constant. Let's look at the impact of each of these changes. If our rents are already at the market rate, what will happen to vacancies if we increase the rents? That's correct, vacancies will increase, because tenants will shop around and find better rent levels at the market rate. How do we reduce vacancy rates? We can either reduce rents, or we can offer better services. Those better services will increase our operating expenses, which may once again be counterproductive with respect to its impact on NOI. As we see, increasing NOI is not as easy as it sounds.

Rather than increasing NOI, we could also decrease the DS payment, and that would increase our DCR. There are a number of ways we could decrease the DS payment, and these changes are not as likely to affect other areas of our cash flow analysis as the changes to NOI would. We could negotiate a lower interest rate which would reduce our mortgage payment. Second, we could increase our down payment, which would decrease the mortgage amount, thus decreasing the mortgage payment. We could also use some alternative financing method other than a fixed rate mortgage. We could use a graduated payment mortgage (GPM), an adjustable rate mortgage (ARM), or even an interest-only mortgage. All these mortgages have additional risks for the borrower which he or she would have to take into consideration when thinking about the alternative financing methods. Their use may in fact increase the DCR enough to make the plan acceptable to the lender.

Breakeven Occupancy Rate

The *breakeven occupancy rate* is the occupancy level at which the property's income will just cover the bills. The bills that must be covered are the debt service and the operating expenses. The ratio appears in Equation 11.8.

Equation 11.8

Breakeven occupancy $= (DS + Op\ Exp)/PGI$

$$= (\$62,185 + \$47,000)/\$126,900 = 0.86 = 86\%$$

This tells the investor that the building needs a vacancy rate of 14% or less in order for the before-tax cash flow to be positive because if the vacancy is greater than 14%, the investor won't have enough NOI to cover the debt service and the operating expense. There is no magic number for breakeven occupancy; however, the lower this ratio is, the sooner the bills will be covered and the higher the vacancy rate that the building will be able to absorb.

Operating Expense Ratio

The operating expense ratio is the amount of annual operating expense divided by the effective gross income. This ratio simply gives us a value that we can use to compare the subject property with other similar properties. As far as what level is desirable for this ratio, lower is preferable to higher. Professional organizations like the Building Owners and Manager Association (BOMA) and the Institute of Real Estate Management (IREM) collect data from members and aggregate those data for members to access. In this way members can compare the operating expense ratio and other ratios of their properties with similar properties to determine if they are managing their buildings effectively and efficiently. If the operating expense ratio of their subject property is much less than the operating expense ratio of similar properties, it may help explain why their vacancy rate is higher than the comparable properties, because they may not be providing similar

levels of maintenance and upkeep. If the ratio is much greater than that of comparable properties, it may indicate that they are providing levels of service that are greater than what the market is demanding.

Equation 11.9

$$\text{Operating expense ratio} = \text{Operating expenses/effective gross income}$$

$$= \$47{,}000/\$118{,}017 = 0.398 = 39.8\%$$

Return on Investment

The next two ratios are return ratios that give investors a picture of the rate of return which is being made on their total investment as well as the return being made on their equity investment. Investors would prefer these ratios to be higher rather than lower. The first of these is called the *return on investment* (ROI), meaning the return on their total investment, or purchase price. The ratio is the net operating income divided by the total investment.

Equation 11.10

$$\text{Return on investment} = \text{NOI/investment} = \$71{,}017/\$835{,}500$$

$$= 0.08499 = 8.5\%$$

Look very carefully at Equation 11.10 for a minute and think about where you have seen it before. It's IRV, from Chapter 10. Specifically, it is R = I/V. The ROI is the same as the cap rate from IRV. The only difference is that in appraisal we called the denominator *value* rather than *investment*. At different times in real estate we refer to that dollar amount as value, as purchase price, as sale price, or as the total investment. They are all proxies, or substitutes, for one another.

Return on Equity

The second return calculation, and the final ratio we look at, is the return on equity, or ROE. This numerator of this ratio, rather than being the NOI, is the before-tax cash flow, and the denominator is the equity the investor has in the property. At the time of purchase, that equity can also be referred to as the *down payment*. For this reason this ratio is sometimes called the cash on cash return.

It is the cash return on the cash investment. It is also sometimes called the *equity dividend rate*. Again, as a return type of ratio, the investor would prefer this to be higher rather than lower.

Equation 11.11

$$\text{ROE} = \text{BTCF/equity} = \$8,832/\$167,100 = 0.053 = 5.3\%$$

The equity in the ROE equation comes from the purchase price minus the mortgage amount indicated in the problem, or $\$835,500 - \$668,400 = \$167,100$.

As is mentioned at the beginning of the chapter, the investor will usually look at the cash flows from operations for a holding period of some number of years. To calculate these ratios, we typically use the values from the cash flow analysis in year 1 of the projected holding period. We do this for two reasons. First, the year 1 values in the cash flow analysis are likely the most accurate since the farther out years are based on some assumptions about growth in rents and operating expenses. Hopefully we make valid assumptions about those growth rates, but they are subject to changes in the market and the economy. The second reason we use year 1 ratios is that some of the values change over time, such as the equity the investor has in the property, and this makes the year 1 ratios more meaningful.

Estimating Cash Flows after Year 1

The cash flows and ratios calculated for year 1 give the investor a nice snapshot of how the property is expected to perform in year 1 of the holding period. The investor's time horizon is typically greater than one year. This is particularly the result of the high transaction costs associated with buying and selling real property. It is hard to recoup the commission expense associated with selling investment property after owning it for only a single year. Also, while the ratios we calculated are very useful for comparing properties, they are missing some important elements of the cash flows that the investor is to receive. Let's look at the ROI, and we'll see what information is lacking from this ratio. The ratio itself, as stated in Equation 11.10, is ROI = NOI/investment. This means that all the cash flow values that come below NOI are left out of consideration. Look at Tables 11.1 and 11.2 to see what information doesn't work itself into the ROI. The impact of financing is missing, because debt service comes after NOI in Table 11.1. All depreciation and tax benefits are left out of ROI because they come after NOI in Table 11.2. Any appreciation, or value increase, is left out of ROI because we are looking only at cash flows from operations.

As you can see, there is a lot of important information that is missing from the ROI.

Similarly, there is much information that is missing from ROE. If you look at Equation 11.11, you will note that the ROE = BTCF/equity. This return calculation does take financing into consideration because BTCF = NOI − DS; however, it is still missing information on tax benefits, rent increases over time, operating expense increases over time, and any appreciation that may take place. For these reasons investors like to take a look at the investment over a longer holding period than one year, and they also like another return type of calculation that captures cash flows for the entire holding period plus this missing information that was just mentioned.

Growth Rates

The investor will make an assumption about the growth in rents over the projected holding period. You will notice in Table 11.4 that we have increased rents at a 3% rate each year over the five-year holding period. In similar fashion the operating expenses have been increased at a 2% annual growth rate. Table 11.4 uses values rounded to even dollars.

Table 11.4 Five years of cash flows

	Year 1	Year 2	Year 3	Year 4	Year 5
PGI	126,900	130,707	134,628	138,667	142,827
−Vacancies	8,883	9,149	9,424	9,707	9,998
EGI	118,017	121,558	125,204	128,960	132,829
−Operating expenses	47,000	47,940	48,899	49,877	50,874
NOI	71,017	73,618	76,305	79,084	81,955
−DS	−62,185	−62,185	−62,185	−62,185	−62,185
BTCF	8,832	11,432	14,120	16,898	19,770
NOI	71,017	73,618	76,305	79,084	81,955
−Interest	46,284	45,135	43,902	42,581	41,163
−Depreciation	24,382	24,382	24,382	24,382	24,382
Tax inc.	351	4,101	8,021	12,121	16,410
−MTR	−0.28	−0.28	−0.28	−0.28	−0.28
Tax liability	−98	−1,148	−2,246	−3,394	−4,595
BTCF	8,832	11,432	14,120	16,898	19,770
+/− Tax liability	−98	−1,148	−2,246	−3,394	−4,595
ATCF	8,734	10,284	11,874	13,504	15,175

Year 2 Cash Flows

As indicated above, the PGI for year 1 is multiplied by 1.03 (3% growth) to obtain the year 2 value of $130,707. The vacancy in year 2 is once again the PGI times the 7% vacancy rate, resulting in a vacancy allowance of $9,149. That value deducted from the PGI leaves an EGI of $121,558 in year 2. Multiplying the first year's operating expenses by 1.02 (1+2% growth) results in operating expenses in year 2 of $47,940, and that value deducted from the EGI leaves an NOI of $73,618. The debt service is constant since we are using a fixed-rate constant payment mortgage, so the $62,185 deducted from the NOI leaves a BTCF of $11,432 for year 2.

Now we return to the NOI to see how much of that the investor has to share with the IRS. The interest expense in year 2 can be calculated after we have calculated the mortgage balance at the end of year 2. You will recall that the principal balance at the end of year 1 was $652,499 (see Solution 11.2), which represented the PV of the remaining 228 monthly payments (240 − 12 = 228). The principal balance at the end of year 2 is the PV of 216 monthly payments (228 − 12 = 216), as indicated in Solution 11.3.

Solution 11.3

5182.10 [pmt]

216 [n]

7/12 = [i/y]

[cpt] [PV] 635448.79

If we now take the principal balance at the end of year 1 minus the principal balance at the end of year 2, that will give us the principal reduction in year 2. The total debt service for the year (which is p + i) minus the principal reduction for the year will give us the total interest paid in year 2.

Equations 11.12

$$\$652,499 - \$635,449 = \$17,050 = \text{Principal reduction}$$

$$\$62,185 - \$17,050 = \$45,135 = \text{Interest paid in year 2}$$

The depreciation expense in year 2 is the same as that for year 1 since we are using straight line depreciation. Once again this is a math book, not a tax book, but remember that the first year you put a building in service you can take only one-half the allowed depreciation expense. I am using the same amount in year 1 as in the other years for simplification purposes only. Check with your accountant or tax attorney for your particular case.

Beyond this point the after-tax cash flow calculation will work the same as it did in year 1. Now that we have seen how the year 2 cash flows are calculated, years 3, 4, and 5 follow exactly the same pattern. You may want to verify the numbers in Table 11.4, and that would be a very useful exercise.

After-Tax Cash Flow from the Sale

At the end of the projected holding period, we factor in a sale price for the property, or what we call a *reversion* in Chapter 10. This future sale price may be calculated in a couple of different ways. We could do an income capitalization at the end of year 5, and that is often the way the reversion is estimated. This would involve IRV, or $V = I/R$. Since the value at time period zero is equal to the NOI for period one divided by R, the value at the end of time period five would be the NOI for period six divided by R. The cap rate used to estimate the value at the end of the holding period is called the *going out cap rate*. This is as opposed to the cap rate involved at the front end of the investment which is referred to as the *going in cap rate*. Another method of estimating the value at the end of the holding period, and the one used in this example, is to take the original purchase price and increase that value at a certain growth rate over the holding period. We estimated the sale price in this example by taking the purchase price of $835,500 and grew that at a 3% growth rate compounded for five years.

Solution 11.4

835500 [PV]

5 [n]

3 [i/y]

[cpt] [FV] 968753

Hence, a sale price of $968,753 appears under sale price in our cash flow analysis. The next value on the analysis is the mortgage balance. The mortgage balance at any point in time is equal to the PV of the remaining payments. We started with a 20-year, or 240-month, mortgage. Five years are now gone, so 15 years are remaining. The principal balance is the PV of 15 years' worth of payments, or $576,539 in our example.

Solution 11.5

5182.10 [pmt]

15 × 12 = 180 [n]

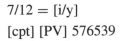

7/12 = [i/y]

[cpt] [PV] 576539

The selling expenses are figured at 5% of the selling price, or $968,573 × 0.05 = $48,429. The mortgage balance and the selling expenses are both deducted from the sale price to leave the before-tax cash flow from the sale (BTCF).

The next step is to go back to the sale price and to deduct the adjusted basis from that value. The *adjusted basis* is defined as the acquisition cost minus any depreciation that has been taken. In this case our acquisition cost was $835,500 and we took depreciation of $24,382 five times, or 5 × $24,382 = $121,910. Our adjusted basis calculation is illustrated in Equation 11.13.

Equation 11.13

$$\text{Adjusted basis} = \$835,500 - \$121,910 = \$713,591$$

Now, as in Table 11.5, we take the sale price minus the adjusted basis and also minus the selling expenses again to arrive at the gain on the sale. The reason we once again subtract selling expenses is that we are now attempting to figure out how much of this BTCF we have to share with the IRS. Uncle Sam says that we don't have to pay tax on our selling expenses, so we get to deduct them before we calculate our tax liability. This gain on the sale is in fact a capital gain and as such receives some preferential treatment as far as the tax rate is concerned. Rather than paying the same rate that we pay on the income from operations, we are permitted to use a 15% rate and a 25% rate. That portion of the gain that comes from the appreciation of property value is taxed at the 15% rate.

Table 11.5   After-tax cash flow from the sale

Sale price	$968,573
−Mortgage balance	−$576,539
−Selling expenses	−$48,429
BTCF(s)	$343,606
Sale price	$968,573
−Adjusted basis	−$713,591
−Selling expenses	−$48,429
Gain on sale	$206,554
× − Gain tax rate × Appreciation + 2nd gain tax rate	$20,055
× Excess appreciation	+$18,371
Tax liability	$38,425
BTCF(s)	$343,606
−Tax liability	−$38,425
ATCF(s)	$305,181

Any additional or excess gain that has resulted from the depreciation is taxed at the 25% rate. In this case we had a total gain of $206,554. The portion that came from appreciation was $968,573 − $835,500 = $133,073. That amount is taxed at the 15% rate. The excess gain over and above that from appreciation was $206,554 − $133,703 = $73,481 and is taxed at the 25% rate.

Equation 11.14

$$\text{Tax from sale} = \$133,703 \times 0.15 = \$20,055 \text{ and } \$73,481 \times 0.25 = \$18,370$$

$$\text{Or } \$20,055 + \$18,370 = \$38,425$$

Deducting the tax liability of $38,425 from the BTCF leaves an ATCF of $305,181.

Net Present Value and Internal Rate of Return

The cash flows are now in place for calculating a rate of return that will take into consideration the elements that are missing from the ROI and ROE ratios. By calculating the ATCF from operations over a five-year period and the ATCF from the sale of the building at the end of the holding period, we have brought much more information into the analysis. We now use these cash flows and come up with a much more complete measure of the investor's return. The return that we use is called the *internal rate of return* (IRR). (This calculation is discussed in Chapter 6.) The cash flows that will be used for the IRR calculation are the ATCF from operations for years 1–5 and the ATCFs at the end of the holding period. The cash outflow at time period zero will be the cash down payment. See Table 11.6.

There are two ways you can calculate the internal rate of return that is present in a set of cash flows. One method is to use the cash flow keys of your financial

Table 11.6   IRR cash flows

Year	ATCF
0	−$167,100
1	$8,734
2	$10,284
3	$11,874
4	$13,504
5	$15,175 + $305,181

calculator as illustrated in Chapter 6. The second method is to do some present value calculations, a little addition and a little subtraction. We look at both methods in this chapter. While the cash flow key method is the fastest once you become accustomed to it, the second method gives the investor the clearest picture concerning what the IRR calculation is really doing and really means.

Let's look at the second method first. The first step is to choose some discount rate to begin with, and it doesn't matter what it is. I like to use the interest rate on the mortgage simply because it is there. So what we do is find the present value of each of the cash flows from our property discounted at the 7% discount rate.

Table 11.7 started out the same as Table 11.6 with the year in column one and the ATCF in column two. The only difference is the year 5 after-tax cash flows were added together so that we have to deal with only a single cash flow. So, $15,175 was added to $305,181, and the result of $320,356 was placed in that cell in the table for the column two year 5 value. Next we calculated the PV of each of the after-tax cash flows and placed them in column three. The $8,734 was called an FV, for one period, a 7% discount rate, and we solved for PV, which turned out to be $8,163. Next the $10,284 was discounted back two periods at the 7% rate for a PV of $9,693. The other three cash flows were treated in a similar manner. The five present values were then added together to get the total present value of the cash inflows. Finally, the net present value (NPV) was calculated. The NPV is the difference between the PV of the cash inflows and the PV of the cash outflows. The NPV calculation is illustrated in Equation 11.15.

Equation 11.15

$$NPV = \$265,549 - \$167,100 = +\$98,449$$

The PV of the cash outflow is in fact the down payment which takes place at time period zero, so it is already in PV form. The NPV of these cash flows is +$98,449,

Table 11.7 NPV at 7% discount rate

Year	ATCF	PV @ 7%
0	−$167,100	−$167,100
1	$8,734	$8,163
2	$10,284	$8,982
3	$11,874	$9,693
4	$13,504	$10,302
5	$320,356	$228,409
Total PV		$265,549
NPV		+$98,449

Table 11.8 NPV at 7% and 20%

Year	ATCF	PV @ 7%	PV @ 20%
0	−$167,100	−$167,100	−$167,100
1	$8,734	$8,163	$7,278
2	$10,284	$8,982	$7,142
3	$11,874	$9,693	$6,872
4	$13,504	$10,302	$6,512
5	$320,356	$228,409	$128,744
Total PV		$265,549	$156,578
NPV		+$98,449	−$10,522

and one of the key elements is that the NPV is positive. The positive NPV means that we are earning more than the discount rate we used, in this case 7%. What we want to do next is to choose another discount rate that will give us a net present value that is negative. Recalling one of our major premises regarding TVM—the higher the discount rate, the lower the PV—we need to choose a higher discount rate to get a lower PV and hence a lower NPV. Let's try a 20% discount rate. Now look at Table 11.7 and calculate the PV of each of the cash flows, this time using a 20% discount rate. (The results are found in Table 11.8.)

You will recall from Chapter 6 that the IRR is the discount rate that makes the NPV equal to zero. If you look at Table 11.8, you see that we have calculated NPVs of +$98,449 and −$10,522, which means that the zero is in between those two values. Given a linear relationship between the NPV and the discount rate, we can then assume that the IRR is somewhere between the two discount rates, 7% and 20%. Given the distances between the two NPVs and zero, it would appear that the IRR is closer to 20% than it is to 7%.

Now that we have 1 + NPV and 1 − NPV, we can use what I call the simple five-step method to estimate the internal rate of return. The steps are listed below:

1. Find the total range in net present values. That is, how far apart are they on the number line? This may be obtained by adding together their absolute values.
2. Divide the +NPV by the total range in net present values.
3. Find the total range in discount rates.
4. Multiply answer 2 by answer 3.
5. Add answer 4 to the discount rate associated with the +NPV, and the resulting answer is the estimate of the IRR.

The five steps used to find the IRR using the data in Table 11.8 are contained in Table 11.9.

Using the five-step method, the estimate of the IRR of these cash flows is 18.74%. Keep in mind that this is an estimate. The farther apart the two discount

Table 11.9   Five-step method of IRR

Step	Calculation
1. Find the total range in NPVs	$98,449 + 10,522 = 108,971$
2. Divide the +NPV by the total range	$98,449/108,971 = 0.9034$
3. Find the total range in discount rates	$20\% - 7\% = 13\%$
4. Answer 2 × answer 3	$0.9034 \times 13\% = 11.74\%$
5. Add answer 4 to the discount rate associated with +NPV	$11.74\% + 7\% = 18.74\% = \text{IRR}$

rates are that we use in the calculation, the greater our margin of error. Since we used discount rates that are fairly far apart, a range of 13%, we might expect our margin of error to be fairly large.

We next use the financial calculator to calculate the IRR as is illustrated in Chapter 6. Using the cash flow keys will allow us to see how far away from the actual IRR our estimate is. The steps are shown in Solution 11.6.

Solution 11.6

[CF] 167100 [+/−] [enter]

[↓] 8734 [enter][↓]

[↓] 10284 [enter][↓]

[↓] 11874 [enter][↓]

[↓] 13504 [enter][↓]

[↓] 320356 [enter][↓]

[↓][IRR] [cpt] 18.29%

As we have just shown, the IRR of the after-tax cash flows for this investment property using the cash flow keys of the financial calculator is 18.29%. If you look at Table 11.9, you can see that the five-step method gives us a very reasonable estimate of the IRR at 18.74%. This is in spite of our using a fairly wide range in discount rates in our estimate.

The IRR calculation suffers from two problems. One is called the *multiple rate of return problem*, and one is called the *reinvestment assumption*. When the cash flows in an IRR calculation have multiple sign changes, where the cash flows go from negative to positive to negative, there can actually be two discount rates that will make the NPV equal to zero. In other words there are two IRRs. The investor must be aware that the potential for such a problem exists.

The second problem, the reinvestment assumption, comes about because the IRR calculation is a compound interest calculation. The IRR calculation assumes that the cash flows are immediately reinvested at the same IRR. This may be an overly optimistic assumption. In the previous problem the process assumes that the $8,734 ATCF in year 1 can be reinvested and earn the same 18.29% rate of return that we earn from the $167,100 initial investment. The reality may be that we can't find another investment that will pay us 18.29% for the much smaller amount of $8,734. Once again, as long as investors are aware of the potential problems that can arise from the limitation of the calculation, they should be able to deal with it.

Before-Tax Equivalent Rate of Return

The IRR we just calculated is an after-tax rate of return because we used after-tax cash flows to estimate it. We can also determine the before-tax rate of return that we would have to earn in order for our return to be equivalent to this after-tax rate of return. To obtain the before-tax equivalent rate of return of an after-tax rate of return, simply divide the after-tax rate of return by 1 minus the tax rate that the investor pays. In the case of our example, divide the 18.29% by $(1 - 0.28)$ as shown in Equation 11.16.

Equation 11.16

BT equivalent $= $ AT rate$/(1-T) = 18.29\%/(1-0.28) = 18.29\%/0.72 = 25.4\%$

As you can see, in order to earn the same return as our 18.29% after-tax rate of return, you would need to earn a before-tax return of 25.4%. Most returns that you see advertised are before-tax rates of return, because you have to pay tax on the earnings. This gives you a method of comparing one with the other. If you want to go in the other direction, that is, you have a before-tax rate of return and you would like to know what the equivalent after tax-rate of return is going to be, just take the before-tax rate of return and multiply it by 1 minus the tax rate as shown in Equation 11.17.

Equation 11.17

AT return $= $ BT return $(1 - T) = 25.4\%$ $(1 - 0.28) = 25.4\%(0.72) = 18.29\%$

Modified Internal Rate of Return

The goal of the modified internal rate of return (MIRR) is to compensate for the drawback of the IRR that assumes the cash flows can immediately be reinvested at the same IRR. The MIRR reinvests those cash flows at a more reasonable rate. Some analysts will use the firm's cost of capital, if we are dealing with a corporate finance department, or the cash flows may be reinvested at the risk free rate of interest. In our example we reinvest them at the same interest rate that the lender is earning—the mortgage interest rate. The investor should be able to earn at least that much and certainly more since he or she taking considerably more risk than is the lender.

Let's go back to the cash flows in Table 11.6. The MIRR asks us to take the cash inflows and compound them forward to the end of the holding period, compounding at a safe rate of interest that we choose. The mortgage interest rate that we used for this problem was 7%, so we compound our cash inflows forward at a 7% rate. Those future values are given in Table 11.10.

Now that we have the total future value of the cash inflows, we simply ask the question, what interest rate takes us from a present value of $167,000 to a future value of $372,446 in five years, as in Solution 11.7.

Solution 11.7

−167000 [PV]

372446 [FV]

5 [n]

[cpt] [i/y] 17.4

The MIRR is 17.4%, and we have worked around one of the major gripes about the IRR—that the cash flow is assumed to be reinvested at the IRR. In this case we have made the assumption that the cash flows are reinvested at a realistic 7%. If there had been other cash outflows during the holding period, those would have been discounted back to present value to be added to the cash outflow at time period zero. Then we would solve in the same way by finding the interest rate that makes the present value of the inflows equal to the future value of the inflows.

Table 11.10   Future value of cash flows

Year	ATCF	Future value
0	−$167,000	—
1	$8,734	$11,448
2	$10,284	$12,598
3	$11,874	$13,595
4	$13,504	$14,449
5	$320,356	$320,356
Total		$372,446

Leverage

Leverage can be defined as the use of borrowed money to finance an investment and the borrowed money's impact on the investment's rate of return. In the example that we look at throughout this chapter, we assume that the investor is going to use an 80% L/V mortgage to finance the purchase. We could just have easily assumed the investor was going to pay cash for the investment. Let's take another look at the investment assuming that the investor would pay cash for the investment and see what the impact on the rate of return is.

To accomplish this, we go back to Table 11.4 and take out anything that has to do with the mortgage. The debt service will go to zero as will the interest expense. The new amounts appear in Table 11.11. The cash flow from sale calculation from Table 11.5 is also affected, and those new values appear in Table 11.11.

You will notice that the before-tax cash flows from operations are approximately $62,000 greater than the before-tax cash flows from Table 11.4. They are greater by the amount of the annual debt service payment that is not being paid in Table 11.10 because we are now free from debt. The after-tax cash flows in Table 11.4 are not greater than those in Table 11.10 by the exact amount of the debt service payment. This is because by using all cash, we have lost the tax benefit of the interest expense deduction. As a result the after-tax cash flows in Table 11.10 are greater by $49,000–$50,000.

Table 11.11   After-tax cash flow with no debt

	Year 1	Year 2	Year 3	Year 4	Year 5
PGI	126,900	130,707	134,628	138,667	142,827
−Vacancies	8,883	9,149	9,424	9,707	9,998
EGI	118,017	121,558	125,204	128,960	132,829
−Operating expenses	47,000	47,940	48,899	49,877	50,874
NOI	71,017	73,618	76,305	79,084	81,955
−Debt service	0	0	0	0	0
BTCF	71,017	73,618	76,305	79,084	81,955
NOI	71,017	73,618	76,305	79,084	81,955
−Interest	0	0	0	0	0
−Depreciation	24,382	24,382	24,382	24,382	24,382
Taxable income	46,635	49,236	51,924	54,702	57,573
x−MTR	−0.28	−0.28	−0.28	−0.28	−0.28
Tax liability	−13,058	−13,786	−14,539	−15,316	−16,120
BTCF	71,017	73,618	76,305	79,084	81,955
+/−Tax liability	−13,058	−13,786	−14,539	−15,316	−16,120
ATCF	57,959	59,832	61,767	63,767	65,834

Table 11.12   Cash flows from sale with no debt

Sale price	968,573
–Mortgage balance	0
–Selling expense	48,429
BTCF(s)	920,145
Sale price	968,573
–Adjusted basis	713,591
–Selling expense	48,429
Gain on sale	206,554
–Gain tax rate	
Tax liability	–38,425
BTCF(s)	920,145
–Tax liability	–38,425
ATCF(s)	881,720

The after-tax cash flow from the sale is also larger using no debt because, of course, we have no mortgage payoff at the end of the holding period. See Table 11.12 for that calculation.

Given that the after-tax cash flows are so much greater than they were using debt, you might assume that the IRR using the after-tax cash flows (IRR-AT) would also be greater. Surprisingly, that is not the case. This is because our cash outflow at time period zero is no longer the cash down payment of $167,100 that we used earlier, but rather it is the entire purchase price of $835,500 since we are using all cash. The IRR calculator calculation is detailed in Solution 11.8.

Solution 11.8

[CF] 835500 [+/−] [enter]

[↓] 57959 [enter][↓]

[↓] 59832 [enter][↓]

[↓] 61767 [enter][↓]

[↓] 63767 [enter][↓]

[↓] 947554 [enter][↓]

[↓][IRR] [cpt] 8.30%

Note that the cash flow used for year 5 is the ATCF from operations of $65,834 plus the cash flow from sale of $881,720 for a total of $947,554. The IRR-AT for this property using all cash is only 8.30%. The same value using the 80% loan-to-value mortgage amortized over 20 years at a 7% rate of interest was 18.29%. This illustrates the use of positive leverage. In this example the IRR has been magnified by using borrowed funds. As long as the after-tax cost of debt is less than the IRR-AT using no debt, the IRR-AT using debt will be magnified. In this case even the before-tax cost of debt, or 7%, was less than the IRR-AT using no debt, or 8.3%. As a result our IRR-AT of 18.29% was magnified, or was greater than the rate using no debt, or 8.3%. Once again, this is called *positive leverage*.

Summary

Is the property that we just looked like a good investment? It is a good investment if we can get over one hurdle, and that is the debt coverage ratio. That ratio is sitting at a paltry 1.14, and most lenders are going to want that ratio to be at least 1.2 or higher.

This cash flow analysis can be used to analyze a single-family house, a four-unit apartment building, a 5,000-unit apartment complex, or a 50-story office building. The analysis does not change. The cash flows become a little more challenging, but the analysis is the same. The entire analysis may be put into an Excel spreadsheet, and the amount of work and the number of calculations that must be done by hand are both greatly reduced. There are also canned software packages that can be purchased to streamline the process. Once you understand what is happening in this chapter, your ability to choose good investment properties should improve dramatically. The level of sophistication that you choose to use in your analysis is entirely your decision. You can use a pad of paper and a financial calculator, you can create an Excel spreadsheet, or you can invest in expensive software programs. In any event you will need to know the difference between before-tax cash flows and after-tax cash flows, between adjusted basis and an adjustable mortgage, and between cash inflows and cash outflows. Hopefully this chapter has brought you to that level.

Quiz for Chapter 11

1. An investor is considering the purchase of an 18-unit apartment building. The building contains six one-bedroom units, six two-bedroom units, and six three-bedroom units. The one-bedroom units rent for $800 per month; the two-bedroom units rent for $950 per month; and the three-bedroom units rent for $1,100 per month. What is the potential gross income of the building? (See Table 11.13.)

   a. $57,600

   b. $237,600

   c. $205,200

   d. $172,800

Table 11.13

PGI	$205,200
–Vacancies	–$10,260
EGI	$194,940
–Operating expenses	–$75,000
NOI	$119,940
–Debt Service	–$99,058
BTCF	$20,882

2. Given the information in Table 11.13, what is the debt coverage ratio of the building being analyzed?

   a. 1.21

   b. 84.8

   c. 38.5

   d. 8

   e. 5.6

3. Given the information in Table 11.13, what is the operating expense ratio?

   a. 1.21

   b. 84.8

   c. 38.5

   d. 8

   e. 5.6

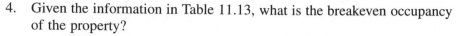
4. Given the information in Table 11.13, what is the breakeven occupancy of the property?
   a. 1.21%
   b. 84.8%
   c. 38.5%
   d. 8%
   e. 5.6%

5. Given the information in Table 11.14 (below), and the fact that the property in question is an apartment building, what is the cost of the improvements?
   a. $1,500,000
   b. $1,200,000
   c. $1,125,000
   d. $119,940

Table 11.14

NOI	$119,940
–Interest	–$89,660
–Depreciation	–$43,636
Taxable income	–$13,357
× –0.28	× –0.28
Tax liability (saving)	$3,740

6. Does the building described in Table 11.14 experience a tax liability or a tax savings?
   a. Tax liability
   b. Tax savings
   c. Both of the above
   d. Neither of the above

7. Given the information in Table 11.15 (below), what is the commission rate (selling expense) as a percentage of the sale price?
   a. 9.8%
   b. 32.5%
   c. 5%
   d. 6%

Table 11.15

Sale price	$1,738,911
–Mortgage balance	–$1,069,536
–Selling expense	–$104,335
BTCF(s)	$565,041

8.   Given the information in Table 11.15 and the fact that the purchase price
     of the property is $1,500,000, what annual value growth rate was used
     to get the sale price if there was a five-year holding period?
     a. 2%
     b. 3%
     c. 4%
     d. 5%

9.   Given the information in Tables 11.13 and 11.14, what is the ATCF from
     operations?
     a. $17,142
     b. $24,622
     c. $20,882
     d. $3,740

10. Using the after-tax cash flows from operations and the after-tax cash
     flow from the sale represented in Table 11.16 (below), and given a cash
     down payment of $150,000 at time period zero, what is the IRR of this
     investment?
     a. 11.73%
     b. 12.73%
     c. 13.73%
     d. 14.73%

Table 11.16

End of year	Cash flows
1	$10,000
2	$20,000
3	$30,000 + $155,000

Risk in Real Estate

The Probability of Achieving an Undesired Outcome

Risk can be defined in a number of different ways. One way of defining risk is that it is the probability of achieving an undesired outcome—that is, the chance that an investor will achieve a rate of return that is different from the expected rate of return. Carrying this thought a little further, the definition of risk could be variability of returns. In this chapter we address risk and its impact on mortgages, both from the lender's perspective and the borrower's perspective. We also see

what the impact of risk is on capitalization rates and hence property values. Finally, we address the different types of risk that affect real estate investors.

Interest Rates and Risk

Interest is a charge for the use of money. Lenders are sometimes referred to as investors because they are investing money in a transaction. Investors, or lenders, want to earn fair compensation, or a fair return, for the money they have invested. This return includes compensation for any risk they are undertaking in their investment.

RISK-FREE RATES

Interest rates are made up of a number of different elements. Risk-free rates of interest, such as those earned on U.S. Treasury instruments such as treasury bills and treasury bonds are said to be made up of two elements. These elements are a real rate of return plus an inflation premium. Let's say we are going to invest in a one-year treasury security. The expected rate of return, or risk-free rate, is summarized in Equation 12.1.

Equation 12.1

$$\text{Risk free rate, } R_f = \text{real rate} + E \text{ (inflation premium)}$$

The real rate of return is simply to compensate the lender for not having his or her money for the coming year. Historically, the real rate of return has been in the 1% to 2% neighborhood on U.S. treasuries. The treasury securities are considered risk free because the federal government will always pay the investor back. If the government doesn't have enough from tax revenue to pay back investors, it will simply borrow more money (issue new treasury securities) to pay them back.

The inflation premium in Equation 12.1 is preceded by the letter E because we are referring to the *expected* inflation for the coming year. We are not considering the CPI (consumer price index) for the previous year because that is history as far as financial markets are concerned. Investors are loaning their money to the government for the coming year so they are interested in the expected inflation during the coming year. When their money is paid back at the end of the year, they will want compensation for the increase in the prices of goods and services that took place during the year they didn't have their money.

THE YIELD CURVE

The *yield curve* is the graphic representation of what is called the *term structure of interest rates*. The term structure of interest rates is the relationship between interest rates and time. When the yield curve is in its normal position, as in Figure 12.1, long-term rates tend to be higher than short term rates. There are a couple of explanations for this. One of these explanations is referred to as *market segmentation*, which says that there is a market for all types of loans. By and large lenders prefer to lend short term because there is less time for the borrower to default. Since lenders would like to get their money back sooner, they have to be encouraged to loan money long term, by the borrower paying a higher rate of interest. Borrowers on the other hand would prefer to borrow long term. It puts off their having to repay the debt until a later date, postponing what is sometimes called *crisis at maturity*, or a default on the borrower's part caused by the borrower's lack of ability to repay the loan. In order to borrow long term, borrowers are willing to pay a higher rate of interest. In both these situations the long-term rates end up higher than the short-term rates.

Occasionally the yield curve assumes an inverted position, as shown in Figure 12.2. This happens when short-term rates are higher than long-term rates. This typically is the result of higher rates of inflation. When inflation is high in the short term, this gets factored into short-term rates. The markets will then predict a reduction in inflation rates in the long term so that short-term rates end up higher than long-term rates.

A second explanation for the yield curve is called *perfect expectations*. This theory holds that the interest rate markets reflect what is going to happen in the future. Long-term interest rates are the geometric average of the intermittent short-term rates. What this is saying is that long-term rates have short-term rates built right into them. That would mean that the expected inflation in coming years is somehow built in to the long-term interest rates and if we just know the

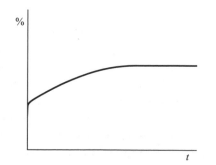

Figure 12.1 Yield curve in normal position

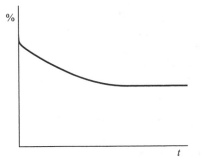

Figure 12.2 Yield curve in inverted position

right tools, we could get the future inflation expectations from these long-term rates. Fortunately, we do know what the tool is, and it is a time value of money calculation, which means that we can solve it with our financial calculator.

SPOT RATES AND FORWARD RATES

In order to find the expected inflation rate, you can reference a source of U.S. treasury yields, such as in the *Wall Street Journal*. In Table 12.1 you will find the yields on one-, two-, and three-year treasuries as of October 5, 2006. You will notice that the one-year rate is 4.78%, the two-year rate is 4.58% and the three-year rate is 4.51%. Given this information, we can see that the yield curve is inverted with short-term rates higher than long-term rates. The current one-period spot rate of 4.78% could be broken down between the real rate of interest and the expected inflation. If the real rate is 1%, then the expected inflation rate would be 4.78% − 1% = 3.78%.

Table 12.1   Spot rates

Maturity	Yield
1 year	4.78%
2 year	4.58%
3 year	4.51%

These rates are referred to as spot rates, because we are standing at time period zero, that is today, and looking at the one-year rate, the two-year rate, and the three-year rate. If we purchased these treasury securities, we would earn 4.78% for one year, or 4.58% each year for two years, or 4.51% each year for three years depending on which security we invested in. One-period forward rates will contain the expected inflation premiums that we are interested in. The one-period forward rate would be the interest rate that the markets predict will be in effect from the end of period one to the end of period two and from the end of period two until the end of period three. Standing at time period zero, we can't purchase a security that will give us a return from the end of period one until the end of period two because that rate will depend on market factors when we get to that time period. The perfect expectations theory states that those future spot rates, or short-term (ST) rates, are already built into the existing long-term (LT) rates.

To calculate those forward rates, we start with $1 and compound it forward given the spot rates in Table 12.1. The calculations are shown in Solutions 12.1, 12.2, and 12.3.

Solution 12.1

−1 [PV]

1 [n]

4.78 [i/y]

[cpt] [FV] 1.0478

Solution 12.2

−1 [PV]

2 [n]

4.58 [i/y]

[cpt] [FV] 1.0937

Solution 12.3

−1 [PV]

3 [n]

4.51 [i/y]

[cpt] [FV] 1.1415

To estimate the forward rate from the end of period one to the end of period two, we ask the question, what interest rate will take us from a present value of −1.0478 to a future value of 1.0937 in one period? That answer is found in Solution 12.4.

Solution 12.4

−1.0478 [PV]

1.0937 [FV]

Table 12.2   Spot rates, forward rates, and expected inflation

Year	Spot rate	Forward rate	Expected inflation
1	4.78%		3.78%
2	4.58%	4.38%	3.38%
3	4.51%	4.37%	3.37%

1 [n]

[cpt] [i/y] 4.38%

The forward rate that is expected by the financial markets from the end of period one to the end of period two is 4.38%. That illustrates to us that the markets expect the rate of inflation to go down. If the real rate is again 1%, then the expected inflation from the end of period one to the end of period two would be 4.38% − 1% = 3.38%, or a reduction of 4.78% − 4.38% = 0.4%.

The one-year forward rate from the end of period two to the end of period three can be estimated in similar fashion using Solution 12.5. We ask what rate will take us from a present value of −1.0937 to a future value of 1.1415 in one period.

Solution 12.5

−1.0937 [PV]

1.1415 [FV]

1 [n]

[cpt] [i/y] 4.37%

The financial markets believe the inflation will decline ever so slightly in year three to 3.37%, 4.37% − 1% = 3.37%, assuming a real rate of return of 1% again.

Based on one-year, two-year, and three-year treasury securities, Table 12.2 contains the spot rates, forward rates, and inflation premiums that are expected in the market today, or as of October 5, 2006. The expected inflation premiums are based on an assumption of a 1% real rate of return.

Mortgage Interest Rates

While a treasury security earns a risk-free rate of return, a mortgage will earn a risky rate of return. The federal government will always pay the investor back, and the mortgage borrower isn't always a sure thing. There are two major types of risk that the lender assumes in generating a mortgage loan. The first of these is default risk and the second is interest rate risk.

DEFAULT RISK

As the name implies, *default risk* is the risk that the borrower may in fact not repay the debt as agreed to in the mortgage note and mortgage document, but rather default on the mortgage before the full debt has been repaid. The interest rate on a mortgage, or risky loan, is summarized in Equation 12.2. We generally use a lowercase r to designate a risky rate of interest as opposed to the upper case R_f which is used to designate the risk free rate of interest.

Equation 12.2

$$r = \text{Real rate} + E \text{ (inflation premium)} + \text{default premium}$$

or:

$$r = R_f + E \text{ (inflation premium)}$$

Both statements in Equation 12.2 say the same thing, since Equation 12.1 states that R_f = real rate + E (inflation premium). That default premium is sometimes referred to as the risk premium. The term *default premium* is used here because we refer to many types of risk, and hence risk premiums, throughout the chapter.

If we check the current mortgage interest rate on a 30-year conventional mortgage, we find that it is about 6.13%. If we compare that with a 25- or 30-year treasury security which is listed as 4.78%, we can extract a default premium of $6.13\% - 4.78\% = 1.35\%$ on a 30-year mortgage. So mortgage lenders are earning about a 1.35% default premium on their 30-year mortgages to compensate them for the additional risk of default. Naturally, lenders try to manage that risk through effective underwriting programs that allow them to eliminate borrowers who are most likely to default on their mortgage loans.

INTEREST RATE RISK

The second major risk from the lender's viewpoint is referred to as *interest rate risk*. This is the risk that market rates of interest will increase while the lender has fixed interest rate mortgages outstanding. This increase in market rates of interest, if they cannot be passed on to the borrowers, will result in the value of the lender's mortgage portfolio (the lender's assets) decreasing. If the value of these assets decreases while the value of the liabilities remains the same, there is a technical term for that, *bankruptcy*. This is the one of the major problems that hit the savings and loan industry in the 1970s and 1980s.

Let's take a look at an example of what interest rate risk means to the value of a mortgage portfolio. XYZ Mortgage Company has a portfolio of 100 mortgages of $100,000 each for a total value of $10,000,000. That portfolio has an average interest rate of 6.5%. Suddenly, or over time (it doesn't make much difference), market rates of interest go up to 8%. The average remaining term on the mortgages is 25 years. What has happened to the portfolio's value? We can analyze this situation by looking at one mortgage, the average mortgage, in the portfolio that is for $100,000 at a 6.5% rate with 20 years remaining. The payment calculation is in Solution 12.6. After calculating the payment we change the interest rate to 8% and solve for the new present value.

Solution 12.6

100000 [PV]

$20 \times 12 = 240$ [n]

$6.5/12 =$ [i/y]

[cpt] [pmt] 745.57

$8/12 =$ [i/y]

[cpt] [PV] 89136.47

We see that the payments are now discounted at the new market rate of 8%, and that reduces the present value of the mortgage from $100,000 to $89,136.47 which reduces the value of the portfolio from $10,000,000 to $8,913,646. One fact that might reduce the size of that value change would be that a mortgage today generally doesn't have an expected life of 20 years. Most mortgages today are expected to be paid off in seven to nine years, either because the property will be sold or because the loan will be refinanced. However, the size of the interest rate shift that lenders saw in the 1970s was greater than the 1.5% shift we use in our example. Lenders saw the mortgage market shift from 8.5% to in excess of 14% in a very short period of time. This increase in market rates had a tremendous impact on the value of savings and loan mortgage portfolios. In times of increasing rates you don't see much refinancing either, so mortgages tend to run for longer periods of time, exacerberating the problem.

Lenders have attempted to create situations where they are not required to bear the full brunt of interest rate risk in the mortgage market. The adjustable rate mortgage (ARM) has been the most useful tool for these purposes over the years. The ARM ties its interest rate to an index, and as that index moves, so does the interest rate on the borrower's mortgage. As the index goes up, the interest rate on the mortgage goes up. As the interest rate goes up, the payments go up. This same tool that protects the lender against market rate increases passes the interest rate risk on to the borrower. Many borrowers have been hit hard by payment increases that were not budgeted for, and these changes have resulted in large numbers of foreclosures.

Appraisal Cap Rates and Risk

Risk also affects appraisal capitalization rates and, as a result, real estate values. The risk associated with commercial/investment property valuation can be found in the capitalization rate used in the appraisal process. Two major types of risk affect the cap rate choice, and they are the lack of liquidity associated with a real estate investment that is not present in a common stock investment and the potential for changing markets associated with a real estate investment. The two types are in fact closely associated with each other. It is the lack of liquidity, or the inability to quickly get out of a real estate investment, that subjects the investor to the potential for changing markets. If the investment was more liquid, investors would not have to worry as much about changing markets because they could simply sell the investment and get out of it.

These changing markets could affect both the NOI of the property as well as the potential selling price of the real estate at the end of the holding period. These two risk factors are present in the cap rate used by an appraiser. While they are most likely not separated out and/or separately calculated, they are present in the rate. Other risks, such as tenant quality, can also come up in appraising one property in comparison with the entire local market for investment properties.

MARKET EXTRACTED CAP RATES

Let's say we are appraising a single-tenant building in an office/warehouse market. The comparables that you have used as an appraiser to come up with your market-extracted cap rate have been of different types. A market-extracted cap rate, you will recall, is one that is extracted from a comparable sale using IRV. Using IRV, the cap rate is calculated as shown in Equation 12.3.

Equation 12.3

$$R = I/V$$

Two of the comps in your analysis are single-tenant buildings, but the third has several tenants. The one with several tenants is probably deemed less risky because of the investor's eggs not all being in one basket, so to speak. If that building is less risky to an investor, should its cap rate be the same as those derived from single-tenant buildings by the appraiser? It should probably be lower than the other two because of the reduction of risk resulting from multiple tenants. Not only would the number of tenants be relevant, but the quality of those tenants is also important. Those tenants with a higher credit rating should certainly be reflected in a lower cap rate. Maybe the tenant of one of the comps is the U.S. Postal Service which has signed a 30-year lease. In that case the income is almost like the income on a treasury security. Rather than saying our cap rate should reflect default or some other type of risk, maybe we should be using a risk-free cap rate.

Hopefully you are getting the feeling of how capitalization rates can be risk-adjusted rates and how different types of risk are applicable to different types of tenants. Riskier properties should be valued using cap rates that reflect those elevated levels of risk. The higher cap rates will result in lower values.

BAND OF INVESTMENT CAP RATES

You will recall from Chapter 10 that the band of investment method of estimating a cap rate uses both the mortgage information and the required rate of return on equity for the investor in building the cap rate. As the expected inflation premium and the default premium associated with the mortgage increase, the mortgage constant will increase, both leading to a higher cap rate. As the required return on equity for a given investor increases, so will the cap rate using the band of investment. Increased risk finds its way into the cap rate both through the mortgage terms and through the return on equity for the investor. It is probably easier to see these risk factors affecting the cap rate in the band of investment method of estimating the cap rate than it is in the market extraction method. At least it is easier to isolate and quantify them. The equation for calculating the cap rate using the band of investment technique is replicated from Chapter 10 in Equation 12.4.

Equation 12.4

$$R = (L/V \times MC) + (E/V \times ROE)$$

As a review, it says that the cap rate is calculated by multiplying the loan-to-value ratio on the mortgage by the annual mortgage constant, plus the equity-to-value ratio times the required return on equity for the typical investor in this type of property. Risk is built into this cap rate in two places. First of all it is built into the mortgage information. We have already discussed how the risk of default premium and the expected inflation premium are built into mortgage interest rates. If that is the case, then those same premiums are built into the mortgage constant. Second, risk factors are built into an investor's required return on equity. Investors certainly will not be happy earning a risk-free rate of return given the types of risk that they are exposing themselves to by investing in the real estate market.

What does the presence of risk premiums in cap rates do to property values? If those risk premiums increase the cap rate, then the obvious impact on property values is that the values will go down. To quote a major premise, the higher the discount rate, the lower the present value. Increases in risk premium will convert to increases in cap rates which will convert to decreases in property value.

Problem 12.1

Let's look at a situation in which a lender has mortgage applications on two different four-unit apartment buildings, property A' and property B', that are right next to each other. They were built in the same year by the same builder. The units within the buildings are the same size, and they generate the same amount of rent per month. The lender finds the credit score and hence the creditworthiness of borrower A to be better than that of borrower B. The lender decides that the risk of default is greater for borrower B than it is for borrower and A, and as a result will charge a $1/2\%$ greater interest rate on the mortgage to compensate for the additional risk. The mortgage to be obtained is an 80% L/V mortgage amortized over 30 years. Borrower A will get the mortgage at a 7.5% rate of interest, and borrower B will pay 8% interest. Both buildings will generate $26,000 of NOI next year, and investors in this type of building are expecting a 12% ROE. What is the impact of the additional default risk on the value of property B versus the value of property A?

We use the band of investment technique for estimating the cap rate in this problem. First we must calculate the mortgage constant. This is done in Solution 12.7 for investor A.

Solution12.7: Mortgage Constant for Investor A

> 1 [PV]
> 360 [n]
> 7.5/12 = [i/y]
> [cpt] [pmt] $0.0070 \times 12 = 0.0839$

The same calculation for investor B is made in Solution 12.8.

Solution12.8: Mortgage Constant for Investor B

> 1 [PV]
> 360 [n]
> 8/12 = [i/y]
> [cpt] [pmt] $0.0073 \times 12 = 0.0881$

These mortgage constants are then inserted into Equation 12.4 to result in the cap rates indicated in Equations 12.5.

Equations 12.5

$$R_A = (0.80 \times 0.0839) + (0.20 \times 0.12) = 0.0671 + 0.024 = 0.0911 = 9.11\%$$

$$R_B = (0.80 \times 0.0881) = (0.20 \times 0.12) = 0.0705 + 0.024 = 0.0945 = 9.45\%$$

The additional default risk resulted in an increase in the cap rate from 9.11% for investor A to 9.45% for investor B. How does the increase in default risk affect the value of the property? This is illustrated in Equations 12.6.

Equations 12.6

$$V_A = I/R_A = \$26,000/0.0911 = \$285,400$$

$$V_B = I/R_B = \$26,000/0.0945 = \$275,132$$

In this case the additional default risk that was present in the increased rate of interest charged to investor B resulted in a property value decline of approximately $10,000, from $285,400 to $275,132. What this really means to investor B is that in order to buy the property, this investor will have to come up with an additional $10,000 in down payment. The seller isn't really going to care if investor B has to pay a higher rate of interest on the mortgage; that is the investor's problem. The seller is still going to want the same $285,400 that building A is selling for because it is an identical building. The additional risk results in the investor having to make a larger cash investment on the property.

Problem 12.1 illustrates how risk that finds its way into capitalization rates can have a detrimental effect on property values.

Standard Deviation of Returns

One method of measuring the risk associated with a real estate investment is to analyze that investment given different economic scenarios and see how the investment returns vary. This is typically measured using the standard deviation of returns. As an example, an investor is looking at a building and determines through economic analysis that the economy could go in one of three directions. The economy could be super duper, it could be okay, or it could be really rotten. These are technical economic terms that you might not be familiar with. Through the cash flow analysis the investor has calculated the IRR associated with each of those projected economic conditions. Table 12.3 contains the economic conditions, the

Table 12.3   Investment A

Economic condition	Probability	IRR
1. Super duper	0.30	18%
2. Okay	0.40	11%
3. Really rotten	0.30	7%

probability of those conditions, and the IRRs associated with each economic scenario. This example is referred to as investment A.

The information contained in Table 12.3 is now used to calculate the expected return and the standard deviation of returns. First we calculate the expected return using Equation 12.7. (Before you look at the equation, don't panic. The terms are explained below.)

Equation 12.7

$$\text{Expected return, } E(R) = \sum (R_j \times P_j)$$

$$E(R) = (18\% \times 0.30) + (11\% \times 0.40) + (7\% \times 0.30)$$

$$= 5.4\% + 4.4\% + 2.1\% = 11.9\%$$

The Greek letter sigma ($\sum$) stands for *summation*, so we multiply the return by the probability associated with that return, and we add them all up. The j in the equation refers to return 1, or return 2, or return 3 and probability 1, probability 2, and probability 3. So the j is just standing in for 1, 2, or 3. In the case of the data in Table 12.3, the expected value, given the three different economic scenarios and the returns associated with those scenarios, is 11.9%. Now that we have the expected value, we can calculate the variance of returns and then the ultimate goal which is the standard deviation of returns.

Equation 12.8

$$\text{Variance} = \sum [R_j - E(R)]^2 \times P_j$$

To calculate the variance, you start in the middle, between the brackets. Take the actual return (R_j) minus the expected (or average) return, and square that difference. Then multiply the result by the probability associated with that return. Then the sigma tells us to sum up all of those values. The variance calculation for this investment is illustrated in Equation 12.9.

Equation 12.9

$$\text{Variance} = (18 - 11.9)^2 \times 0.30 + (11 - 11.9)^2 \times 0.40 + (7 - 11.9)^2 \times 0.30$$
$$= (37.21)\,0.30 + (0.81)\,0.40 + (24.01)\,0.30 = 11.16 + 0.32 + 7.2$$
$$= 18.68$$

The variance itself doesn't tell us a whole lot about the investment. Rather it is the standard deviation that gives us some information. The calculation of the variance allows us to get to the standard deviation because the standard deviation is the square root of the variance.

Equation 12.10

$$\text{Standard deviation} = \sqrt{18.68} = 4.32\%$$

What this says is that the expected return given the three economic scenarios has a standard deviation of 4.32%. The standard deviation is a measure of variability of returns or a measure of risk. The standard deviation in this form is best used in comparing investment alternatives. If we were to analyze the standard deviations of two similar investments that we are considering and if they have similar expected returns, an investor would select the investment with the lower standard deviation in order to avoid the additional risk.

Let's analyze a second investment option and compare it with our original investment from Table 12.3. This time we have the same potential economic scenarios and the same probabilities of each of them taking place, but the expected IRRs associated with the scenarios are 15% given a super duper economy, 11% given an okay economy, and 8% given a really rotten economy. Calculate the standard deviation of returns for this investment, which we refer to as investment B.

Equation 12.11

$$E(R) = (15\% \times 0.30) + (11\% \times 0.40) + (8\% \times 0.30)$$
$$= 4.5\% + 4.4\% + 2.4\% = 11.3\%$$

As shown in Equation 12.11, the expected return of investment B is 11.3%. We can now move on to the variance and standard deviation calculations.

Equation 12.12

$$\text{Variance} = (15 - 11.3)^2 \times 0.30 + (11 - 11.3)^2 \times 0.40 + (8 - 11.3)^2 \times 0.30$$

$$= 13.69 + 0.09 + 10.89$$

$$= (13.69)\,0.30 + (0.09)\,0.40 + (10.89)\,0.30$$

$$= 4.11 + 0.036 + 3.27$$

$$= 7.42$$

The variance of returns for investment B is 7.42. Once again, the square root of the variance is equal to the standard deviation.

Equation 12.13

$$\text{Standard deviation} = \sqrt{7.42} = 2.72\%$$

Now the standard deviation for investment A can be compared with the standard deviation for investment B, as shown in Table 12.4.

In looking at Table 12.4 it is apparent that investment A has the higher expected rate of return, which would make it more attractive to an investor. It also has the higher standard deviation which would signal greater risk to the investor. Both of these pieces of information are important to the investor, but they each may lead the investor to a different conclusion.

COEFFICIENT OF VARIATION

There is one more measure of risk that can clear up problems of weighing rate of return versus standard deviation, and that is called the *coefficient of variation*. What it does is that it gives us a measure of risk per percentage point rate of return.

Table 12.4   Comparison of standard deviations of investments A and B

Investment	E(R) Expected return	Standard deviation
A	11.9%	4.32%
B	11.3%	2.72%

Equation 12.14

$$\text{Coefficient of variation} = \text{Standard deviation}/E(R)$$

$$\text{Coefficient of variation}_A = 4.32/11.9 = 0.36$$

$$\text{Coefficient of variation}_B = 2.72/11.3 = 0.24$$

Since investment A has a higher coefficient of variation, it is considered riskier than investment B because it has a higher measure of risk per percentage point rate of return.

Partitioning of IRR

Another way we can measure the risk of an investment is to partition the IRR into two parts. We are interested in seeing how much the IRR is dependent on the cash flows from operations and how much of the IRR is dependent on the cash flow from the sale of the building. When a larger portion of the IRR comes from the cash flow from the sale, that would be considered a riskier investment than one in which a larger percentage of the IRR comes from the cash flows from operations. The cash flows from operations are received sooner by the investor than the cash flow from the sale, and as a result they are considered less risky. There is less time until the cash flows are received for changes in market and economic conditions to take place so these cash flow estimates are more certain than that coming from the sale which is more uncertain.

Table 12.5 is the summary of cash flows contained in Table 11.6 (in Chapter 11). You may recall that the IRR of these cash flows was 18.29%. Let's partition this rate of return to determine what percentage is coming from the cash flows from operations and what percentage is coming from the cash flow from the sale. We need to find the present value of the cash flows from operations using the IRR as the discount rate.

Table 12.5   After-tax cash flows

Year	ATCF
0	−$167,100
1	$8,734
2	$10,284
3	$11,874
4	$13,504
5	$15,175 + $305,181

This calculation is found in Solution 12.9.

Solution 12.9

    [CF] 0 [enter]

    [↓] 8734 [enter][↓]

    [↓] 10284 [enter][↓]

    [↓] 11874 [enter][↓]

    [↓] 13504 [enter][↓]

    [↓] 15175 [enter][↓]

    [↓][NPV] I = 18.29 [enter] [↓]

    [NPV] [cpt] 35356.43

Now we find the present value of the cash flow from the sale discounted at the IRR, which is summarized in Solution 12.10.

Solution 12.10

    305181 {FV]

    5 [n]

    18.29 [i/y]

    [cpt] [PV] 131770.24

The present value of the cash flow from operations and the present value of the cash flow from the sale of the property are now added together as shown in Equation 12.15.

Equation 12.15

$$\text{Total PV of cash flows} = \$35{,}356.43 + \$131{,}770.24 = \$167{,}126.67$$

To get the percentage of the IRR coming from the cash flow from operations, simply divide the present value of the cash flows from operations by the total present value of all of the cash flows as shown in Equation 12.16.

Equation 12.16

$$\% \text{ of IRR from operations} = \$35{,}356.43/\$167{,}126.67 = 0.212 = 21.2\%$$

To obtain the percentage of the IRR coming from the sale of the property divide the present value of the sale price of the property as calculated in Solution 12.10, by the total present value of the cash flows that was calculated in Equation 12.15.

This operation is illustrated in Equation 12.17. Alternatively, we can simply take 1 minus the result of Equation 12.16. In both cases we obtain 78.8%.

Equation 12.17

$$\text{\% of IRR from sale} = \$131{,}770.24/\$167{,}126.67 = 0.788 = 78.8\%$$

This measure can also be used in comparing one investment with another to determine which investment is more dependent on sale cash flow. Those investments receiving a greater percentage of their return from the sale are considered riskier, as stated previously.

Quiz for Chapter 12

1. If the real rate of return is 1%, what are the expected rates of infla-
    tion and the default premium associated with the following securities?
    The one-year treasury rate = 4.6%, and the one-year corporate bond
    rate = 6.1%.
    a. Inflation premium = 3.6%; default premium = 2%
    b. Default premium = 2%; inflation premium = 3.6%
    c. Inflation premium = 3.6%; default premium = 1.5%
    d. Default premium = 1.5%; inflation premium = 3.6%

2. XYZ Federal Savings has a mortgage portfolio containing mortgages
    with a face value of $1,500,000. They earn an average interest rate of
    7% and an average term of 25 years and are payable monthly. If the
    mortgages are expected to be paid off in the full 25 years (that is, no
    prepayments), and the market rate of interest goes to 7.5%, what is the
    new value of the portfolio?
    a. $1,500,000
    b. $65,383
    c. $1,750,000
    d. $1,434,616

3. Li has just taken out an adjustable rate mortgage (ARM) from her
    favorite lender for an amount of $140,000 amortized over 30 years at a
    6.25% rate of interest. At the end of the first year her interest rate went
    up to 6.5%. What is her monthly payment in the second year of the loan,
    assuming no payment caps and no negative amortization?
    a. $862.00
    b. $884.41
    c. $884.90
    d. $862.48

4. Kate is appraising your apartment building, and she tells you that she is
    going to use the band of investment method of estimating a capitalization
    rate. You have told her that you are refinancing the building and that
    you are applying for a 75% loan-to-value mortgage with a 7% rate and
    a 30-year amortization. She finds most investors in this type of building
    are expecting a return on equity of 14%. What cap rate will Kate be using
    in her income capitalization approach if she uses the band of investment
    technique to estimate her cap rate?

  a. 9.49%

  b. 7%

  c. 8.75%

  d. 10%

5. You are looking into an investment with the following potential internal rates of return (IRR) and the given probabilities that they will occur. What is the expected IRR given the probabilities?

IRR	Probability
10%	20%
14%	30%
16%	30%
18%	20%

  a. 14.5%

  b. 14.6%

  c. 14.0%

  d. 15.0%

6. What is the variance of the returns in question 5?

  a. 8.61

  b. 4.23

  c. 2.31

  d. 1.96

7. What is the standard deviation of the returns from question 5?

  a. 1.4%

  b. 2.41%

  c. 2.06%

  d. 2.93%

8. Bill is analyzing two real estate investment opportunities that have come his way. The first one has an expected return of 16% and has a standard deviation of returns of 3.5%. The second investment has an expected rate of return of 14% and has a standard deviation of 2.8%. If Bill is using rate of return as his benchmark, he chooses the first investment because it has a higher rate of return. If Bill's decision rule is based on standard deviation, he chooses the second investment because it is less risky. If Bill uses the coefficient of correlation as his decision rule, which investment does he choose?

a. First investment since it has less risk per percentage point rate of return

b. Second investment since it has less risk per percentage point rate of return

c. Either one would be acceptable to Bill

d. Neither one would be acceptable to Bill

9. Dave is analyzing a real estate investment with the cash flows found in Table 12.6. He has found that the IRR of the after-tax cash flows is 13.73%. He has decided that in order to do an effective risk analysis, he should partition the IRR and determine what percentage of the IRR comes from the cash flows from operations. What percentage of the IRR is coming from the cash flows from operations?

Table 12.6

Year	Cash flows
0	(150,000)
1	$10,000
2	$20,000
3	$30,000 + $155,000

a. 29.8%

b. 28.9%

c. 70.2%

d. 71.1%

10. In question 9, what percentage of the IRR is coming from the cash flow from the sale of the property?

a. 29.8%

b. 28.9%

c. 70.2%

d. 71.1%

CHAPTER 13

Leases

This Is the Lease of Your Problems

A *lease* is the contract between the landlord, or building owner, and the tenant. It establishes the rights and responsibilities of both parties to the agreement. The primary items of interest in the lease are the term, or how long the lease is in effect, and the rental rate, or how much rent the tenant is obligated to pay. The lease will also indicate whether the rental payments will be gross rental payments or net rental payments. Since the lease is a contract, it must contain the essential elements of a valid contract. These essential elements are offer and acceptance, competent parties, legality of object, and consideration. Since it is a real estate contract, there are two additional elements. First the contract must be written, and second it must contain a description of the property in question.

Appraisers and investors are interested in the information contained in the lease because the information will be the primary indicator of the market value and the investment value of the property. Both of these values are dependent on the duration of the lease, the quality of the tenant, and the amount of rent to be generated by the property.

Gross Rent and Net Rent

Gross rent is the gross amount that the landlord or owner of the building will be receiving. When landlords receive the gross amount, that indicates that they will have to pay the operating expenses out of that rental amount. If the rent they receive is the net amount, that means that the tenant will be paying the operating expenses because this is already the landlord's net amount. To keep these straight, think back to the cash flow analysis in Chapter 11. In order to obtain the net operating income, we had to deduct vacancy and rent loss from the potential gross income, and we also had to deduct operating expenses, as shown in Table 13.1. If the landlord were to receive a net rental payment, that would imply that he or she does not have to pay operating expenses, but of course someone has to pay them. In the case of net rental payments being made to the landlord, the tenant must pay the operating expenses.

Residential Rent

Residential rent is typically stated as a monthly rental amount. The apartment can be rented for $1,000 per month. Rent is also usually due at the beginning of the month. If we refer back to Chapter 6, we see the lease payments as an annuity

Table 13.1   **Before-tax cash flow**

PGI	$126,900
–Vacancies	$8,883
EGI	$118,017
–Operating expenses	$47,000
NOI	$71,017
–Debt Service	–$62,185
BTCF	$8,832

due, since the payments are made at the beginning of the month. By analyzing the value of the rental payments, we can see why the landlord would be upset if we, as the tenants, were consistently late with our rent payments. If we were to look at the value of a one-year lease with payments of $1,000 per month and using a discount rate of 10%, we can find that value in Solution 13.1.

Solution 13.1

-1000 [pmt]

12 [n]

10/12 = [i/y]

[cpt] [PV] 11374.51 × 1.0083 = $11,469.30

The lease has a value of $11,469.30. When we compute the PV of the annuity, the calculator assumes it is an ordinary annuity unless we tell the calculator that we are going to use the beginning of the period payments. In Solution 13.1, I didn't tell the calculator that, so the value of $11,374.51 must be multiplied by 1 plus the rate of interest for one period, in this case 1 plus (10/12 = 0.83%) or 1.0083. There is also a [BGN] key on your calculator that will move the payment from the end of the period to the beginning of the period, but I will let you read your manual about that. I prefer to simply multiply the present value of the ordinary annuity by 1 plus the rate of interest for one period. The resulting value is the present value of the annuity due, or the present value of the lease.

Notice that if our payments were consistently late by one month during the term of the lease, then we would have an ordinary annuity, with payments at the end of the month. What would be the value of the lease then? It would be worth $11,374.51. That is why the landlord insists that we make our lease payments in a timely manner. If we don't, the landlord is losing value or wealth.

OFFICE AND WAREHOUSE RENT

Office and warehouse rent is typically quoted in price per square foot per year. If the stated office rental rate is $14 per square foot and the space to be rented is 1,500 square feet, that would equal the value stated in Equation 13.1. First the annual rental amount is calculated followed by the monthly amount.

Equation 13.1

$$\text{Annual rent} = \$14 \times 1,500 = \$21,000 \text{ per year}$$

$$\text{Monthly rent} = \$21,000/12 = \$1,750 \text{ per month}$$

This rental rate may be a gross figure, or it may be a net figure. If it is a gross rental amount, the landlord would be responsible for paying the operating expenses as explained previously. If it is a net rental amount, the tenant would be responsible for paying the operating expenses.

RETAIL RENT

Retail rent can work differently from either of the others already mentioned. In retail leases we may have something referred to as *percentage rent*. In a rental situation with percentage rent the tenant first customarily pays what is called *base rent*. This would simply be the rent needed to open up the shop. Then there may be percentage rent that is added on top of the base rent. That percentage is generally a percentage of sales volume during the month. In that way the more successful the store is, the more successful the landlord is also. The percentage will vary depending on the business enterprise that the tenant is involved in. The range of percentages is most often in the 5–10% of sales range. The difference between the base rent and the total rent paid is referred to as *overage rent*.

STEPS

A tenant may sign a multiyear lease with the annual rental rates established at the time the lease is signed. The rental rates may very well increase at different times during the lease, maybe every year, maybe less often. These increases, or steps, may be in the form of dollars per square foot, or they may be tied to the consumer price index (CPI).

Leased Fee Value versus Leasehold Value

If the landlord entered into a long-term lease without steps, then the tenant may be able to obtain value for his leasehold interest. This value gain for the leasehold interest would be in direct proportion to the value loss that would be experienced by the leased fee (landlord's) interest. Let's look at an example in which the landlord may lose value. Look at the formula for the value of the leased fee estate, Equation 13.2, and then, the value of the leasehold estate, in Equation 13.3.

Equation 13.2

$$\text{Value of leased fee} = \text{PV of NOI}_j + \text{PV of reversion}$$

In simple terms, the value of the leased fee estate, the landlord's interest, is equal to the present value of the NOI for j periods, plus the present value of the reversion, or selling price, at the end of the holding period.

Equation 13.3

Value of the leasehold = PV of any rent savings

The value of the leasehold estate, or the tenant's interest, is equal to the present value of any rent savings (versus the market rent) that may be earned.

Let's say that the tenant signs a five-year lease. The contract net rent is $14 per square foot for 1,500 total rentable square feet. There are no steps in the lease. After the first two years the market goes through a small change, and the market rent is now $16 per square foot. What happens to the leasehold interest? If we assume a 10% discount rate, the value of the leasehold interest is contained in Solution 13.2.

Solution 13.2

−3000 [pmt]

3 [n]

10 [i/y]

[cpt] [PV] 7460.56

The leasehold interest has a value of $7,460.56. Since the tenant is locked in at the $14 rate for five years, after two years if the market rate goes to $16 per square foot, the tenant will be experiencing a rent savings of $2 per square foot for the last three years of the lease. That $2 per square foot × 1,500 square feet results in a rent savings of $3,000 per year. The present value of the rent savings is the value of the leasehold interest.

The value gain that accrues to the tenant because of the fixed-rent long-term lease is identical to the value loss experienced by the landlord as a result of the lease. The contract rent which is $2 per square foot lower than what the market rent is means that the leased fee interest is going to have a lower present value than it would have if the contract rent was at the market level. The present value of that rent loss is equal to the same $7,460.56. The value that one party to the lease gains is the same value that the other party to the lease loses.

Problem 13.1

Let's look at a comprehensive problem illustrating the value loss and value gain associated with a long-term lease. This time the subject property is a small office building of 5,000 square feet. The lease is a five-year lease with a contract rental rate of $12.50 per square foot for the entire five-year period. After three years the market rent climbs to $14 per square foot. Using a 10% discount rate and a going out cap rate of 8%, calculate the value of the leasehold interest, the value of the leased fee interest, and finally the value of the leased fee interest if the rental rate was at the market level at the end of year 3. All three value estimates are to be calculated at the end of year 3.

Solution 13.3

−7500 [pmt]

2 [n]

10 [i/y]

[cpt] [PV] 13016.53

As indicated in Solution 13.3, the leasehold interest has a value at the end of year 3 of $13,016.53. There is a rent savings in each of the last two years of $1.50 × 5,000 = $7,500. Discounted at the 10% discount rate gives the rent savings a present value of $13,016.

In order to calculate the value of the leased fee interest we have to calculate the present value of the NOI for the two-year period plus the present value of the reversion at the end of period two. The reversion value, or projected sale price, can be calculated using IRV. You will recall from Chapter 10 that $V_0 = I_1/R$. The value at time period zero is equal to the NOI for period 1, the coming period, divided by the cap rate. We want to estimate the value at the end of period three, so we will need to use the NOI for period four, the coming period. The NOI = 5,000 × $12.50 = $62,500. If the rent was at the market rate, the NOI would be $14 × 5,000 = $70,000. The market rent is typically used to estimate the value of the reversion, so V = 70,000/0.08 = $875,000. The value of the leased fee interest then is contained in Solution 13.4.

Solution 13.4

875000 [FV]

62500 [pmt]

2 [n]

10 [i/y]

[cpt] [PV] − 831611.57

The value of the leased fee interest comes in at $831,611. If the rent was at the market rate, the value of the leased fee interest would be as shown in Solution 3.5.

Solution 13.5

   875000 [FV]

   70000 [pmt]

   2 [n]

   10 [i/y]

   [cpt] [PV] − 844,628.10

If the rent was at the market rate of $14 per square foot rather than the lower contract rate of $12.50 per square foot, the value of the leased fee interest would be $844,628. That represents a value difference of $844,628 − $831,611 = $13,016, which just happens to be the value of the leasehold interest. Is that another wow moment? I think so.

Average Rent and Effective Rent

If a lease has contract rent of $10 per square foot in year 1 and then contains steps of a $1.50 increase each year over the remaining four years of the five-year lease, the rents would appear as shown in Table 13.2. Average rent is a simple arithmetic average of each of the annual rental rates, and for this lease, the calculation would look like Equation 13.4.

Equation 13.4

$$\text{Average rent} = (10 + 11.50 + 13 + 14.50 + 16)/5 = 13$$

Given the rental values based on the beginning contract rent of $10 per square foot and annual steps of $1.50 per foot, the average rental rate for the lease is $13 per square foot.

The effective rent takes into consideration the time value of money. The calculation involves finding the present value of each of the rental rates and then taking

Table 13.2   Rent per square foot

Year	Rent per square foot
1	$10.00
2	$11.50
3	$13.00
4	$14.50
5	$16.00

the total present value and amortizing it over the lease term. Using the rental rates from Table 13.1, we would discount $10 back one period, $11.50 back two periods, $13 back three periods, $14.50 back four periods, and $16 back five periods. Let's use a 9% discount rate for our calculations. To simplify the calculation we can use the cash flow keys on the calculator as shown in Solution 13.6.

Solution 13.6

[cf]

10 [enter] [↓][↓]

11.50 [enter] [↓][↓]

13 [enter] [↓][↓]

14.50 [enter] [↓][↓]

16 [enter] [↓][↓]

[NPV] I = 10 [enter]

[↓] NPV [cpt] 48.20

Remember, the values not in [ ] above show up in the display. The [characters] are your keystrokes. The rental amounts have a total present value of $48.20. That amount is now called a *present value*, and we calculate the payment to amortize to obtain the effective rent as shown in Solution 13.7.

Solution 13.7

48.20 [PV]

5 [n]

10 [i/y]

[cpt] [pmt] − 12.72

The effective rent of this series of rental amounts is $12.72 versus the average rent of $13. The rental amounts in years 1 and 2 have a greater impact on the present value than do the rents for years 4 and 5, which is why the effective rent is lower than the average rent.

Problem 13.2

Let's look at another five-year lease situation with net rents of $13, $15, $15.75, $16.60, and $17.50 in years 1 through 5 of the lease. Calculate both the average rent and the effective rent for the rental amounts stated.

Equation 13.5

>   Average rent $= (13 + 15 + 15.75 + 16.60 + 17.50)/5 = \$15.57$

The effective rent is calculated in Solution 13.8 and Solution 13.9.

Solution 13.8

[cf]

13 [enter] [↓][↓]

15 [enter] [↓][↓]

15.75 [enter] [↓][↓]

16.60 [enter] [↓][↓]

17.50 [enter] [↓][↓]

[NPV] I $= 10$ [enter]

[↓] NPV [cpt] 58.25

Solution 13.9

58.25 [PV]

5 [n]

10 [i/y]

[cpt] [pmt] $- 15.37$

The effective rent of this second series of rental amounts is $15.37 per square foot per year.

Quiz for Chapter 13

1. Dan is managing a small office building, and the lease states that the rent can be payable monthly, at the rate of $2,500 per month and that it covers a period of two years. Given a discount rate of 10%, what is the current value of the lease?

    a. $60,000

    b. $54,177

    c. $54,626

    d. $22,461

2. Bev has purchased a warehouse, and the building has a five-year lease with rent payments constant for all five years at $10,000 per year. At the end of year 3 the market rent increases to $12,000 per year. Given a discount rate of 10%, what is the value of the leasehold interest at the end of year 3?

    a. $3,471

    b. $4,000

    c. $20,826

    d. $20,280

3. In question 2, what is the value of the leased fee interest today, at time period zero if we assume the reversion is zero?

    a. $40,000

    b. $37.907

    c. $45,489

    d. $35,907

4. The net rent per square foot on your office building for the next three years is $10.25 per square foot, $11 per square foot, and $12.50 per square foot. What is the average rent per square foot?

    a. $11.00

    b. $11.25

    c. $11.50

    d. $11.75

5. What is the effective rent for the next three years on the office building in question 4 given a 10% discount rate?

a. $11.00
b. $11.25
c. $11.35
d. $11.18

6. The local drug store asks you to analyze its new lease with the strip center that it rents space from. The base rent is $7 per square foot of the 1,500-square-foot store, plus there is percentage rent at the rate of 4% of annual sales. The store has averaged annual sales of about $500,000 per year. How much rent can it expect to pay for the coming year based on the lease requirements?
   a. $10,500
   b. $20,000
   c. $30,500
   d. $35,000

7. How much of the annual rent in question 6 is overage rent?
   a. $10,500
   b. $20,000
   c. $30,500
   d. $35,000

8. The lease for your office space is a five-year lease, and it quotes annual per square foot rental rates of $13, $13.75, $14.25, $15, and $16.50 for years 1 through 5, respectively. What is the average rent per square foot?
   a. $14.00
   b. $14.25
   c. $14.50
   d. $14.75

9. What is the effective rent per square foot of the lease described in question 8 using a discount rate of 10%?
   a. $14.25
   b. $14.34
   c. $14.44
   d. $14.54

10. If you are renting 1,500 square feet of space in question 8, what is the present value of the lease if your discount rate is 10%?
    a. $81,567
    b. $75,767
    c. $72,987
    d. $67,777

Final Exam

1. Tony had his 22nd birthday this week, and he has decided he'd like to be a millionaire by the time he retires at age 65. If Tony can set aside equal amounts each month until he retires in a 10% account, how large would his monthly payments have to be to have $1 million by the time he retires?
    a. $8,450.05
    b. $116.72
    c. $1,937.98
    d. $516.00

2. I want to be a millionaire when I retire at 65 and I've just had my 57th birthday. How much do I have to set aside each month until I retire in my 10% account to have my $1 million?
    a. $8,450.05
    b. $516.00
    c. $6,840.83
    d. $15,174.00

3. If you borrow $120,000 in the form of a 25-year mortgage amortized monthly at the 7% annual rate, what is your monthly payment?

a. $848,14

b. $798.36

c. $719.46

d. $773.16

4. What is the principal balance after two years on the mortgage described in question 3?

a. $117,473

b. $112,896

c. $116,195

d. $100,839

5. If I deposit $4,000 today in an investment paying 10% annual interest and I withdraw $800 per year, how many withdrawals will I be able to make, if those withdrawals are made at the end of the year?

a. 5

b. 5.27

c. 7

d. 7.27

6. You've decided to go to graduate school, and you've calculated that you will need $8,500 per year for each of the three years you expect to be there. If you intend to enroll five years from today, given an interest rate of 9%, how much money should you set aside today?

a. $21,516

b. $13,983

c. $25,500

d. $16,573

7. Your driveway is 30 feet by 42 feet. If you cover it with a three-inch layer of concrete, how many cubic feet of concrete will you need?

a. 630 cubic feet

b. 1,260 cubic feet

c. 415 cubic feet

d. 315 cubic feet

8. Sylvia purchased a home earlier this year for $167,750 and took out a mortgage for $142,375 at 8% for 30 years. What was the loan-to-value ratio on the mortgage, and what is her down payment as a percentage of the purchase price?

    a. 75%, 25%

    b. 85%, 15%

    c. 90%, 10%

    d. 85%, 10%

9. Your cousin Kara recently purchased a new home for $179,500. The lot is worth $36,000 according to the appraiser. The lot size is 75 feet × 140 feet. What is the cost per square foot of the lot?

    a. $12.76

    b. $3.20

    c. $3.43

    d. $4.99

10. Ghulam purchased his home a year ago for $275,000 and has been told by an appraiser that it is currently worth $297,000. What has been the rate of appreciation the home has experienced over the last year?

    a. 6.5%

    b. 7%

    c. 7.5%

    d. 8%

11. Dennis has an opportunity to purchase a duplex for $325,000. He intends to finance the purchase with an 80% loan-to-value mortgage amortized over 30 years at a 7% rate of interest. If he buys the duplex and the value remains at $325,000 for one year, how much equity will Dennis have in the duplex at the end of the first year?

    a. $65,000

    b. $256,596

    c. $72,089

    d. $67,641

12. When Adrienne sold her home, she paid a 6% commission of $14,700. What was the sale price of Adrienne's home?

    a. $235,000

    b. $245,000

    c. $255,000

    d. $265,000

13. Dennis, from question 11, sold his duplex three years after he purchased it for $382,550. What was the compound annual appreciation that Dennis earned during his three-year holding period?

a. 3.6%

b. 4.6%

c. 5.6%

d. 6.6%

14. Karen asked a local real estate broker to come out and do a market analysis on her house because she was thinking of selling. The broker told her that the home should be listed for $235,900 and that he would be charging a 5% commission on the sale. If the home sells for 95% of the listing price, how much will Karen have to pay the broker for the commission?

   a. $11,795

   b. $11,205

   c. $13,446

   d. $10,615

15. Jason just signed a purchase agreement to sell his condo for $215,000. He bought it three years ago for $185,000. What was his annual average rate of appreciation over the three years?

   a. 5.4%

   b. 5.0%

   c. 16.2%

   d. 4.0%

16. Frances is selling her home after being transferred to another city for her job. She would like to net $175,000 from the sale of her home after paying a 6% commission to the broker. What sale price does the home have to sell for in order for Frances to receive her desired net proceeds?

   a. $185,500

   b. $186,170

   c. $186,500

   d. $185,170

17. Partha is selling a manufacturing building that has been in his family for years. The broker informed him that the commission would be 5% on the first $500,000 in sale price, 4% on the second $500,000 in sale price, and 2% on anything in excess of $1,000,000. If the building sells for a sale price of $1,250,000 how much commission does Partha have to pay?

   a. $50,000

   b. $45,000

   c. $25,000

   d. $47,500

18. The service station located two blocks from your home is installing a new fuel tank. The tank is 15 feet long and has a diameter of 6 feet. How many cubic feet of fuel does the tank hold?
    a. 282.6 cubic feet
    b. 423.9 cubic feet
    c. 141.3 cubic feet
    d. 372.6 cubic feet

19. Elise recently purchased the NW 1/4 of section 12 to house her horses and set up a training ring. She paid $475,000 for the land. How much did Elise pay per acre?
    a. $2,968
    b. $11,875
    c. $5,937
    d. $3,958

20. A half-acre lot on the outskirts of the city is listed for $8 per square foot. The commission on the listing contract is 7% of the sale price. If the lot sells for 85% of the listing price, what is the amount of the gross commission on the sale?
    a. $20,734
    b. $12,196
    c. $17,624
    d. $10,367

21. Denny took a listing on a four-unit apartment building with a list price of $425,000. The property sold for 95% of the list price. The net proceeds to the seller were $375,487 after the commission was paid. What was the commission rate charged on the sale of the four-unit building?
    a. 5%
    b. 6%
    c. 7%
    d. 8%

22. Tim is hoping to purchase a condo for $225,000, and he intends to get a mortgage of $157,500 at a 7% interest rate amortized over 25 years. What is the loan-to-value ratio on the mortgage?
    a. 60%
    b. 70%
    c. 80%
    d. 90%

23. A sum of $50,000 is invested today to provide a man with an annual income for 20 years; the first payment is to be received in one year. Given an interest rate of 5%, how much will the annual payments be?
    a. $1,512
    b. $2,500
    c. $3,500
    d. $4,012

24. How much money do you have to invest today in order to be able to spend $500 in two years and $700 in four years if you can earn 10% on your investment?
    a. $413.22
    b. $341.51
    c. $478.11
    d. $891.33

25. If your starting salary is $37,000 and you receive a 5% raise each year for the next 20 years, what will your salary be in year 20?
    a. $74,000
    b. $98,172
    c. $89,172
    d. $79,821

26. Kate is buying a condo; the purchase price is $315,000, and she is taking out a 90% loan-to-value mortgage to finance the purchase. The interest rate on the loan will be 7.25%, and it will be amortized over 30 years. What are Kate's monthly principal and interest payments on the mortgage going to be if it is a fixed-rate mortgage?
    a. $1,933.97
    b. $2,148.86
    c. $23,422.66
    d. $1,951.89

27. Five years from now Kate decides to sell her condo from question 26. If the property has gone up in value by 3% per year compounded annually, what is the expected sale price of the condo?
    a. $362,250
    b. $324,450
    c. $365,171
    d. $364,651

28. What is the mortgage balance when Kate sells her condo in question 27?
    a. $283,500.00
    b. $167,461.81
    c. $267,563.83
    d. $274,908.99

29. What is Kate's total equity in her condo when she sells it in question 27?
    a. $50,171
    b. $81,671
    c. $97,607
    d. $31,501

30. Pat bought a new house and closed on it last week for the price of $345,000. He took out a 75% loan-to-value 30-year mortgage to finance the purchase. He will be making payments of $1,635.48 for principal and interest each month on the loan. What is the rate of interest Pat is paying on the mortgage?
    a. 5.0%
    b. 5.5%
    c. 6.0%
    d. 6.5%

31. If Pat decides to sell the house in question 30 after 10 years, what will be the amount of his mortgage payoff?
    a. $258,750
    b. $219,358
    c. $242,218
    d. $238,219

32. The home that Maxine bought a couple of years ago cost $169,500 at the time of her purchase. She obtained a mortgage of $135,600 amortized over 25 years at a 5.5% rate of interest. What is the amount of her monthly mortgage payment?
    a. $823.70
    b. $832.70
    c. $827.30
    d. $837.20

33. What is the loan-to-value ratio on Maxine's mortgage in question 32?
    a. 125%
    b. 90%

c. 80%

d. 75%

34. Four years ago the country club took out a mortgage to finance the construction of a new club house. The total amount financed came to $2,500,000, and it had a 20-year term and an interest rate of 7%. What is the current principal balance on the mortgage?
    a. $19,382

    b. $2,457,638

    c. $2,235,043

    d. $2,480,634

35. What portion of the country club's (question 34) next payment, payment 49, will go toward principal reduction?
    a. $19,382

    b. $13,037

    c. $6,344

    d. $15,286

36. Dale took out an ARM three years ago for $179,500 at a 6% rate of interest with a 30-year amortization. His interest rate readjustment is coming up later this month, when the mortgage will be exactly three years old. He has been told that the treasury bond index, which is the index against which his mortgage is benchmarked, will be 4.5%. The margin on his loan is 2%. What will the new mortgage payment on his loan be after the interest rate is readjusted assuming that there are no payment caps on the mortgage?
    a. $1,130.64

    b. $1,058.21

    c. $1,076.19

    d. $920.51

37. Mary Jo recently bought a townhouse in a new development in town. When she went to the bank to apply for a mortgage, she found out that the bank had recently introduced biweekly mortgages. She thought that sounded interesting, so she asked what the payment would be on such a mortgage for $180,000 at 6% interest with a 30-year amortization. What will the biweekly payment be?
    a. $497.85

    b. $549.36

c. $1,079.19

d. $539.60

38. Gina has just finished her first year in the real estate brokerage business. She has sold $3,750,000 worth of real estate. Her broker told her at the beginning of the year that she would get 50% of the commission on her first $1,500,000 in real estate sales and 60% on all sales thereafter. If her sales were at an average commission rate of 3% of the sale prices, how much did Gina make in her first year?

    a. $63,000

    b. $56,250

    c. $67.500

    d. $112,500

39. Which of the following is not an equation?

    a. $100 = 4 \times 25$

    b. $100 = 1,000 \div 10$

    c. $100 = 1,010 - 10$

    d. $100 = 90 + 10$

40. Your cousin Kara recently purchased a home for $179,500. The lot is worth $36,000 according to the appraiser. The lot size is 75 feet × 150 feet. What is the square footage of the lot?

    a. 75 square feet

    b. 11,250 square feet

    c. 150 square feet

    d. 15.96 square feet

41. Laura is paying her broker a 7% commission to sell her house. How would you express Laura's expected net proceeds after her commission is paid?

    a. Sale price × (1 + 0.07)

    b. Sale price/(1 + 0.07)

    c. Sale price × (1 − 0.07)

    d. Sale price/(1 − 0.07)

42. Sharon purchased a new home for the price of $322,500 and took out a 25-year 6.5% interest rate mortgage for $258,000 to finance the purchase. She will have to pay loan costs that total $5,000 to take out the mortgage. What is the APR that the lender will have to disclose to Sharon at the closing?

a. 6.71%
b. 6.675%
c. 6.75%
d. 6.875%

43. What is the loan-to-value ratio of the mortgage in question 42?
    a. 60%
    b. 75%
    c. 80%
    d. 90%

44. Equity is equal to _____ – mortgage balance.
    a. Principal balance
    b. Market value
    c. Down payment
    d. Total interest

45. The mortgage you took out this morning to purchase a new home required you to make a down payment of $45,000. If you took out an 80% loan-to-value mortgage, what was the purchase price of your home?
    a. $56,250
    b. $180,000
    c. $450,000
    d. $225,000

46. What was the amount of your mortgage in question 45?
    a. $56,250
    b. $180,000
    c. $450,000
    d. $225,000

47. The type of mortgage that starts at a certain rate of interest but can have the interest rate and the payments increase at different points in time is referred to as:
    a. A shared appreciation mortgage
    b. An adjustable rate mortgage
    c. A constant payment mortgage
    d. A reverse annuity mortgage

48. Your sister purchased a home five years ago for the price of $199,500. Today the assessor told her that the property was worth $254,618. What has been her annual compound rate of appreciation on the home?

a. 3%

b. 4%

c. 5%

d. 6%

49. When Kent took out his shared appreciation mortgage, the bank reduced his interest rate by 25% in exchange for 25% of the appreciation that would take place over the next five years. If Kent paid $275,500 for the home and after five years its value has increased to $325,000, how much must Kent pay to the lender to meet the terms of the mortgage?

a. $49,500

b. $12,500

c. $12,225

d. $12,375

50. If the market rate of interest when the loan was originated in question 49 was 12% and the mortgage had a loan-to-value ratio of 80% amortized over 30 years, what was Kent's monthly payment during the first year of the loan?

a. $1,773.39

b. $2,267.06

c. $1,617.22

d. $2,615.02

51. Kristi's mortgage was originated five years ago for $176,600 to be amortized over 30 years at 5.75% interest. If Kristi makes regular payments on the loan until it is satisfied, how much total interest will Kristi pay on the loan?

a. $176,600

b. $371,012

c. $304,635

d. $194,412

52. Given the mortgage in question 51, what portion of payment number 3 is principal?

a. $1,030.59

b. $844.44

c. $186.15

d. $195.16

53. Given the mortgage in question 51, how much principal will Kristi pay over the life of the loan?

a. $176,600
b. $371,012
c. $304,635
d. $194,412

54. If you take out a mortgage for $217,900 amortized over 25 years at a 6% rate of interest and the lender charges you 2 points plus a 1% origination fee, what is the lender's effective rate of return?
   a. 6.25%
   b. 6.375%
   c. 6.32%
   d. 6.5%

55. What is the APR that must be disclosed to the borrower in the mortgage described in question 54?
   a. 6.25%
   b. 6.375%
   c. 6.32%
   d. 6.5%

56. In the cost approach to determining value, the depreciated cost of the improvements is added to the value of the _____ in order to obtain the value estimate.
   a. The total construction cost of the improvements
   b. The historical construction cost of the improvements
   c. The depreciated cost of the improvements
   d. The cost of the land

57. Betty is appraising a 2,000-square-foot colonial style house that has four bedrooms. One of the comparables that Betty chose to use in her sales comparison approach was another colonial with similar square footage, four bedrooms. The property was otherwise very similar to the subject property, but it had a swimming pool in the backyard, and the subject did not have a pool. The comparable sold for $245,000, and the appraiser thinks the market value of the pool is about $25,000. What is the indicated value of the subject property?
   a. $245,000
   b. $270,000
   c. $220,000
   d. $232,500

58. Ben, your boss at the appraisal firm, has just given you an assignment to appraise a single-family home, and he wants you to use the gross rent multiplier to get its value. The subject should bring in about $1,450 per month if it were to be rented out. The very best comparable you can find was rented for $1,350 when it sold earlier this month for a price of $165,000. What is the indicated value of the subject property using the GRM form of the income approach and the given comparable?

    a. $122.22

    b. $177,219

    c. $164,900

    d. $153,620

59. Which of the following is critical in the value estimate using the income approach and IRV?

    a. Net investment income

    b. Investment value

    c. Discount rate

    d. Capitalization rate

60. The appraiser is going to use the band of investment method of estimating a cap rate. He is going to use the mortgage constant for a 75% loan-to-value mortgage amortized for 25 years at a 6% interest rate and a required return on equity for the investor of 13%. What is the annual mortgage constant that should be used in the formula for estimating the cap rate?

    a. 0.0064

    b. 0.0325

    c. 0.0773

    d. 0.0880

61. The potential gross income minus the vacancy and rent loss allowance is called what?

    a. NOI

    b. PGI

    c. BTCF

    d. EGI

62. The amount of cash flow that the investor earns in a year after all operating expenses, debt service, and income taxes have been paid is called what?

    a. NOI

    b. BTCF

c. ATCF

d. IOU

63. Amanda has invested $150,000 in a small office building, and it is generating after-tax cash flows of $5,000 in year 1, $6,000 in year 2, $7,000 in year 3, $8,000 in year 4, and $9,000 in year 5 plus a $225,000 reversion, or sale price, at the end of year 5. Given Amanda's required rate of return of 10%, what is the net present value of the cash flows of the building?
a. $14,523
b. $15,523
c. $16,523
d. $17,523

64. You are analyzing a potential investment in an office building, and you notice that the before-tax cash flow is positive. What does that tell you about the debt coverage ratio?
a. It is greater than 1
b. It is less than 1
c. It is equal to 1
d. Nothing

65. If the one-year spot rate for treasuries is 4.5% and the two-year spot rate is 4.25%, what is the indicated forward rate from the end of period one to the end of period two?
a. 4.75%
b. 4.25%
c. 4.0%
d. 3.75%

66. An investment opportunity has three potential outcomes. It could earn a return of 22% if the economy does really well, and you think there is a 25% probability of that happening. If the economy is just average, the return should be 15%, and the probability of that is 40%. If the economy does very poorly, you will earn only a 4% return, and there is a 35% probability of that taking place. What is your expected return?
a. 11.5%
b. 12.9%
c. 13.3%
d. 10.5%

67. Given the expected return you calculated from the information in question 66, what is the standard deviation of the returns from the same question?

    a. 4.5%

    b. 5.2%

    c. 6.3%

    d. 7.1%

68. You were talking about this book around the office, and your boss suggested that you help her solve a problem she had been working on. A property your company is considering investing in has an IRR of 18%. The cash flows from operations have a present value of $425,000, and the cash flow from the sale of the property will be $975,000. What percentage of the IRR comes from operations, and what percentage comes from the sale?

    a. 30.3% from the sale and 69.7% from operations

    b. 43.6% from the sale and 56.4% from operations

    c. 69.7% from the sale and 30.3% from operations

    d. 56.4% from the sale and 43.6% from operations

69. Fred purchased a small office building that has a potential gross income of $145,500, a 6% vacancy rate, and net income of $24,700. What are the operating expenses in year 1?

    a. $115,800

    b. $112,070

    c. $151,800

    d. $121,070

70. Blair just took a listing on a 4,000-square-foot retail building and is putting together a cash flow analysis. The lease states that the store has a base rent of $8 per square foot and a percentage rent of 4% of annual sales revenue. If the store has sales revenue of $1 million, what is the total rent for the next year?

    a. $32,000

    b. $52,000

    c. $72,000

    d. $92,000

71. Lauren's company is looking for new office space. She is looking at a building that is in a good location for her needs, and the lease terms include rent for the first five years of $10.50, $10.50, $12.00, $13.75, and $14.25, respectively, per square foot. What is the average rent per square foot per year?

    a. $10.50

    b. $11.40

    c. $13.10

    d. $12.20

72. What is the effective rent on the building that Lauren is considering in question 71, given a 10% discount rate?

    a. $45.48

    b. $12.00

    c. $12.20

    d. $10.50

73. How much overage rent is there in the lease in question 70?

    a. All of it

    b. $40,000

    c. $32,000

    d. $72,000

74. You are measuring a home for a listing, and the main body of the house is a rectangle that is 35 feet × 45 feet, and there is a year-round porch off the back that is 10 feet × 14 feet. What is the square footage of the main floor?

    a. 1,575 square feet

    b. 140 square feet

    c. 1,435 square feet

    d. 1,715 square feet

75. The state deed transfer tax rate in your state is $3.30 per $1,000 of sale price, and you just closed on the purchase of your first home, for which you paid $265,900. You paid $53,180 in cash and the balance with a 30-year mortgage at 6%. What amount of state deed tax did you pay at closing?

    a. $701.90

    b. $175.56

    c. $877.47

    d. $656.27

Glossary

accelerated depreciation   Depreciation in excess of straight line depreciation for tax purposes, not currently allowed for real property.

accrued expense   An expense that has been earned, but not fully used up.

acquisition cost   The same as the purchase price of property.

acre   A unit of measure of land made up of 43,560 square feet.

adjustable rate mortgage (ARM)   A mortgage that has an interest rate that is adjusted to the market rate of interest periodically. It shifts some of the interest rate risk to the borrower.

adjusted basis   A term in investment property that refers to acquisition cost minus any depreciation that has been taken.

adjustment interval The time period between interest rate adjustments in an ARM.

after-tax cash flow (ATCF) Either the cash flow from operations or the cash flow from the sale of a building. It is the amount of the cash flow available to the investor after paying all expenses and all taxes.

amortization schedule A breakdown and summary of the principal and interest payments on a mortgage as well as the principal balance over time.

annual compounding One of the compounding periods over which time value of money calculations can be calculated. Others include quarterly, monthly, and daily compounding.

annual percentage rate (APR) The effective cost of money to the borrower after all loan fees and interest paid to the lender have been accounted for.

annuity A series of equal payments that comes at regular intervals.

annuity due An annuity in which the payments come at the beginning of a period.

appraisal An informed estimate or opinion of value. It is also the process of valuing property.

appreciation The increase in property value resulting from inflation in the market.

area The surface size of a plane, it can be in square feet, square inches, or acres.

baseline The horizontal line from which government rectangular survey legal descriptions are measured; similar in concept to the lines of latitude.

before-tax cash flow (BTCF) The cash flow available to the investor after paying operating expenses and debt service, but before settling taxes.

beneficial financing Mortgage or contract for deed financing that has an interest rate that is lower than the current mortgage interest rate. It could be a below-market rate contract for deed or a below-market interest rate mortgage assumption.

biweekly mortgage   Rather than having monthly mortgage payments, biweekly mortgages have payments due every two weeks.

breakeven occupancy   The percentage of occupancy needed in an investment property so that there is sufficient income to cover just the mortgage payments and the operating expenses.

capital gain   A gain on one's capital investment. In the case of investment property it comes from a combination of property value appreciation and depreciation taken for tax purposes.

capital gain tax rate   The tax rate that applies to capital gain income. Current tax law applies a 15% rate to gains coming from appreciation and 25% to gains in excess of appreciation.

capitalization rate   The rate that is divided into the net income of a piece of property. It results in a value estimate in the income approach to appraisal.

cash equivalency   The process of adjusting a comparable sale for the presence of below-market-rate financing in the appraisal process.

cash flow from sale   The one-time cash flow from the sale of property which comes at the end of the holding period.

cash flows from operations   Cash flows that come each year of a real estate investment from the operations of the building. They are assumed to come at the end of the year.

closing   A gathering of interested parties at which the promises made in the purchase agreement are executed.

closing agent   The person who conducts the proceedings of the closing and calculates the closing statements.

closing statement   The document that sorts out the expenses and prepayments associated with a real estate transaction.

coefficient of variation   A statistical measure that puts the standard deviation, or variation in cash flows, in a per unit of rate of return format. It is a measure of risk.

commission The form of compensation that a broker or salesperson receives in exchange for the service provided to buyers and sellers. It is typically a percentage of the sale or exchange price of a piece of property.

common denominator To facilitate the addition or subtraction of fractions, a common denominator is required. It is most easily established by multiplying the two denominators together.

composite rate In an ARM this is the combined value of the index rate and the margin.

compound growth rate A rate of increase per year or per month that, when multiplied by a beginning value, will yield a new value. The value increases at a greater rate than a nominal rate because of the interest that is earned on both the beginning value and the interest that is earned on the previously earned interest.

compound interest See *compound growth rate*.

contract for deed A sales and financing agreement in which the buyer of property makes payments directly to the seller with no lending institution involved. In some states this is called a *land contract*.

contract rate The contract rate of interest is the rate that is stated in the contract. The contract may be a contract for deed, or it may be a mortgage contract.

cost approach One of the three approaches for determining value in a real estate appraisal.

credits The values in a closing statement that are either prepaid and the payer wants credit for having paid them or is money that is coming to either the buyer or the seller.

debits Values in a closing statement that the person being debited owes or is responsible for paying.

debt coverage ratio (DCR) Gives an indication of how much cushion there is in NOI over and above the debt service. Lenders typically want a DCR of 1.2 or greater.

decimal equivalent This is achieved by dividing the numerator into the denominator in a fraction, or by shifting the decimal point two places to the left in a percentage. The decimal equivalent of $1/2$ is 0.5, and the decimal equivalent of 25% is 0.25.

default risk The risk that the borrower may default on loan payments prior to the debt being satisfied.

depreciation There are two types of depreciation, one that is used in appraisal and one that is used for investment property. In appraisal it is a loss in value resulting from any cause. In investment property it is the theoretical wearing out of the property over time. It reduces an investor's taxable income. Currently straight line depreciation is used. The useful life for residential property is 27.5 years, and for commercial property it is 39 years.

discount points One discount point is equal to 1% of the mortgage amount. Discount points are cash paid at the time of closing, and their impact is that they increase the yield to the lender.

discount rate The rate used to calculate a present value. The higher the discount rate, the lower the present value.

discounted cash flow (DCF) A form of the income approach used by an appraiser to estimate the value of income-producing property. The value is equal to the present value of the property's NOI plus the present value of the reversion. Both types of cash flows are discounted over the projected holding period.

effective gross income (EGI) The amount equal to the potential gross income minus the vacancy and rent loss allowance in the cash flow analysis of investment property.

effective rate of interest The rate that the borrower is paying once all loan fees have been factored into the cost.

equation States a relationship between numbers or values using an equal sign. The values on each side of the equal sign are equivalent to each other.

equity The market value of a property minus the mortgage balance.

equity-to-value ratio One minus the loan-to-value ratio. If the loan-to-value ratio is 80%, then the equity-to-value ratio is 20%. This ratio is used in the band of investment method of estimating a capitalization rate.

expected return   The weighted average return on an investment using the probability of different market conditions taking place.

financial calculator   A calculator programmed to make time value of money calculations given financial inputs. Those inputs can be present value, future value, payment, term, and interest rate.

fixed-rate mortgage   A mortgage that has the same interest rate over the entire term of the mortgage.

floors   In an adjustable rate mortgage, the lowest interest rate level that the loan could have.

forward rate   An interest rate that may be changed in the future, such as the one-year rate in effect from the end of period one to the end of period two, or the end of period two to the end of period three.

fraction   A part of a whole. The denominator states how many parts are in the whole, and the numerator states how many of those parts we are dealing with. The fraction 1/4 says we are looking at a whole with four parts, but we are dealing with only one of those parts.

functional obsolescence   A form of appraisal depreciation that can result from a poor floor plan, from a feature that no longer serves the same purpose it once did, or from a feature that is no long desired in the marketplace, such as a shag carpet or an oil-fired furnace.

future value (FV)   One of the inputs in a time value of money calculation. It is the value of an amount of money at some point in the future.

government survey system   A form of legal description that describes land using a grid system of principal meridians and baselines. Land is divided into townships and sections.

gross lease   A lease in which the rent that is paid is the gross amount to the landlord, and the landlord is responsible for paying the operating expenses out of that rent.

gross rent multiplier (GRM)   A form of the income approach in which the GRM is extracted from a comparable sale by taking the sale price and dividing it by the gross rent. The rent is usually monthly in the case of single-family residential property and annual rent for other property types.

growth rate   The rate at which cash flow items, such as rents or operating expenses, are growing.

highest and best use   Referring to a parcel of land, the most economically profitable way to use the property or the use that generates the highest dollar return for the land.

holding period   The period of time that an investor expects to hold, or own, a piece of property.

improvements   Improvements to land include buildings, access, and utilities.

income approach   One of three approaches to determining property value. The other two are the sales comparison approach and the cost approach.

income capitalization   One form of the income approach. It makes use of the IRV formula, in that $V = I/R$. This says that the value of the property is equal to the property's NOI divided by the capitalization rate.

index   An interest rate series against which the interest rate on a mortgage is measured.

inflation premium   A premium built into interest rates because investors want to be compensated for any inflation in the cost of goods and services that takes place while their investment is outstanding.

interest rate risk   The risk long-term lenders take that the market rates of interest will go up and that they will be locked into the lower rate. The increase in market rates will have a negative impact on the value of the mortgage.

investment property   Property that is used in a trade or business or held for the production of income.

IRV (income rate value)   The appraisal method that is often used in the income approach. It spawns two equations, $I/V = R$ and $I/R = V$, where $I = NOI$, $R = $ cap rate, and $V = $ value.

land   The earth's surface, everything above the earth's surface and everything below the earth's surface to the center of the earth. Air rights are limited to 1,000 feet in an urban area and 500 feet in a rural area.

lease   A contract between the landlord and the tenant in which the landlord conveys to the tenant the right of possession of a piece of property.

legal description   A precise method of describing a parcel of land that would be upheld in a court of law.

loan-to-value ratio   The mortgage amount divided by the property value.

locational (economic) obsolescence   The loss in value that results simply from the location of a property. If a major employer in a small town were to close and many people had to put their homes on the market at the same time, they would all lose value due to locational, or economic, obsolescence.

lot and block   A form of legal description used in urban areas, sometimes referred to as a subdivision plat.

lot size   The surface area of the lot typically stated in square feet.

margin   Used in an ARM and added to the index to get the composite rate, or the new interest rate, on the mortgage.

marginal tax rate (MTR)   The tax rate on the next dollar earned by an investor.

market value   The price of a property that a reasonable buyer would be willing to pay and a reasonable seller would be willing to accept.

measurement and boundaries   See *metes and bounds*.

metes and bounds   A form of legal description in which a parcel of land's entire perimeter is detailed starting at a point of beginning. This point is referenced to some monument, which may be as precise as a surveyor's monument placed in the earth's surface or something as imprecise as a old oak tree or a large block of granite.

mixed number   A number containing both a whole number and a fraction.

monthly compounding   Uses the interest rate on a monthly basis and in a time value of money problem.

monument   See *metes and bounds*.

mortgage   A loan secured from a lender that uses property as security for the debt. The borrower will typically make payments over a 20-, 25-, or 30-year period.

mortgage balance   The unpaid principal amount on a loan.

mortgage constant   The payment necessary to repay the debt of one dollar over time. It is calculated just like a mortgage payment, only rather than using the mortgage amount as the present value, you use 1 as the present value. It is used in the band of investment method of estimating a capitalization rate.

mortgage registration tax   The tax charged by the state to register a new mortgage document.

negative amortization   Results from a payment that is not sufficient to cover the interest due on a mortgage. The unpaid interest gets added on to the principal balance.

net lease   Provides the net amount to the landlord so any operating expenses will be paid by the tenant.

net operating income (NOI)   The the income available to the investor after both vacancy and operating expenses have been deducted. It is the income that an appraiser is going to value.

net present value (NPV)   The difference between the present value of the cash inflows and the present value of the cash outflows.

net proceeds   The net amount that the borrower receives after any loan fees are deducted from the total loan amount.

nominal rate   The same as the stated rate or the contract rate.

operating expense ratio   Calculated by taking the operating expenses divided by the effective gross income as a cash flow analysis.

operating expenses   The expenses needed to operate a building for one year.

ordinary annuity   An annuity in which the payments come at the end of the period.

origination fee   A fee paid by the borrower to the lender to cover the paper-work costs associated with the loan application. It has the effect of increasing the effective rate on the loan.

part, percent, whole   Explains the relationship between these three elements algebraically. The following equations are inferred; part/whole = %, part/% = whole, and % × whole = part.

partially amortized loan   A loan that is not fully paid off with the monthly payments, but currently has a principal balance yet to be paid.

payment cap   In an ARM a payment cap would establish an upper limit beyond which the monthly payment could not go. The impact on the loan may be negative amortization.

payment to amortize   In a TVM problem the payment to amortize would be the payment needed to repay a debt over time. The payment is made up of both principal and interest.

percentage   Refers to a whole that is divided into 100 parts, and we are just referring to a portion of those parts. Example: 25%—the whole has 100 parts, and we are looking at 25 of them.

percentage rent   Often charged in a retail lease and refers to a percentage of sales a store makes that would be paid to the landlord as part of the rent.

physical deterioration   A form of appraisal depreciation that refers to the chipped paint and cracked plaster on a property.

point of beginning   In a metes and bounds legal description, this is the point where the description of the perimeter of the parcel of land begins and ends.

points   See *discount points*.

potential gross income (PGI)   The amount of income that the investment property could generate given two assumptions: The building is occupied 100% of the time, and tenants always pay their rent.

prepaid expense   An expense that has already been paid but the good or service has not been fully used up. Prepaid expenses appear on transaction closing statements.

prepaid interest   A term sometimes applied to the concept of discount points.

present value (PV)   One of the variables in a time value of money calculation. It refers to the value of an amount of money today at time period zero.

principal balance   The unpaid principal amount on a loan at a point in time. The initial principal balance is the amount borrowed. The principal balance at any point in time is equal to the present value of the remaining payments.

principal meridian   The north/south line in the government survey system.

principal plus interest (P+I)   The payment to amortize is made up of principal plus interest. A mortgage payment is an example of a principal plus interest payment.

principal reduction   Every time a mortgage payment is made, the principal portion of the payment goes to reducing the principal balance. This is principal reduction.

prorated items   Expenses that are split between the buyer and the seller in a closing statement.

quarter section   The government survey system divides land into sections, which contain 640 acres of land. A quarter section contains $640 \times 1/4 = 160$ acres.

real estate   Land plus improvements.

real property   Refers to the rights of ownership, sometimes called the bundle of rights, which include the right to use and enjoy, the right to possess, the right to mortgage, the right to lease, and the right to convey.

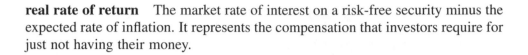

real rate of return   The market rate of interest on a risk-free security minus the expected rate of inflation. It represents the compensation that investors require for just not having their money.

reconciliation   The process of converting three value estimates to a single value estimate in an appraisal. It is usually a weighted average calculation.

rectangle   A geometric shape with four sides, 90-degree angles at the corners, and two parallel sides that are longer than the other two parallel sides.

rectangular survey system   See *government survey system.*

replacement cost   In the cost approach of the appraisal process the replacement costs are the construction costs associated with replacing the building with one of similar size and similar utility.

reproduction cost   In the cost approach of the appraisal process the reproduction costs are the construction costs associated with replacing the building with one that is exactly the way the first building is today.

return on equity (ROE)   Sometimes called the cash-on-cash return or the cash return on the cash investment. ROE is the before-tax cash flow divided by the equity investment.

return on investment (ROI)   The return on the investor's total investment and equal to the NOI divided by the investment, or purchase price.

reverse annuity mortgage (RAM)   A mortgage arrangement that allows the borrower to convert equity into a cash flow stream. Designed for retirees, it provides a series of payments from the lender to the borrower.

reversion   Refers to the sale price of a real estate investment at the end of the projected holding period.

risk   The probability of achieving an undesired outcome or the variability of returns.

sales comparison approach   One of the three approaches for determining value in the appraisal process. The subject property is compared to similar properties that have already been sold to estimate the subject's value.

scientific notation   A method of stating a number in relation to a power of 10. The number 2,000 would be 20×10^2.

section   In the government survey system, consists of 640 acres. There are 36 sections in a township.

shared appreciation mortgage (SAM)   The borrower gives up part of the equity over a period of years in exchange for an interest rate reduction at the outset of the loan.

sinking fund payment   One of the time value of money calculations, it is the payment needed to accumulate some amount of money in the future.

spot rate   An interest rate that could be obtained today for a one-year, two-year, three-year loan or investment.

standard deviation   A statistical measure of risk. Approximately 68% of the observations should be within 1 standard deviation of the expected value in a normal distribution.

state deed tax   Tax levied against grantees when they record the deed to their property.

straight line depreciation   The same amount of depreciation expense each year. Simply divide the value of the improvements by the useful life.

subdivision plat   See *lot and block*.

teaser rate   The interest rate for the first year of an ARM. Generally a little lower than the rate on a fixed-rate mortgage in order to tease, or attract, borrowers.

term   Referring to a mortgage, the period of time over which the payments will be made.

time value of money (TVM)   The concept that money has differing values over time. The variables used in TVM calculations are present value, future value, number of periods, interest rate or discount rate, and payment.

title insurance   Protects a buyer from undisclosed title defects that may arise.

township The government survey system divides land into six-mile by six-mile parcels of land called townships. These are divided into 36 one-square-mile sections.

township and range system See *government survey system*.

trapezoid A four-sided object with two parallel sides.

vacancy rate The percentage of units in the building that are not occupied.

volume The amount of interior space within a fully enclosed cube, box, or cylinder.

yield curve The graphical representation of the relationship between interest rates and time. The yield curve can either be in its normal position, in its inverted position, or it may be flat, in which case the one-year rate, two-year rate, three-year rate, and so on are all equal.

Quiz Answers

Chapter 1

1. c. $75 \times 150 = 11,250$ square feet
2. a. $20 \times 20 = 400$ square feet
3. d. $22 \times 24 \times 8 = 4,224$ cubic feet
4. b. $7 + 6 - 4 = 9$
5. c. $(50 + 80) \times \frac{1}{2} \times 100 = 6,500$ square feet
6. b. $(15 \times 15) \times 3.14 = 706.5$ square feet
7. c. $(14 \times 14) \times 3.14 \times 30 = 18,463.2$ cubic feet
8. a. $(30 \times 40) + (10 \times 10) = 1,200 + 100 = 1,300$ square feet
9. c. $30 + 30 + 10 + 10 + 40 + 40 = 166$ feet
10. d. $80 \times 165 = 13,200$; $\$65,000 \div 13,200 = \$4.92$; $\$65,000 \div 80 = \$812.50$

Chapter 2

1. $4/4 = 1$, $4/3 = 1\,1/3$, $4/5$, $5/8$, $16/12 = 1\,4/12 = 1\,1/3$,
   $7/6 = 1\,1/6$
2. $2/4 = 1/2$, $1/6$, $3/28$, $1/8$

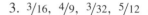

3. $3/16$, $4/9$, $3/32$, $5/12$

4. $12/4 = 3$, $6/6 = 1$, $5/15 = 1/3$, $12/8 = 1\,4/8 = 1\,1/2$,
   $15/4 = 3\,3/4$, $6/8 = 3/4$

5. 0.75, 0.67, 0.20, 1.5, 2.25, 4.75

6. 75%, 67%, 20%, 150%, 225%, 475%

7. b. 142375/167750 = 0.85 = 85% L/V; 1 − 0.85 = 0.15 = 15% down
   payment

8. c. 167750 − 142375 = 25375

9. b. 220000 − 206800 = 13200/220000 = 0.06 = 6% or
   206800/220000 = 0.94 and 1 − 0.94 = 0.06 = 6%

10. d. 220000 − 215686 = 4314/220000 = 0.02 = 2% or
    220000/215686 = 1.02 − 1 = 0.02 = 2%

Chapter 3

1. b. $475,000 × 0.06 = $28,500

2. c. $475,000 − $28,500 = $446,500

3. c. $225,000 × 0.07 = $15,750 v 0.50 = $7,875 × 0.50 = $3,937.50

4. a. $195,000 × 0.06 = $11,700.60 = $7,020

5. d. $500,000 × 0.06 = $30,000; $500,000 × 0.04 = $20,000; $500,000 ×
   0.02 = $10,000; $30,000 + $20,000 + $10,000 = $60,000

6. c. $60,000/$1,500,000 = 0.04 = 4%

7. b. $171,000 − $164,500 = $6,500/$164,500 = 0.04 = 4%, or
   $171,000/$164,500 = 1.04 − 1 = 0.04 = 4%

8. b. $179,700 − $164,500 = $15,200/$164,500 = 0.092/2 = 0.046 = 4.6%

9. d. $144,000/(1 − 0.05) = $144,000/0.95 = $151,578

10. a. $175,000/(1 − 0.055) = $175,000/0.945 = $185,185

Chapter 4

1. d. 70.41 × 100 = 7,041

2. b. $35,000/7041 = $4.97, $35,000/6500 = $5.38,
   $35,000/7500 = $4.67, $35,000/7000 = $5.00

3. c. 22

4. d. $640 × 1/4 × 1/4 × 1/4 = 10$

5. b. $640 × 1/4 × 1/4 = 40$, $640 × 1/4 × 1/4 = 80$, $40 + 80 = 120$

6. a.

7. c. 640 × 4 = 2,560 acres

8. d. 2,560 × $2,000 = $5,120,000 × 0.60 = $3,072,000

9. b. 100 × 100 = 10, 000, (60 × 20) × 1/2 = 600,
   10, 000 + 600 + 600 = 11, 200 square feet.

10. a. 15

Quiz Answers

Chapter 5

1. a.
2. c.
3. b.
4. c. $138,000 ÷ 1,000 = 138$; $138 × \$2.30 = \$317.40$
5. b. $140,000 ÷ 1,000 = 140$; $140 × \$3.30 = \$462.00$
6. b. $\$8,500,000 ÷ \$365,000,000 = 0.023 = 2.3\%$
7. b. $\$163,000 × 0.0233 = \$3,797$
8. b. $\$325,000 × 0.01 = 3,250$; $3,250 × 1.02268 = 3,323.71$
9. c. $\$325,000 − \$76,000 = \$249,000$; $\$249,000 × 0.0009 = 224.10$;
   $304 − 224.10 = 79.90$
10. d.

Chapter 6

1. c. -10000 [PV], 3 [n], 5.5 [i/y], [cpt] [FV] 11,742.41
2. b. -150 [pmt], $20 × 12 = $ [n], $8/12 = $ [i/y], [cpt] [FV] 88,353.06
3. d. 75,000 [FV], 12 [n], 10 [i/y], [cpt] [pmt] 3,507.25
4. c. $-1,000$ [pmt], 25 [n], 8 [i/y], [cpt] [PV] 10,674.78
5. b. 35,000 [PV], 15 [n], 4 [i/y], [cpt] [FV] 63,033.02
6. a. 95,000 [PV], $30 × 12 = $ [n], $6/12 = $ [i/y], [cpt] [pmt] 569.57
7. b. 95,000 [PV], $30 × 12 = $ [n], $6/12 = $ [i/y], [cpt] [pmt] 569.57,
   [rcl] [n] $- 120 = $ [n] [cpt] [PV] 79,501.44
8. a. -659 [pmt], $7/12 = $ [i/y], 240 [n], [cpt] [PV] 84,999.47
9. c. 45,000 [FV], 5 [n], 8 [i/y], [cpt] [PV] 30,626.24
10. d. $-5,000$ [pmt], 4 [n], 5 [i/y], [cpt] [PV] 17,729.75

Chapter 7

1. c. 150,000 [PV], 360 [n], $6.5/12 = $ [i/y], [cpt] [pmt] 948.10
2. b. 150,000 [PV], 360 [n], $6.5/12 = $ [i/y], [cpt] [pmt] [rcl] [n] $- 60 = $
   [n] [cpt] [PV] 140,416.47
3. d. 170,000 [PV], 300 [n], $7/12 = $ [i/y], [cpt] [pmt] 1,201.52 [rcl] [PV]
   $170,000 × 0.96 = 163,200$ [PV] [cpt] [i/y] $0.62 × 12 = 7.46$
4. a. 170,000 [PV], 300 [n], $7/12 = $ [i/y], [cpt] [pmt] 1,201.52 [rcl] [n] $- 60 = $
   [n] [cpt] [PV] 154,975.66; [2nd] [CLR TVM], 154,975.66 [FV] 1,201.52
   [pmt] $- 163,200$ [PV] 60 [n] [cpt] [i/y] $0.67 × 12 = 8.01$
5. b. 145,000 [PV], 360 [n], $7.5/12 = $ [i/y], [cpt] [pmt] 1,013.86 [rcl] [PV] ×
   $0.98 = $ [PV] [cpt] [i/y] $0.64 × 12 = 7.71$
6. b. $130,000/162,500 = 0.80 = 80\%$
7. a. 864.89, b. 125,745.05, c. 172,446.30, d. 46,701.25

8. b. 215,000 [PV], 360 [n], 6/12 = [i/y], [cpt] [pmt] 1,289.03; [rcl] [n] − 60 = [n] [cpt] [PV] 200,066.87; [2nd] [CLR TVM] 200,066.87 [FV], 1,289.03 [pmt], −215,000 × 0.985 = −211,775 [PV], 60 [n], [cpt] [i/y] 0.53 × 12 = 6.36

9. d. 195,000 × 0.75 = 146,250 [PV], 25 × 12 = 300 [n], 6.25/12 = [i/y], [cpt] [pmt] 964.77, [rcl] [n] − 36 = [n] [cpt] [PV] 138,232.96

10. d. 220,000 × 0.75 = 165,000 [FV], 15 × 12 = [n], 7.25/12 = [i/y], [cpt] [pmt] 509.35

Chapter 8

1. c. 225,000/162,00 = 1.381; 1.381 − 1 = 0.381 = 38.1%
2. d. 185,000 × (1 − 0.15) = 185,000 × 0.85 = 157,250
3. b. −194,500 [PV], 6 [n], 3 [i/y], [cpt] [FV] 232,243.17
4. a. (345,000 − 70,000)/39 = 275,000/39 = 7,051.28
5. c. (220,000 − 44,000)/27.5 = 176,000/27.5 = 6,400
6. a. −122,000 [PV], 455,000 [FV], 19 [n], [cpt] [i/y] 7.27
7. a. 163,500/137,900 = (1.186 −1)/4 = 0.186/4 = 0.046 = 4.6%
8. d. 133,000/(1 − 0.15) = 133,000/0.85 = 156,470.59
9. c. 175,000/123,900 = 1.412; 1.412 − 1 = 0.412 = 41.2%
10. a. 245,000 [PV], 5 [n], 4 [i/y], [cpt] [FV] 298,079.96

Chapter 9

1. d
2. d
3. d
4. a
5. c
6. a
7. a
8. a
9. c
10. a

Chapter 10

1. c. 1,200 × $65.75 = $78,900 × (1 − 0.19) = $78,900 × 0.81 = $63,909
2. b. $55 × 250 = $13,750; $145,000 − $13,570 = $131,250
3. a. $162,500/$1,500 = 108.33; 108.33 × $1,400 = $151,667

Quiz Answers

4. d. 179,000/1,650 = 108.79 × 0.50 = 54.44; 149,750/1300 = 115.19 × 0.15 = 17.28; 187500/1,700 = 110.29 × 0.35 = 38.6; 54.44 + 17.28 + 38.6 = 110.12

5.
PGI	$154,800
–Vacancies	–$10,836
EGI	$143,964
–Operating expenses	–$57,600
NOI	$86,364

6. c. 4,000 × $12,50 = $50,000 × (1 − 0.09) = $50,000 × 0.91 = $45,500 − $17,300 = $28,200

7. a. 33,300/370,000 = 0.09; 24,000/300,000 = 0.08; 23,100/280,000 = 0.083; 0.09 × 0.45 = 0.041; 0.08 × 0.35 = 0.028; 0.083 × 0.20 = 0.017; 0.041 + 0.028 + 0.017 = 0.086

8. d. R = (0.80 × 0.0758) + (0.20 × 0.16) = 0.0607 + 0.032 = 0.0927 = 9.27%

9.
PGI	$124,800
–Vacancies	–$9,984
EGI	$114,816
–Operating expenses	–$44,800
NOI	$70,016
–DS	–$45,830
BTCF	$24,185

755,300 × 0.80 = 604,240 [PV]

360 [n]

6.5/12 = [i/y]

[cpt] [pmt] 3,819.21 × 12 = 45,830

10. c. [CF] 0 [enter]

   [↓] 5,000 [enter][↓]

   [↓] 5,500 [enter][↓]

   [↓] 5,575 [enter][↓]

   [↓] 6,120 [enter][↓]

   [↓] 101,150 [enter][↓]

   [↓][NPV] I = 1 [enter] [↓]

   NPV = [cpt] 77,103.86

Chapter 11

1. c. [(6 × $800) + (6 × $950) + (6 × $1,100)] × 12 = $205,200
2. a. $119,940/$99,058 = 1.211

3. c. $75,000/$194,940 = 0.385 = 38.5%
4. b. ($99,058 + $75,000)/$205,200 = 0.848 = 84.8%
5. b. $43,636 × 27.5 = $1,199,990
6. b.
7. d. $104,335/$1,738,911 = 0.06 = 6%
8. b. −1,500,000 [PV], 1,738,911 [FV], 5 [n], [cpt] [i/y] 3.0
9. b. 20,882 + 3,740 = 24,622
10. c. [CF] 150,000 [+/−] [enter] [↓]

   10000 [enter] [↓][↓]

   20000 [enter] [↓][↓]

   185000 [enter] [↓][↓]

   [IRR] [cpt] 13.73

Chapter 12

1. c. 4.6% − 1% = 3.6% E(inflation); 6.1% − 1% − 3.6% = 2% Default premium
2. d. 1,500,000 [PV], 300 [n], 7/12 = [i/y], [cpt] [pmt] 10,601.69 7/5/12 = [i/y] [cpt] [PV] 1,434,616
3. b. 14,000 [PV], 360 [n], 6.25/12 = [i/y], [cpt] [pmt] 862.00, [rcl] [n] − 12 = [n] [cpt] [PV] 138,359.49 6.5/12 = [i/y] [cpt] [pmt] 884.41
4. a. 1 [PV], 7/12 = [i/y], 360 [n], [cpt] [pmt] 0.0067 × 12 = 0.0798 = MC; R = (L/V × MC) + (E/V × ROE); R = (0.75 × 0.0798) + (0.25 × 0.14) = 0.0949
5. b. 0.20(10) + 0.30(14) + 0.30(16) + 0.20(20) = 15.0%
6. a. $(10 − 14.6)^2$ 0.20 + $(14 − 14.6)^2$ 0.30 + $(16 − 14.6)^2$ 0.30 + $(18 − 14.6)^2$ 0.20 = 8.61
7. d. $\sqrt{8.61}$ = 2.93
8. b. 3.5/16 = 0.2188, 2.8/14 = 0.20
9. a. [cf] 0 [enter] [↓] 10,000 [enter] [↓][↓] 20,000 [enter] [↓][↓] 30,000 [enter] [↓][↓] [NPV] I = 13.73 [enter] [↓] npv = [cpt] 44,648.97 ÷ 150,000 = 0.298
10. c. 155,000 [FV], 3 [n], 13.73 [i/y], [cpt] [PV] 105,367/150,000 = 0.702

Year	Cash flows
0	(150,000)
1	$10,000
2	$20,000
3	$30,000 + $155,000

Quiz Answers

Chapter 13

1. b. −2500 [pmt], 24 [n], 10/12 = [n], [cpt] [PV] 54,177.14
2. a. −2000 [pmt], 2 [n], 10 [i/y], [cpt] [PV] 3,471.07
3. b. −10000 [pmt], 5 [n], 10 [i/y], [cpt] [PV] 37,907.87
4. b. 10.25 + 11.00 + 12.50 = 33.75, 33.75 ÷ 3 = 11.25
5. d. 10.25 [FV], 1 [n], 10 [i/y], [cpt] [PV] 9.32; 11 [FV], 2 [n], 10 [i/y], [cpt] [PV] 9.09; 12.50 [FV], 3 [n], 10 [i/y], [cpt] [PV] 9.39; 9.32 + 9.09 + 9.39 = 27.80; 27.80 [PV], 3 [n], 10 [i/y], [cpt] [pmt] 11.18
6. c. 7 × 1,500 = 10,500; 500000 × 0.04 = 20,000; 10500 + 20000 = 30,500
7. b.
8. c. 13.00 + 13.75 + 14.25 + 15.00 + 16.50 = 72.50; 72.50 ÷ 5 = 14.50
9. b. C[F][↓] 13 [enter][↓][↓] 13.75 [enter][↓][↓] 14.25 [enter][↓][↓] 15 [enter][↓][↓] 16.50 [enter][↓][↓] [NPV] I 10 [enter][↓] NPV [cpt] 54.38; [2nd][CLR TVM] 54.38 [PV], 5 [n], 10 [i/y], [cpt][pmt] 14.345
10. a. 13 × 1500 = 19,500; 13.75 × 1500 = 20,625; 14.25 × 1500 = 21,375; 15 × 1500 = 22,500; 16.50 × 1500 = 24,750; C[F][↓] 19500 [enter][↓][↓] 20625 [enter][↓][↓] 21375 [enter][↓][↓] 22500 [enter][↓][↓] 24750 [enter][↓][↓] [NPV] I 10 [enter][↓] NPV [cpt] 81,567.69

Final Exam Answers

1. b. 1,000,000 [FV], 12 × 43 = [n], 10/12 = [i/y], [cpt] [pmt] −116.72
2. c. 1,000,000 [FV], 8 × 12 = [n], 10/12 = [i/y], [cpt] [pmt] −6,840.83
3. a. 120,000 [PV], 25 × 12 = [n], 7/12 = [i/y], [cpt] [pmt] −848.14
4. c. Continuing on from the keystrokes in answer 3, [RCL] [n] − 24 [=] [n], [cpt] [pv] 116,195
5. d. 4,000 [PV] −800 [pmt] 10 [i/y] [cpt] [n] 7.27
6. b. −8,500 [pmt] 3 [n] 9 [i/y] [cpt] [pv] 21,516
   21,516 [fv] 5 [n] 9 [i/y] [cpt] [pv] 13,983
7. d. [30 × 42 x 25] = 315
8. b. 142,375/167,750 = 0.85; 1 − 0.85 = 0.15; 85%, 15%
9. c. 75 × 140 = 10,500; 35,000/10,500 = 3.43
10. d. 297,000/275,000 = 1.08 − 1 = 0.08 = 8%
11. d. 260,000 [pv], 25 × 12 = [n], 7/12 = [i/y] [cpt] [pmt] [rcl] [n] − 12 = [n], [cpt] [pv]; 257,828; 325,000 − 257,828 = 67,641
12. b. 14,700/0.06 = 245,000
13. c. −325,000 [pv] 382,550 [fv] 3 [n] [cpt] [i/y] 5.58
14. b. 235,900 × 0.95 = 224,105 × 0.05 = 11,205
15. a. 215,000 − 185,000 = 30,000; 30,000/3 = 10,000; 10,000/185,000 = 5.4
16. b. 175,000/0.94 = 186,170
17. a. 0.05 × 500,000 = 25,000; 0.04 × 500,000 = 20,000; 0.02 × 250,000 = 5,000; 25,000 + 20,000 + 5,000 = 50,000
18. b. $3.14 \times 3^2 \times 15 = 423.9$
19. a. 475,000/160 = 2968.75

20. d. 43,560/2 = 21,780; 21,870 × 8 = 174,240; 174,240 × 0.85 = 148,104; 148,104 × 0.07 = 10,367
21. c. 425,000 × 0.95 = 403,750; 375,487/403,750 = 0.93; 1 − 0.93 = 0.07 = 7%
22. b. 157,500/225,000 = 0.70
23. d. 50,000 [pv], 20 [n], 5 [i/y] [cpt] [pmt] 4012.13
24. d. 500 [fv], 2 [n], 10 [i/y] [cpt] [pv], 413.22; 700 [fv], 4 [n] 10 [i/y] [cpt] [pv] 478.11; 413.22 + 478.11 = 891.33
25. b. −37,000 [pv] 5 [i/y] 20 [n] [cpt] [fv] 98,172
26. a. 315,000 × 0.90 = 283,500 [pv] 30 × 12 = [n] 7.25/12 = [i/y], [cpt] [pmt] 1,933.97
27. c. −315,000 [pv] 3 [i/y] 5 [n] [cpt] [fv] 365,171
28. c. Continuing on from answer 26 keystrokes, [rcl] [n] − 60 = [n] [cpt] [cpv] 267,563.83
29. c. 365,171 − 267,563 = 97,607
30. d. 345,000 × 0.75 = 258,750 [pv] 360 [n] − 1635.48 [pmt] [cpt] [i/y] 0.54 × 12 = 6.5
31. b. [rcl] [n] − 120 = [n] [cpt] [pv] 219,358
32. b. 135,600 [pv] 300 [n], 5.5/12 = [i/y] [cpt] [pmt] 832.70
33. c. 135,600/169,500 = 0.80
34. c. 2,500,000 [pv] 240 [n] 7/12 = [i/y] [cpt] [pmt] 19,392.47 [rcl] [n] − 48 = [n] [cpt] [pv] 2,235,043.14
35. c. 2,235,043.14 × 0.07 = 156,453.02; 156,453.02/12 = 13,037.75 = interest; 19,382.47 − 13,037.75 = 6,344.72; (P + I) − I = P
36. a. 179,500 [pv], 6/12 = [i/y] 360 [n] [cpt] [pmt] [rcl] [n] − 36 = [n] [cpt] [pv] 172,470.01; 6.5/12 = [i/y] [cpt] [pmt]
37. a. 180,000 [pv] 30 × 26 = [n]; 6/26 = [i/y] [cpt] [pmt] 497.85
38. a. 1,500,000 × 0.03 = 45,000; 45,000 × 0.50 = 22,500; (3,750,000 − 1,500,000) = 2,250,000; 2,250,000 × 0.03 = 67,500; 67,500 × 0.60 = 40,500; 22,500 + 40,500 = 63,000
39. c.
40. b. 75 × 150 = 11,250
41. c.
42. c. 258,000 [pv] 300 [n] 6.5/12 = [i/y] [cpt] [pmt] 1,742.03; [rcl] [pv] − 5,000 = [pv] [cpt] [i/y] 0.56 × 12 = 6.71, 6.75%
43. c. 258,000/322,500 = 0.80
44. b. market value
45. d. 45,000/0.20 = 225,000
46. b. 225.000 × 0.80 = 180,000
47. b. an adjustable rate mortgage
48. c. −199,500 [pv], 254,618 [fv], 5 [n], [cpt] [i/y] 5%

49. d. $325,000 - 275,500 = 49,500 \times 0.25 = 12,375$

50. a. $275,500 \times 0.80 = 220,400$ [pv] 360 [n] 9/12 = [i/y] [cpt] [pmt] 1,773.39

51. d. 176,600 [pv], 360 [n], 5.75/12 = [i/y], [cpt] [pmt] 1,030.59;
    $1,030.59 \times 360 = 371,012$; $371,012 - 176,600 = 194,412$

52. c. Continuing on from the payment calculation in answer 51, [rcl] [n] − 2 =
    [n] [cpt] [pv] 176,230.35; $176,230.56 \times 0.0575 = 10,133.25$;
    $10,133.25/12 = 844.44$; $1,030.59 - 844.44 = 186.15$

53. a. 176,600

54. c. 217,900 [pv] 300 [n], 6/12 = [i/y], [cpt] [pmt] 1,403.90 [rcl] [pv] ×
    $0.97 = 211,363$ [pv] [i/y] $0.53 \times 12 = 6.32$

55. b. 6.375

56. d. The cost of the land

57. c. $245,000 - 25,000 = 220,000$

58. b. $165,000/1,350 = 122.22 \times 1,450 = 177,219$

59. d. capitalization rate

60. c. 1 [pv], 300 [n], 6/12 = [i/y], [cpt] [pmt] $0.0064 \times 12 = 0.0773$

61. d. EGI

62. c. ATCF

63. b. [cf] 150,000 [+/−] [enter] [↓] 5000 [enter] [↓][↓] 6000 [enter] [↓][↓]
    7000[enter] [↓][↓] 8000 [enter] [↓][↓] 234000 [enter] [↓][↓] [NPV] I 10
    [enter][↓] [cpt] 15,523

64. a.
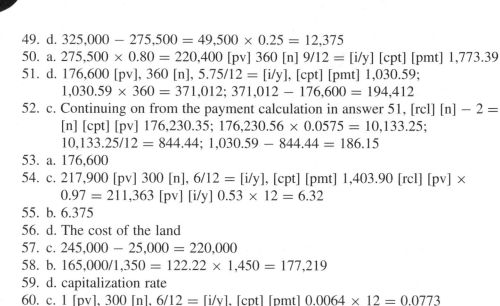

65. c. −1.045 [pv], 1.0868 [fv] 1 [n] [cpt] [i/y] 4.0%

66. b. $(22 \times 0.25) + (15 \times 0.40) + (4 \times 0.35) = 12.9\%$

67. d. $= (22 - 12.9)^2\ 0.25 + (15 - 12.9)^2\ 0.40 = (4 - 12.9)^2\ 0.35, = 20.7 +$
    $1.76 + 27.72, = 50.19; \sqrt{50.19} = 7.1$

68. c. $425,000 + 975,000 = 1,400,000$; $425,000/1,400,000 = 0.303$ op;
    10 0.303 = 0.697 sale

69. b. $145,500 \times 0.94 = 136,770$; $136,770 - 24,700 = 112,070$

70. c. $8 \times 4,000 = 32,000$, $1,000,000 \times 0.04 = 40,000$; $32,000 + 40,000 =$
    72,000

71. d. $(10.50 + 10.50 + 12 + 13.75 + 14.75)/5 = 12.20$

72. b. [cf] 0 [+/−] [enter] [↓] 10.50 [enter] [↓][↓] 10.50 [enter] [↓][↓] 12.00
    [enter] [↓][↓] 13.75 [enter] [↓][↓] 14.25 [enter] [↓][↓] [NPV] I 10 [enter]
    [↓] [cpt] 45.48; NPV = 45.48; 45.48 [pv] 5 [n] 10 [i/y] [pmt] 12

73. b. 40,000

74. d. $35 \times 45 = 1575$, $10 \times 14 = 140$, $1,575 + 140 = 1,715$

75. c. $265,900/1,000 = 265.9$; $265.9 \times 3.30 = 877.47$

INDEX

Index

Index